TRUTH KNOWLEDGE BLISS

Discourses of
Sadguru Sri Sri Arjun

English version by
Rabindranath Mohanty

INDIA • SINGAPORE • MALAYSIA

ISBN 979-8-88783-569-3

Sadguru Sri Sri Arjun (1933-1989)

This work is dedicated to Sadguru Sri Sri Arjun

Contents

Acknowledgement

This is a collection of selected discourses by Sadguru Sri Sri Arjun delivered mostly during 1981 to 1989 on self-knowledge and allied topics. Sadguru Sri Sri Arjun used to conduct classes thrice in a week at Sunabeda in his quarters and impart knowledge to the disciples mainly on Divya Darshan. As he was an employee of H.A.L, he was taking classes after his duty hours. He could easily influence people by his magnetic personality. He could explain any intricate spiritual topic very lucidly and convincingly that left the listeners spell bound. He was of the view that today's man with scientific mind should try to explore if there is any way better and more effective than those shown to us long time back. Divya Darshan is nothing but divine experience. It imparts true knowledge. Everything in this Creation is a manifestation of Brahman who is the Supreme Truth, and who is eternal and all-pervasive.

What is then true knowledge? What is true Dharma? Sadguru Sri Sri Arjun says, "Knowing the Law of Eternity is true knowledge and observing the same is true Dharma. He further preached, "Acquire knowledge and divine virtues; practice Dharma (righteousness) to attain peace, bliss and freedom which is everyone's goal of life.

Some disciples had jotted down some portions of Sadguru's discourses which proved to be useful afterwards. A few recordings in the form of cassettes were also available. From all these sources, as many as 20 small books were published in Odia under Divyadhara series. The present two books in English are more or less translation of the Divyadhara series. By the blessings of Sadguru and encouragement from the honourable President Sri Gurudip Singh ji and also the distinguished members of the Central Committee of Divya Darshan Sangha, I ventured to work on this project. The topics have been re-arranged in two books titled 'Ignorance Sins Sufferings' and 'Truth Knowledge Bliss'.

It is a well-known fact that it is difficult to accurately express in a foreign language the subtle spiritual thoughts of Sadguru. However I have tried to meticulously stick to the essence of the subject and maintain the simplicity that is characteristic of Divya Darshan. The whole purpose of this book is to spread the teachings of Sadguru Sri Sri Arjun far and wide in a simple language without using any scriptural jargon so that even a beginner can grasp the subject of self-knowledge fully and fast.

I am grateful to Divya Darshan Sangha and Divya Darshan Charitable Trust for their unstinted support to this project. I must acknowledge the spontaneous help and inspiration received from Er. Bhagabat Prasad Mishra of Bhubaneswar who has made a deep study, re-arranged the topics, and thoroughly edited the book. I also thank M/s Notion Press, Chennai for their professional expertise and sincere involvement without which the book would not have come to light.

I own all mistakes that might have crept in. Suggestions and comments from our readers are always welcome so that we can improve upon our work next time. Best wishes and regards,

Rabindranath Mohanty

Bhubaneswar (Odisha, India)

mail-rnmiob@gmail.com

mob: 9439749074

Foreword

Ignorance is the cause of sufferings. Ignorance breeds sins; sins breed sufferings. Life is a continuous journey from ignorance to knowledge, from sufferings to bliss. Many of us do not know why we are born and what the purpose of life is. Not knowing about the self is the real ignorance. Sadguru Sri Sri Arjun said, "This is no life at all. To know Him who has infused life into this life is true life."

Sadguru Sri Sri Arjun, the exponent of Divya Darshan (The Philosophy Divine) taught the mankind the secret of a divine life and exhorted, "If you want to live, be dutiful; if you want peace and happiness, possess divine virtues; if you desire liberation, acquire self-knowledge." Knowing the Law of Eternity is knowledge and observing the same is Dharma (righteousness).

Pointing out to the latent divinity in every being, he emphasized, "You are absolutely divine. Therefore, pursue divine knowledge; desire only divinity; engross yourself in divine thoughts and then only divine bliss will be bestowed upon you."

Sadguru Sri Sri Arjun said, "I have come to wake you up. Time will prove it. Whether you accept me as your Guru or not, it is immaterial, but a time will come when your children and grandchildren will accept me and Divya Darshan. Remember that whatever knowledge the Vedas, Upanishads and Gita have been trying to impart, that knowledge is yet to reach the people at large. Divya Darshan has come with that purpose that is to reach out to the people with simple explanation."

He further said, "This is no life at all. To know the infuser of life is true life. He gave a waking call to the mankind to cast off ignorance, acquire true knowledge and develop divine qualities." Repetitively reminding us of our True Self, he exhorted,

"Oh mankind! Forgetting your True Self and mistaking this stage for your abode and unreal role for your 'Self', how long will you continue to be tortured in the frying cauldron of lust and greed, pride and prejudice? Arise; enkindle the flame of awareness within. Get ready to return to your peaceful, immortal and heavenly abode and get back your Eternal, True and Pure Self. Then only you will free yourself from all miseries and fear. Remember! **You are the immortal and emancipated soul**."

He further said, "This is the need of the hour to break your slumber and to arouse you to reach your goal of attainment of bliss. You have taken innumerable births before. You have enjoyed a lot in your craving for sensual pleasures. But due to ignorance, there is no end to human miseries. It must be remembered that without self-knowledge, bliss and liberation shall remain unattainable."

Sri Rabindranath Mohanty, Vice-President of Divya Darshan Sangha had earlier worked on Sadguru's teachings to make English version of Divya Darshan: The Philosophy Divine (2017). He had also written the biography of Sadguru Sri Sri Arjun under the title, "Diamond in the hills" (2019). The response of the readers to the above two books has been quite encouraging.

We are glad that he has now done the English version of Sadguru's discourses in (Odia) in the form of twin books namely, "**Ignorance Sins Sufferings**" and "**Truth knowledge Bliss**". We place on record our sincere appreciation of his splendid efforts to spread Sadguru's divine knowledge far and wide. We conclude here with a prayer,

"Let everyone welcome knowledge and dispel the darkness of ignorance. Let peace and bliss prevail in the world. Let noble thoughts of righteousness, service, truth and love come to everyone from every side. Let the World be a still better place to live in." Om Shanti (peace), Shanti (peace), Shanti (peace).

Central Committee

Divya Darshan Sangha

18th July, 2022

Sadguru Sri Sri Arjun (1933-1989)

His Holiness Sadguru Sri Sri Arjun (1933-1989), was born on 18.07.1933 at Gudiabandha (a village near Gunupur of Rayagada District in Odisha) to Sri Odiya Gomango and Srimati Chandrama Devi.

He had studied up to class VIII. He had an analytical mind with unusual inquisitiveness and strong grasping capacity. He had a strong inclination towards science and technical studies. But he was not interested in the routine syllabus-bound school education. He was good in carpentry, drawing, dance, music, painting, sculpting, drama, astrology, palmistry, Ayurveda, and magic etc.

After his school education, he underwent training on Turner trade at ITI, Cuttack, but could not complete the course. He worked as carpentry teacher for about 7 years. He resigned and set up a furniture shop and electric appliance repair shop. In 1967, he joined HAL Sunabeda as a carpenter till his departure in 1989.

Once while reading a science book, he came across a topic on X-ray. A scientist had written, "On passing electricity through a vacuumed tube, he had observed a feeble ray inside the tube. He could not cognize it fully. But he had a conviction that there was a fourth state of matter." This term, "fourth state of matter" made Him inquisitive. There are normally three states of matter, i.e. solid, liquid and gaseous. The fourth state, if any, was not discussed or comprehended. He started inquiring into the fourth state of matter.

He had tremendous respect for knowledge. Once his mind was inclined towards fourth state of matter, he got inclined towards the subtlest subject of spirituality. He reasoned that, behind the Creation, there is some invisible power. This thought haunted him again and again. All his previously nurtured obsessions slowly vanished. He became keen to know the Eternal Truth.

In the year 1948, when he was 15 year old, he came across Socrates' words; **"Ignorance is a great sin."** At that time he was a student of class VIII. This statement spontaneously triggered an awakening in him. He accepted Socrates as his Guru. He heartily concurred with this statement of Socrates and uttered the same several times as if it were a great *mantra* for him. He was convinced that by acquiring knowledge only, ignorance could be dispelled. That means, not acquiring knowledge is a sin. Sins are committed due to ignorance. By welcoming divinity, man can get rid of all sins and attain divinity. By knowledge only man can raise himself to a greater height, i.e. even to the stage of the Supreme. The divine knowledge is therefore essential. He accepted and adored him as his spiritual master (Guru).

In 1963, while going through the Bible, he was greatly impressed with the teachings of **Lord Jesus** and accepted him as his Guru. **"Ask, you will get; seek, it will be revealed; knock, the door shall be opened."** These sermons of Lord Jesus Christ inspired him to ask, seek and knock which were essential for any seeker of knowledge to go farther and farther.

In 1965, he happened to come across **Lord Buddha's** teachings. He could understand and appreciate what truth is. Lord Buddha had envisioned sorrows and sufferings everywhere. Sorrow is entangled with birth and death. Sorrow is there with decay or disease. Sorrows according to him follow everyone just as the wheels of the bullock cart follow the hooves of the bullocks. According to Lord Buddha there are four noble truths. First, there is suffering. Second, there is a cause behind the origin of suffering. Third, suffering which has come shall also go. Fourth, as there is a cause for the suffering, there is also a cause for its cessation. Once the cause is known the sufferings shall vanish. He stated that, "Craving is the cause of sufferings." Annihilation of cravings will lead to cessation of sufferings. Annihilating cravings means extinguishing the fire of desires. That is the state of *Nirvana*. Hence Lord Buddha's first discourse at Sarnath is known as the Fire Discourse. He accepted Lord Buddha as his Guru.

In a nutshell, Socrates represented knowledge and truth; Jesus represented love and forgiveness; Buddha represented truth and non-injury (love). He appreciated and realised the essence of these teachings. He accepted the three masters as his Guru and drew inspiration from their teachings.

He had also accepted various sages, Vedas and Vedanta, Prakriti and Param-Brahman as his Guru. By seeing, hearing and deeply meditating, he could go deep into any subject. Thus out of his seven Gurus, the last Guru is Brahman. Brahman being omnipresent, omniscient and omnipotent makes everything possible.

He got the insight that the universe is full of energy; knowledge is energy and by knowledge-power all other powers are understood, appreciated and acquired. Whether it is energy or matter, the fourth state of matter must be identical and homogeneous. He developed a conviction that the higher state of consciousness starts from this stage. Why it happens? How it happens? Who is the cause behind all these happenings? All these questions repeatedly haunted him and he started inquiring into these questions.

Normally the scientists who deal with physical science do not believe in God. According to them, the matter is converted to energy and vice versa. This is the natural law which is final, they believed. According to them there is no need to believe in another power called God. There is no such existence as God.

But Sadguru Sri Sri Arjun's thinking was different. He did not want to put a stop to further enquiry. He wanted to unfold things more and more. According to him, it is true that matter is converted to energy and vice versa. But how does this conversion take place? For this process of transformation, there has to be some independent principle, law or some power that is at work. That principle, remaining independent of matter and energy but residing in the matter and energy, must be governing the process of transformation. In other words, there is some external impressed force that remains internally but independently to trigger the process of change everywhere from matter to energy and vice-versa. The spiritualists call it God, Brahman, Atman or Self. The energy that is talked about in the domain of physical science is termed by spiritualists as *Apara Shakti* (lower energy). There is still a higher power called Para Shakti which causes and controls *Apara Shakti*. With such inquisitive mind, he continued with his spiritual pursuits, till he realised the Truth.

He was a house-holder and yet by his persistence, inquisitiveness and continuous spiritual practice, attained enlightenment in the year 1967. Post realisation, He propounded his unique philosophy, namely, **Divya Darshan** which focuses on consciousness, knowledge, truth, love and bliss, other concepts like Theory of Change, Theory of Colours, Theory of Rebirth etc. He established Divya Darshan Sangha and started accepting disciples from 1976. He toured extensively in the interior districts of Odisha to spread the knowledge of Oneness. Divya Darshan stands on three pillars. First, one should do his duties diligently to the best of one's abilities; second, one should practice divine qualities like Tyaga, Sanyama, Sadhana, Seva, Satya, Prema and Kshama to live harmoniously in society; third, one must develop an intense longing for self-knowledge which alone will lead to self-realisation. Sadguru has shown the path to be a good social being to peacefully live in society and at the same time realise Self.

Sadguru Sri Sri Arjun says, "If you want to be free from sins, change your mind. Because when the mind changes everything else changes. It is ignorance that breeds sins. Sins breed sufferings. Therefore acquire the light of knowledge to dispel the darkness of ignorance. If you want to live, be dutiful; if you want peace and happiness, possess divine qualities; if you want liberation, acquire self-knowledge. Without self-knowledge, liberation is impossible. You have forgotten your Self which means you have lost your Self. Regain your lost paradise. You are forever immortal and free."

*****.

Prologue

[1]What is Divya Darshan? Before coming to this, it is relevant to discuss something about the situation and trend of the present society. We all are suffering from something or other. No one can deny it. But the question is why are we suffering? This means there are some lapses on our part somewhere. Many think that they are observing some dharma daily and regularly observing some laws. If a man really observes the laws and conducts himself properly, he will not suffer. Our sufferings indicate that we are committing lapses here and there.

We have read from scriptures and puranas that in the Satya Yug people were living in peace and happiness. It is Kali Yug now. People are suffering. If man so wills, he can change the situation. Man does not like to suffer but he suffers as if suffering is beyond his control. If we commit wrongs, how can we get peace? We must think for a while what are the causes of sufferings? Everyone is committing mistakes in some way or other. Telling lies has been a regular habit for many. But nobody likes to be called a liar. Everybody loves truth. We all tell more truths and less lies. This means, while telling truth, we at times do not tell complete truth. The consequence is suffering. People do possess some knowledge about truth, but they have forgotten. They are not aware that more knowledge about truth is

---

[1] *Odia Divyadhara Vol11 Page 19*

essential. According to the great Greek philosopher Socrates, "Knowledge is there in everyone but is forgotten to a large extent."

We have taken innumerable births in the past. Man has immense knowledge and power. But in this birth when he has taken a specific form, knowledge pertaining to that specific form only finds expression in him. In other words, in a human form, knowledge pertaining to a human being is seen in him. In the past, man was a divine being but now that he is a man, only human qualities are seen in him. In other words, man has forgotten his past divine knowledge and divine powers. However, those divine powers and divine knowledge remain in him in a dormant state. If man constantly tries to recollect that knowledge, he will have more such knowledge and power.

When I (Sadguru Sri Sri Arjun) am speaking to you, you are nodding your heads in acceptance. What does it mean? It means you are having that knowledge, but you have forgotten. When I teach you something, you are remembering that knowledge. That is why you are nodding your heads in approval. This means your forgotten knowledge is recollected.

According to Vedanta, "You are scions of immortality. You are divine. You are the Self-Absolute." The Vedas also have given us the four Mahavakyas which bear the essence of Advaita Philosophy.

- Prajnanam Brahman. (Pure Consciousness is Brahman)
- Tattvamasi. (Thou art That)
- Aham Brahmosmi. (I am Brahman)
- Ayamatma Brahman. (This Atman is Brahman)

Due to ignorance, we are not able to realise this Supreme Truth.

Hence you should not underestimate anybody. Those, who are able to speak out, remember things. Those, who are unable to express, have forgotten. In course of time, they will also remember if they contemplate well. But everyone has the potential.

Now in the whole world, suffering is on the rise despite all technological development and availability of all modern amenities. Where is the deficiency? What does Divya Darshan say in this regard? In the olden days, sages were living in ashrams and they were imparting right knowledge to the aspirants. The kings and emperors were patronizing the ashrams. But now-a-days, ashrams are very few in number. The system of Gurukul is almost extinct. People are facing towards darkness. People have distanced themselves from the spiritual knowledge laid down in the Vedas and Vedanta. Resorting to more falsehood than truth is a common malady. If we tell lies, our children will also speak more lies. On the wall you can see a picture wherein there are two persons standing; one of them is facing towards light and the other towards darkness. He, who faces towards darkness, will undergo sufferings whereas he, who faces towards light, will enjoy peace, happiness and bliss. Choice is yours. Whether you would like to face towards light or towards darkness?

Due to alienation from true knowledge, the entire world is moving towards sorrows and sufferings. Absence of true knowledge is ignorance only. No one welcomes sufferings. But everyone is proceeding towards darkness. Often, we commit mistakes knowingly or unknowingly. We rarely try for corrections as a result of which we are bound to suffer. Should we not find out ways to get rid of sufferings? Nobody wants to die. Everyone wants to live in peace and happiness.

Divya Darshan says, “Wherever you are, whatever lies you may be telling, whatever sins you might have committed, from now onwards turn your face towards light and proceed.” That is the surest path to happiness, peace, bliss and freedom. Facing towards light implies facing towards truth and knowledge. In due course, we shall merge with light, the source of all lights.

Some people are so much addicted to telling lies that they feel, it is not possible to live without telling lies.

Divya Darshan gives answer to this. Divya Darshan asks, "How are you living, whether by truth or falsehood?" An example is cited below. A gang of robbers have looted somebody. True, it is a wrongdoing. But while distributing the booties, they distribute equally by observing truth. Otherwise, their gang will break away. There will be misunderstanding and infighting. A thief, after stealing, gives the money with all sincerity and truthfulness to his wife for maintenance of his family. He is also taking shelter of truth. Therefore, we survive due to truth. We speak truth to the extent of 75%; take to falsehood to the extent of 25%. But we have to take extra care to remember falsehood and stick to the same otherwise we may be caught during cross verification. Truth, on the other hand, is spontaneous. No extra effort is necessary to express truth.

When our son commits some wrongdoing, we prevent him from repeating that. Why do we do this? It is because we want truth. Why do we not wish that our children should be a cheat or a rogue? It is because everyone is inclined towards truth, justness and righteousness. We survive by truth. Where does suffering come from? Whenever we commit mistakes or take to falsehood, suffering comes. Had we refrained ourselves from those negative qualities, we would have lived in peace and happiness. It is seen that suffering dogs us always and from time immemorial. Now also it is on the increase. When people approached Lord Buddha, he used to ask them, "Are you suffering or not? If you are suffering why don't you seek remedies?"

He, who takes preventive steps, will get rid of sufferings. Lord Buddha had explained four truths regarding suffering.

- There remains suffering. It is a truth. Because everyone suffers.
- There is also cause of suffering. Because nothing happens without cause.
- Suffering was not there. It has come. It must go away.
- If one knows the cause of suffering, one can get rid of suffering.

Since man does not enquire about the cause of suffering, he cannot prevent it; he suffers. Suffering comes because of typical mind-set. The sages and scriptures have been telling the mankind, "You are Self-Absolute. Self is Bliss-Absolute. There is no suffering for the Self. Being possessed of Jiva feelings, you are not able to realise that you are none other than the Self. You think, you are a jiva or a human. Therefore, the feelings of jiva have overwhelmed you. If you could realise that you are the Self-Absolute, you will not suffer."

Mandukya Upanishad discusses in detail about the Consciousness and its manifestations. The Supreme Consciousness has been explained in four stages. First is body consciousness. Divya Darshan in this regard explains that when any form comes into being, some qualities befitting that form would be there in the form. In a human, human qualities are seen. In a monkey, the qualities are different, and it must behave like a monkey because of its inherent qualities. When fire is created, the properties of fire such as light and heat are seen in the fire. Similarly, water has all the properties of water. Then only we call the same as water. The entire visible universe can be bracketed under body consciousness.

The second is Dream Consciousness. Consciousness also functions outside form or without any form. In the Dream Consciousness, sense organs, mind and intellect are quite active. The dreamer wanders here and there, climbs up mountains, swims across river without the involvement of the physical body. When we dream or fall asleep, we do not maintain link with our respective bodies.

The third is Sleep Consciousness. When we are asleep, there is neither any desire nor any greed, neither any dream nor any thought. This is state of bliss. Consciousness is all-pervasive; it is present even in rocks and rags, earth and air but in a sleeping state.

The fourth is Self-Consciousness that transcends all forms and qualities but is present everywhere. Self-Consciousness manifests as the other three states such as waking, dream and sleep consciousness. We all live in consciousness; we are always covered by consciousness. We are always linked with Self; you are also Self; I am Self. But you are not able to realise it. Divya Darshan says, although that Consciousness is in every being, you are not able to know Him as you have not evinced interest in the same. He, who makes spiritual efforts to realise Him, can realise Him. He, who has got strong inquisitiveness, would know. He must go through scriptures and also approach wise men who have realised Self. If you do not have inquisitiveness, how will you know? You always think that you are a man (or woman). There are also persons who are not conscious about the fact that they are humans. That is why, they behave like brutes. But we all possess divine qualities and divine knowledge. We all possess powers of Atman. If you acquire knowledge about Self, you can realise yourself. Therefore, always be inquisitive to acquire self-knowledge. He, who tries to know, can know the Paramatman, the Supreme. We are all one with Atman; sense of inquisitiveness is our instinct. A blind man also can acquire knowledge if he has inquisitiveness. Self expresses itself through forms and qualities. Inquisitiveness is ingrained in us so that we can get release from the outer coverings such as forms and qualities.

You are Self. You are all-pervasive, i.e. not confined only to the body. You are infinite and ever free. But since you consider yourself as a man, you are doing all your actions in a whimsical manner to fulfil your immediate needs considering them as right and final. Divya Darshan says, “You are erring a lot.” As long as you do not acquire complete knowledge, you will be committing mistakes. To attain perfection, God has bestowed inquisitiveness upon everyone which must be fully utilized.

The sages have made great contributions for our well-being. They have shown us various paths like Karma Yoga, Bhakti Yoga and Jnana Yoga. Through Yoga man can establish union with the Paramatman.

Divya Darshan lays more emphasis on Jnana Yoga. Upanishads say, “God is Sat-Chit-Ananda.” That Supreme Truth is Sat. He is Chit; Chit is Knowledge-Absolute. By that knowledge, when you will know your self, you will attain bliss. But because you do not know Self, you are not able to attain bliss. Whatever pleasure you enjoy now is temporary. Permanent bliss is altogether different from this temporary pleasure. The body, mind, intellect and conscience are all temporary. One must transcend all these. Beyond the intellectual sheath there is blissful sheath. The blissful sheath must also be transcended to be in infinite bliss. On the other hand, any material happiness is transient and finite. According to Jagadguru Shankaracharya, Brahman is the only reality, Jagat is unreal.

Divya Darshan says that in this Creation change is always going on. How do changes occur? You were an infant; became youth and will become old: thereafter you will leave this physical body. There was no cloud in the sky. Cloud appeared. It will disappear after some time. There was no tree. Tree was born. The Supra-Causal factor behind all changes is the Supreme Truth who is unchangeable and eternal. Realization of this Supreme Truth is eternal bliss. This means, you will be free from all bondages. Divya Darshan says that if one has not acquired self-knowledge, one cannot get bliss and freedom. Coming to mythology, Bhasmasur had appeased Lord Shiva and got a boon. But ultimately by that boon he destroyed himself. All possessions are meaningless without self-knowledge. Devotion without knowledge is no devotion. Karma without knowledge is no karma.

By mere mechanical worship, God cannot be attained. One must become simple to attain God. Lord Jesus, pointing to an infant once asked to his disciples, "Can you be as simple as this infant?"

To be simple is a difficult challenge. How can we certify someone as simple unless we have full knowledge about him? Divya Darshan says that every moment you should try to acquire knowledge. By that, you can become simple and pure. People boast of their own religions. But most of them have not read and understood the import of their respective scriptures.

For example, the most sacred scripture of the Hindus is the Vedas. But very few people have read the Vedas. Very few people are interested in these scriptures. Without reading and understanding the scriptures and without instructions from Sadguru, how can one realise the Truth? In the Vedas and the Upanishads, exceptionally good explanations are there about God's all-pervasive existence and His manifestation. We are not evincing interest to learn all these. We argue over the existence and role of God without possessing even fundamental knowledge. None can realise Him without right knowledge. You can speak about God because you have some knowledge. Same way, if you acquire further knowledge, you can also know how He exists, how He is blissful and how He, the Supreme, manifests as everything. That knowledge is available in scriptures. That is why Divya Darshan has been emphasizing on knowledge.

In the scriptures, there is mention about pancha yajna (five sacrifices). Brahman yajna is the most important yajna which means daily contemplation on Brahman by reading scriptures and meditating on Self so as to acquire self-knowledge. Through this process, contact can be established with Brahman, and one can remember Him while realizing truths one after another. Brahman is the Supreme Truth or Absolute Truth. Knowing the truth is knowledge. This is Brahman yajna.

Jnana (Knowledge) will raise you to the state of bhava. True devotion comes after bhava state. Thereafter, comes Mahabhava. In the state of Mahabhava, love rules supreme. When such sattvic love comes, the jiva starts loving Brahman or Atman. That leads to union between the two, jiva and Brahman. Love culminates with immergence with the Supreme. Without knowledge all these states cannot be realised. Therefore, outward worship or performing some rituals in a mechanical manner is not true bhakti. Shrimad Bhagavad-Gita speaks about desire-less devotion. Desires and devotion do not go together. Desire-less devotion will not come unless one acquires true knowledge about Brahman who is omnipotent, omniscient and omnipresent. By knowledge only, one will know what devotion is; what devotion with desire and without desire is. The children say, "There is God." An adult says, "There is God." An old man says, "There is God." The sages and realisers say, "There is God." In all these cases, the levels of knowledge about God are different.

Without knowledge, Brahman cannot be realised. Due to sheer ignorance people say that God does not exist. Divya Darshan therefore preaches knowledge about why we live, how to live with peace, harmony and happiness in the society, and how to get rid of worldly sufferings.

Divya Darshan says, "Our mind seeks peace." For this we must know and do what we should do. Our intellect also seeks peace, but we are not evincing interest in the knowledge that will bring us peace and bliss. Our conscience prompts us for freedom. But we are not interested to acquire that knowledge that will bring us freedom. We think of freedom but choose to remain under the clutches of our mind.

There are gradations of knowledge. From mind stage, one has to go to intellect stage, from intellect stage, one has to go to conscience stage and ultimately one has to be with Atman after transcending mind, intellect and conscience. This is Mahabhava state when Brahman shall be realised.

But people without attaining that state, claim that they have realised God. They claim to be great devotees because they have been doing outward worship regularly and sincerely. But this is not correct. This is an unpleasant truth. By mere outward worship one cannot realise Brahman, the Supreme. The fact is that He is the Supreme Truth. There is no such specific method of worship to attain Brahman. Whatever we speak about Brahman is not Brahman. He, who is the cause of our speech, is Brahman. Speech cannot reach or point out Brahman. The power that propels speech is Brahman. Brahman is the cause behind everything. Mind cannot reflect upon Brahman. Mind itself is a manifestation of Brahman. Brahman is not contemplable. But what do we do? We carve out God according to our whims and fancies and perform some rituals. This is sheer ignorance. Brahman is there in everything everywhere. He is in the mountains and valleys as well as in the void.

This visible universe is the first quarter of Brahman. There are three other quarters which are invisible. But we do not completely know even the first quarter. Hence there are so many controversies and debates over the very existence of God. To realise Brahman, one must know all the four quarters. He, who knows all the four quarters, has understood Brahman to some extent.

Even there are persons who claim that their Vishnu is bigger than Shiva. Some claim that their Shiva is bigger than Vishnu. Brahma, Vishnu and Maheswar are related to the physical or gross Creation. Upanishads say that during the time of deluge Brahma, Vishnu, Maheswar, the Sun and the Moon etc. will all be merged in the Hiranyagarbha. Everyone will be merged in the Supreme Truth i.e. Brahman who is the ultimate. But the ignorant man remaining in the first step only tries to imagine Brahman who is in fact beyond imagination. Divya Darshan says, "Make constant enquiries. He, who is inquisitive, will realise Him." But instead of knowing and practicing one's own religion, people try to find out faults with other's religion. I (Sadguru Sri Sri Arjun) am not speaking about any specific religion. I am talking of humanity as a whole and the Law of Eternity. I have a photo of Lord Jesus in my house, whom I regard as Guru. For this some people think that I am a Christian. For realization of Brahman, one must know both the aspects of God i.e. God with form and without form. Then only you have known Brahman to some extent. Without jnana, all these intricacies cannot be comprehended. Therefore, jnana is your strength, jnana is your life. By jnana only, the Truth can be unravelled. The more you know the Truth, the more you will have love and devotion towards the Truth.

Lord Jesus spoke about love. But people of today are not able to understand its depth. Had people understood the real meaning of love, the world today would not have been so much affected by strife and hatred. Just liking or being attracted towards some appearance or quality is not love. It is infatuation. More often, infatuation is mistaken for love. Infatuation is a tamasic quality like some other qualities such as desire, anger, greed, pride and jealousy. But, love is much superior to mere liking some physical appearance or quality. Love is between self and self. True love is unconditional self-surrender. Where there is true love there is no ego or selfishness. There is no narrowness. If love would have been properly understood by us, peace would have prevailed instead of war. If we face and proceed towards darkness, destruction is inevitable. Divya Darshan says, "Jnana is true light by which you can know yourself and even God."

Divya Darshan says that merely professing some religion and occasionally performing some prescribed rituals is not true Dharma. Whatever is done for realization of Self is Dharma. Observance of the Law of Eternity is Dharma. To possess divine qualities such as renunciation, restraint, spiritual practices, service, truth, love and forgiveness is Dharma. Making self-enquiry is Dharma. Inquisitiveness and contemplation to acquire self-knowledge is also Dharma. "I am the Atman-Absolute". This realization must be there. In absence of this, how anybody will observe Dharma? We misconstrue performance of an occasional ritual for Dharma. We misconstrue donation towards any noble cause for Dharma. We consider providing for water facilities, building educational institutions or hospitals for Dharma. Yes, those are all good things which should be done to acquire Punya. But these are only ancillary things of Dharma. True Dharma is to attain self-realization. We have forgotten the goal of our life. Divya Darshan preaches mankind to know the goal first and thereafter try for attainment.

Divya Darshan reiterates some basic questions as follows.

- Why do you eat?
- Answer- To survive or live
- Why do you want to live?
- Answer- To get peace and happiness
- Why do you want peace and happiness?
- Most of the persons cannot reply to this question.

The answer is-That is our True Self. By seeking peace and happiness we instinctively seek our True Self. Atman is pure, transparent and Bliss-Absolute. All humans are born to realise the True Self who is Bliss-Absolute. That is why we undertake continuous journey birth after birth and pass through the tunnels of innumerable lives and deaths. But this truth is not understood by many and therefore people thoughtlessly take to wrong routes and enormously waste their time. What can be a greater sin than this? The Greek philosopher Socrates said, "Ignorance is a great sin."

After knowing the destination if we proceed towards the destination, we can one day or other reach there. People are breathlessly running for fulfilment of mundane desires without knowing the real destination or goal of life. Selfishness and greed goad them away from the goal. There is a shortcut and straight route to realization of True Self. That route is Dharma. One must catch the path of Dharma to reach the goal of self-realization. But whatever Dharma people say they observe, is not true Dharma since there is no specific goal targeted except fulfilment of desires. In the so called Dharmic acts or rituals, the very intention to reach there or to attain True Self is absent due to ignorance about the goal of life. Since this basic knowledge is absent, there are many deviations or defects in the observance of Dharma. The result is that the goal remains unreachable and therefore, the purpose of human life gets lost. He, who moves on the path of Dharma, will not wander here and there for some personal material gains. He walks firmly towards his goal of self-realization. This is called real spiritual practice. Day and night, he should be eager to attain his goal. He, who firmly sets himself on this path, attains self-realization sooner or later. In this birth or in a few more births, he will attain his True Self. He, who has deviated from the path of Dharma, will never reach his goal of God-realization even after innumerable births. He will continue to suffer.

You might have read Avadhut Gita. The original name of Avadhut was Dattatreya born to Sati Anasuya. Dattatreya was an incarnate of Lord Vishnu. According to Avadhut, "you have taken many births and enjoyed quite a lot. In earlier births, you might have been a king or a Deva. You also might have been a lower creature in some births. After enjoying varieties of things, at last you have become a human. If in this birth also your craving does not wane and you go on seeking pleasure, then when will you seek and realise your Self?"

Divya Darshan says, in order to get rid of sufferings, everyone should acquire self-knowledge by knowing one truth after another. All sages and scriptures have all along been speaking about the Supreme Existence. But we are not trying to respond to their calls. Why is it so? It is due to sheer ignorance. Facing towards darkness, we wander all along through our endless imaginations. But rarely do we evince interest in knowing the truth about our own life.

In this context, what is our duty now? We must seek the light of knowledge. Thereby, we can discriminate between good and bad, beneficial and baneful. Neither do we fully know what is good nor do we know what is bad. By acquiring knowledge, we can know the matter as well as the spirit. We can know the Creation as well as the

Creator. We can know ourselves as well as others. It is by knowledge alone that we know about love and devotion. We can know what is to be done and what not. Unless we know about God, we will not have devotion towards Him. We respect someone only after knowing about him. An ignorant person does not know how to pay respect to others. He also does not know how to pay respect to God. He does not know what devotion is. He only tries to imitate others. A thief also visits temple and promises God that he will offer coconuts if his attempt to steal becomes successful. It cannot be called real devotion. I (Sadguru Sri Sri Arjun) repeat, devotion comes after knowing about God. When somebody shall know more and more about the greatness of God, he will understand that God is his very life. He is all in all and He is everything. Then only he will surrender to Him.

Those, who have some knowledge about God, will believe God. Others will disbelieve. Spiritual knowledge covers vast range of subjects. There is God. This is the first stage. The ultimate stage is- "I am Brahman." When the ultimate state is realised, there is none other than the Self. But after acquiring a little knowledge about God, some people feel complacent.

Divya Darshan says that it is not necessary to ascribe any form to God. God eternally and blissfully exists as Truth. Truth is there everywhere and in everything. For example, water is composed of Hydrogen and Oxygen. Hydrogen is truth. Oxygen is truth. Their product water is also truth. The proportion in which Hydrogen and Oxygen combine to form water is also truth. Every stage is a manifestation of God. The more we know the truth, the more we utilize and get benefited. It is not necessary to see God by our eyes. It is not possible also. God manifests as all forms and qualities in the Creation. We are not able to know this due to ignorance. It must be understood that Brahman remains as Truth everywhere. Many do not understand this. Before we fall asleep, we never set time for waking up. During sleep also we are not aware of anything like time. Who wakes us up? We are breathing even if we never pay attention to the same. Breathing process goes on of its own. How and by whom our food gets digested? There is some power who is there as Truth in everything, in all forms and qualities. To realise Truth, truth is essential. Brahman has become heart that expands and contracts. Brahman has become Oxygen. Even when we cook rice, some truths are involved. The quantity of water, quantity of rice, the amount of heat, amount of fuel etc. are required along with time. Then only rice can be cooked. He, who knows the truth, gets benefited by the truth that is God. Without taking interest to know the truth, we search for God here and there for fulfilment of desires.

Truth is there inside and outside. First, knowledge is to be welcomed. Without knowledge, truth cannot be realised. After gaining knowledge about truth, personal traits will also change. In absence of knowledge, how will the latent qualities be known? After realization of Truth, all delusions will vanish.

There is nothing like untruth. Not realizing truth is untruth. Not realizing truth is ignorance. Not realizing truth is darkness. There is nothing like darkness. Absence of light is darkness. There is light; there is darkness. There is truth; there is untruth. Hence how to describe God? Is He truth or untruth? In reality, there is nothing like untruth. Absence of truth or not realising truth is untruth. This Creation is made of truth. Truth is ever present and all pervasive. Brahman is Truth-Absolute. The more you know truth, the more you come nearer to Brahman and shall ultimately attain Him, the Supreme. To attain the Supreme state, whatever is done is called Yoga or spiritual practice.

We should follow the scriptures and the preaching of sages. We should sincerely try to receive true knowledge from Sadguru and spread the same for the whole of humanity.

*****

About the monogram:

[2]On the top of the Divya Darshan monogram, it is written "Ignorance is great sin". At the bottom, it is written- "Surrendering to Truth." In the monogram, there are seven segments with seven colours such as- Renunciation (Violet colour), Restraint (Indigo), Spiritual Practice (Blue), Service (Green), Truth (Yellow), Love (Orange) and Forgiveness (Red colour). Brahman manifests as all these; but man, due to ignorance, is not able to comprehend this. If God is realised, all sufferings will vanish. The sages have given us so many scriptures, but we are not able to understand and appreciate them. We are not able to feel the presence of God. The monogram of Divya Darshan represents the whole Creation. It represents both the Creator and His Creation.

According to the scriptures, Brahman willed to be many. When Brahman manifests as many, He forgets His True Self due to Maya. How to get back to the True Self then? Hence before becoming many, He kept Himself aside as Guru which means jnana. He, who will make efforts to know Brahman, can know Brahman by the help of jnana (Knowledge). In other words, he can realise his True Self. The monogram of Divya Darshan represents the entire Creation and the Creator in a very subtle form.

---

[2] *Odia Divyadhara Vol 15 Page 26*

It is true that suffering is there. Everyone suffers. In order to get rid of sufferings, something or other has to be done. Divya Darshan explains how to get rid of sufferings. What line of action or what route is to be pursued to get rid of sufferings? Making efforts to reach the goal is sadhana. The sages have been showing various paths. Divya Darshan tries to explain the Law of Eternity that governs the whole Creation. This Law is not new. It is eternal. There is 'Om' at the centre of the monogram.

In the preliminary stage, it is explained that it is a seven coloured flower. At the centre there is kesar (pistil). The kesar is profusely replete with fragrance. The seven colours contain many other colours. He, who will get attracted towards this flower, will not like to come out of it. He will be absorbed in it. True knowledge and divine qualities are given more importance through this monogram of Divya Darshan.

Whatever man does to get rid of sufferings is sadhana. One must possess the seven divine qualities in order to get rid of sufferings. It starts with renunciation. Through restraint and spiritual practices, one gains knowledge. Knowledge is already there in you. Divya Darshan aims to revive the forgotten knowledge in you. Through divine qualities also one acquires knowledge. Karma Yoga, Bhakti Yoga and Jnana Yoga are all inbuilt in the monogram. Renunciation, restraint and spiritual practice represent Karma Yoga. Service represents Bhakti Yoga. Truth, love and forgiveness represent Jnana Yoga.

Every person wants to get rid of sufferings. One should therefore try to acquire the related knowledge by which one can reach the blissful state. He, who seeks knowledge, gains knowledge. Divya Darshan shows the way to acquire true knowledge. If you go under water and do tapah (penance) or enter into the fire, what shall you get? You may get something, but you cannot gain knowledge. By doing so, you will never attain Self-Knowledge which is the goal. Hence, the spiritual path of Divya Darshan is unique. Divya Darshan explains knowledge in three stages.

- Knowledge for individual living
- Knowledge for harmonious social living
- Knowledge for realization of Self.

Without the first step of knowledge, how can one survive? One must acquire knowledge to do some work. Try to be self-dependent. There should be discipline in your life. Bhakti makes one disciplined. One must live in the society in peace and happiness. Divya Darshan teaches true knowledge that enables one to realise Self. By possessing divine qualities, man can get divine blessings and gain true knowledge. He, who follows the above, can realise True Self and get liberated. This is complete Yoga. For this, knowledge is indispensable. Whatever all you are doing is sadhana. But since you are not aware of the goal, you are not able to realise your Self. You must possess strong inquisitiveness for this. It is a great sin not to try to know. By knowing spiritual knowledge, you will be stronger and shall move forward. You will be in a position to cross any hurdle that may come on your way. The invisible divine power always supports you when you proceed on the spiritual path. Have faith on Him. He will create all necessary favourable circumstances for you. My blessings are always with you.

*****

The Supreme Truth

[Here we shall discuss about Truth. It is not limited to the truth we practice daily and perceive generally. This is about the Truth which does not change. For example, we see lightning; it flashes for a moment and then vanishes; if somebody, who has not seen that particular lightning, wants to see it, it may not be possible because it no longer exists. So how do we treat this? As a truth or untruth? It is truth for the person who saw it and not true for the person who has not seen. The lightning was a truth, but for that particular moment only. But Truth should be true for all time. Divya Darshan has classified truth into four types. This phenomenon of lightning is classified under 'Temporal Truth'. Everything in this world is subject to change. Only the time period varies. But the maker of this world does not change. Hence Adi Sankaracharya had said "Brahman satya jaganmithya." Hence Brahman alone is the Supreme Truth.

Sadguru says, it is difficult to comprehend Truth. It is elusive. But it is very near to us. Everything we see around is the manifestation of Truth only. Although we experience it every day in different forms, we are not able to know it due to our ignorance.]

[3]In earlier classes, I (Sadguru Sri Sri Arjun) have discussed about Truth so many times. You too know something about Truth. Truth is beginningless and endless too. Truth is all-pervasive and ever

---

[3]*Odia Divyadhara Vol 18 Page 46*

present. The sages leaving aside all material pleasure were making intense spiritual practices to attain Truth. They have been teaching mankind through various scriptures about Truth. Realization of Truth is the goal of human life. I am going to tell you something about what Truth is.

We all live on Truth whether we know it or not. Everything has come from Truth and finally gets merged in Truth. Truth is always complete. It is the Dharma of every human being to take to Truth, observe and honour Truth. Truth is ever present in Nature also. All changes in Nature occur due to Truth. The Law that is operative in the Nature is Dharma. This is called Law of Eternity which is based on Truth.

People follow some rules and laws in the material world for material pleasure. But they fail to notice the ever operative Law in the kingdom of Nature. By taking shelter of Sadguru, the disciple learns about the Truth that manifests everywhere as everything. He, who does not try to acquire knowledge about Truth, very often does wrong or opposite things for which he suffers. He, who follows Sadguru's sayings, follows Truth. Such a person is not afflicted by Maya. He lives peacefully and happily even in this material world. It is Satya Yug for him who follows Truth. That means he lives with God. He attains God. His life becomes blissful.

He, who considers himself as big and does everything according to whims and caprices, is a tamasic person who undergoes sufferings births after births. But the truthful person lives with ease. Things for him become easy. He, who takes shelter of Truth, gets energy and power from Truth to accomplish difficult things. Even impossible things become possible.

He, who takes shelter of the Devas, will come to possess divine powers. He, who takes shelter of Brahman, will possess all powers. Brahman is the source of all powers. Brahman has manifested as the Devas. Everyone owes its existence to Brahman. The Devas observe the law of Eternity sincerely. Brahman resides as Atman in all beings. Taking shelter of Truth means living with God. Brahman remains as Truth in everything or manifests as everything. Those, who remain in truth, are adorable. They do not suffer. They accept everything as God's gift. As told earlier, various divine powers are known as Devas. He, who takes shelter of Brahman, comes to possess the divine powers.

Those, who are spiritualists and live on truth, are respected by others. He, who sincerely makes spiritual efforts, will attain God. It may not happen that the children of a spiritual master would possess the same level of knowledge and divine powers as their father. They will grow according to their karma and live their lives accordingly. He, who is devoted to Sadguru, will not be fickle; he shall be cool, composed and reactionless.

Truth has no quality or shape. It is the basis of the Creation. God is Truth-Absolute. Sadguru has no specific home, no caste or creed. Asking questions to Sadguru about this terrestrial world is a sin.

By respecting Guru, you are getting His good wishes and blessings. Many people speak of God but they do not know clearly who God is. He is a divine power who should be meditated upon with divine qualities and feelings at heart. The power you worship is none other than Guru. But you are not aware of this. That is why you are not getting His blessings. You should purify yourself so that you will rise stronger and brighter.

Guru possesses the master key to all fortunes. By merely getting all scriptures by heart, you may not attain Him. To attain the divine powers, you must live with Guru and conduct yourself accordingly. Guru has become Guru by his righteous conduct. If you conduct yourself righteously, you can become a Guru. Therefore, your conduct is especially important for attainment of the highest state.

*****

[4]Truth can be realised by knowledge. In other words, knowledge is nothing but realizing the truth. Also, knowledge is the power to realise the truth. If there is limited knowledge, truth remains veiled. Whatever you know about the material world is about temporary things. Hence that knowledge is also changeable. But the knower is permanent. He, who knows the Self, will not suffer. When you realise the truth, you can understand and get rid of the illusion. You can know from what such illusion has emanated. At that time, man gets overwhelmed by Truth. Even if he remains in the world of illusions, he is not affected by them. Those, who are truthful and conscientious, will not get affected by the Maya. Maya casts its spell on mind and intellect. But a realiser is above mind and intellect. Therefore, Maya cannot touch the realiser.

You are being governed by Truth. In reality, you are the Truth. Maya has come from Truth. Lila is nothing but your manifestation. You are different from Lila. Mind, intellect and conscience are also different from Lila. The spider is not caught in the web it has made. He, who knows the Truth, will find Truth everywhere and in everything. Truth manifests as many, called *Lila*. Where there is

[4]Odia Divyadhara Vol 20 Page 36

Truth there is also *Lila*. The noumenon and the phenomenon are not different from each other. The noumenon is invisible.

Whatever we perceive by mind and intellect are all Maya. Whatever remains for a short period is Maya. But due to ignorance, we get attracted towards Maya and cling to it as if it is the only truth. On the other hand, the wise persons realise the Truth as well as the Maya. He enjoys his own *Lila*. To explain about Brahman, it becomes necessary to take the examples of the objects created by Him. You can realise Him only in certain circumstances.

Truth can be realised by means of Truth only. Without the help of Truth, how can you say Truth as Truth? The Supreme Truth manifests as innumerable truths. Unless different truths are understood and appreciated, how can one know the Supreme Truth who is the basis of all? I can understand God. This is a truth. I cannot understand God. This is also a truth. Absence of truth is falsehood. There is nothing like falsehood. Falsehood is conditioned by Truth. Everything is truth. Since the wise persons had realised Truth, they experienced Truth everywhere in all circumstances. Wise men know what we think and what we do. Since they are always established in Truth, they do not react to any action of ours. They remain in blissful state on realizing the Supreme Truth. Since we are yet to acquire that level of knowledge, we are away from Truth. We are carried away by illusions all around us. But the realisers see nothing except Truth.

Mundaka Upanishad explains about *para jnana* and *apara jnana*. *Para jnana* is higher knowledge whereas *apara jnana* is lower knowledge. By inquisitiveness, one moves from lower knowledge to higher knowledge and realise the Supreme Truth. An inquisitive mind will not be confined to idol worship. He will be keen to delve deep into the infinite ocean of the Supreme Truth that manifests as everything in the Creation

Those, who are not evincing interest to know the Supreme Truth, are ignorant. Everything can be attained on realization of the Supreme Truth. It is the first and foremost duty of every human being to realise the Supreme Truth.

*****

[5]*[Truth cannot be attained easily. If chased, it moves farther. Remember, He is very near to you. He is the heart of your heart and life of your life. Everything in you is manifested by Him. You are not able to understand Him due to your ignorance. Once you welcome Him, He will spontaneously come to you in different forms. Finally, you will realise, "He is I and I am He." In other words, "I am the Brahman; Aham Brahmosmi."(Amritbindu-42)]*

I am just giving some hints on Truth. That, which eternally exists, is Truth. He, who has realised that Eternal Existence, is also Truth. What he has realised is also Truth. This means, whatever we come across in this visible universe, is Truth. There exist so many things in the universe which are invisible, but we experience all those by our knowledge. Those are also truths. Therefore, everything is truth. This truth has been explained in different phases. We see someone from his birth to death; but thereafter we cannot see him. A seedling becomes a tree; it grows old and dies; thereafter we cannot see the tree. Lightning comes and goes immediately; we see it for a fraction of a second. Whatever we see are truths. Whatever we see even for a moment is also truth.

---

[5]*Odia Divyadhara Vol 13 Page 8*

Trying to explain the inexplicable Truth, Divya Darshan divides truth in four categories.

- Temporal Truth
- Partial Truth
- Truth
- Supreme Truth

Every form is truth. Every form possesses some quality. Quality is also truth. He, who has caused and conditioned the forms as well as the qualities therein, is the Supreme Truth.

We are all dreaming. The dreamer is truth. The dream consciousness is truth. Remaining in the background, He, who impels all these effects, is also truth. He, who has created the man (dreamer), is truth. But forms, qualities and the dreams are all temporary. Hence, they are categorized under temporal truth. Lightning comes under temporal truth. But the basis of all these who caused and conditioned all these effects is the eternal Supreme Truth.

When somebody is telling the truth, it is truth. When somebody is telling lie, it is also truth. Whatever, whether visible or invisible, happens in this Creation is truth. Everything is truth. I do exist. It is truth. He is there. It is truth. Due to ignorance, we do not have clear and full understanding of truth. I am a human being. It is truth. But we do not try to know the causal factor (Truth) from whom all these truths have come into being. He is called Brahman or the Supreme Truth. Due to ignorance man does not know himself and others.

That Truth has become Lord Rama, Lord Krishna and Lord Vishnu. The same Truth has become plants, animals and humans. They have all come into being by and from Energy or Power. Ornaments made of gold are gold only. Things made of clay, is earth only. Therefore, everything is truth. Ignorance also is truth.

How can we realise truth when we do not have knowledge about truth? Even man's imaginations are limited to the extent he knows truth. If anyone chases after truth, how shall he get the truth, where and how? Truth pervades everywhere and is there in everything. Your thought or imagination is truth. The object or subject of your imagination is also truth. Truth is within and without. If mind just imagines something out of ignorance, by that how can one realise Truth? By acquiring true knowledge only, Truth can be realised. Falsehood is also truth. After knowing the truth, we call any deviation or nonconformity as false. In other words, without knowing what is right or true, we cannot tag anything as false. Therefore, classifying something as false is based on our knowledge of what is true. Ignorantly if somebody searches for Truth, Truth will move farther from him. But for the wise, Truth is very near; it is not only near but is both inside and outside.

If we do not know how to cook rice, it will be difficult. If somebody knows how to cook, he can do so easily. This means the knowledge to cook the rice brings him closer to rice. He, who does not have that knowledge, rice is far away from him. For cooking rice, so many other truths are involved. Fire is truth. Water is truth. Fuel is truth. Oxygen which is truth is essential since without Oxygen, fuel will not burn. Like this, so many linkages of truth are involved in preparation of rice. For example, water comprises Hydrogen and Oxygen. For becoming Hydrogen, so many truths are there behind, including atomic structure comprised of Electrons, Protons and Neutrons. Going forward, Hydrogen is an essential component of several other products which are used by us. Similar is the case with Oxygen. Thus, truth is very near to all of us. All forms and all qualities are truths which rest on many other ancillary truths. Truth pervades everywhere and in everything. Examples are endless.

To explain what Brahman is, the sages have described four steps. The visible universe is just one step of Brahman. There are three subtle steps. Divya Darshan explains these four steps as Temporal Truth, Partial Truth, Truth (Causal) and Supreme Truth (Supra-Causal). The more one acquires knowledge, the more one perceives truths in the gross as well as the subtle, inside as well as outside. A person, who cannot understand anything even after seeing the gross world, is ignorant. A man knows that he is a man. But he does not know why he is born, and after death where he will go. This is due to ignorance.

When one is not able to know the visible world of matters, how will he understand the other three steps which are subtle? In other words, the manifestations of Brahman must be understood to finally realise the Supreme Brahman. Guru's Grace is always there for realization of Truth. But a disciple should have adequate interest to realise Truth.

Due to ignorance you are not able to recognize Him. Once you sincerely welcome Him, He will appear before you in some form or other. But how do we welcome Him? The answer is- To get attracted towards Him, to know about His greatness, to know about His benevolence, to have devotion towards Him and to surrender to Him. These are the signs of welcome.

"What is the ultimate Truth of my life? His glories and grandeurs are ineffable. I must know Him." When this attitude comes, it amounts to welcoming Him. There should be love and respect towards Him coupled with sincerity and humility. When such feelings come, man shall be able to know one truth after another. Truth will spontaneously come to him. Where is Truth? Truth is near me. Truth is in my family. Due to ignorance, we are not able to know.

You might have known the story of Prahlad, son of Hiranyakashipu. Prahlad was a great devotee of Lord Narayana (Hari). Prahlad was seeing Hari everywhere. But the demon Hiranyakashipu was not able to digest the unusual type of devotion his son had towards Hari. He became angry. He questioned Prahlad, "Whether Hari is there in this pillar?" Prahlad confidently replied in affirmation. Thereafter Hiranyakashipu violently hit the pillar with his mace. In no time, from out of the pillar, Hari appeared in the form of Narasingha (Half lion and half human) and tore Hiranyakashipu into pieces.

Yes, God can spontaneously incarnate anywhere and from anything. No preparatory time is necessary for Him. He is always complete in all respects and ever ready to protect him who takes refuge in Him.

In this instance, the pillar is a truth. The atoms and molecules which are there in the pillar are also truths. Atoms and molecules have lot of energy stored in them. Atoms are the forms of energy. They have also powers to attract each other and therefore different forms are created. To eliminate Hiranyakashipu, whatever truth was required at that time, the same manifested through the pillar by His Will. In other words, He willed and became Narasingha to kill Hiranyakashipu.

In a magic show when a magician shows some tricks and we cannot understand the same, we get surprised. If somebody tries to know the trick behind the surprising show, he can very well realise that there is no element of surprise in it, but it is just a tricky and timely manipulation of things. It is so simple.

In this Creation whatever we come across, has been possible only by knowledge. Knowledge manifests as forms and qualities. Due to ignorance, we are not able to know. Knowledge is truth. Knowledge manifests as this visible and invisible Creation. Truth manifests as the visible and invisible Creation. It is told earlier that Truth is God. Truth is Brahman. It means, Brahman has created the entire Creation, visible and invisible. To put it in a different language, Brahman has manifested as everything in this Creation. The Creation is a manifestation of Brahman.

When we undergo C.T. training or B.Ed. training, we become teachers. When we acquire engineering degree or diploma, we become engineers. Those, who acquire spiritual knowledge, can know that it is Brahman who has manifested as the Creation. Man can know everything after acquiring knowledge on Brahman. Brahman is omnipotent. He can do everything. The more one knows Brahman, the more one comes to possess powers. I am not clarifying everything about self-knowledge. I am giving some hints only.

Brahman became 'Om', and then became Devas and thereafter humans. We surrender to the Devas. But wherefrom Devas have come? The answer is 'Om'. 'Om' is Brahman. One, who wants to transcend everything and reach the highest state, must become a man first. He must elevate himself higher and higher from man to Devas and from Devas to 'Om'. Thereafter, he can realise the Supreme Brahman. The more he knows, the more powerful he becomes. Therefore, once you invoke truth, the truth will spontaneously come to you. Thus, when you will go on knowing one truth after another, a stage will come when you will realise that there is nothing further to know.

Finally, a stage will come when you will realise that 'He is I' and 'I am He'. "I am the Brahman; Aham Brahmosmi." Scriptures say, "By knowing whom, nothing remains to be known; by attaining whom, nothing remains to be attained; He is to be known. Everything has emanated from the Supreme Truth." He is outside us; He is very much inside us also. He, who realises Him, becomes That. In other words, the realiser is Brahman.

Why you are not able to affirm this now? It is because your knowledge about truth is incomplete. You are in human form now. Your knowing the truth is limited to human stage. The animals are in lower stage of knowledge. It is the level of knowledge that is an indicator of the stage of evolution of somebody. At the highest level of knowledge, one can say that he is Brahman.

Therefore, the animals suffer more than the humans. The Devas undergo least sufferings. The Devas are also affected by the tri-qualities. When someone transcends the tri-qualities, he attains the unqualified or Nirguna state which is beyond 'Om'. Thereafter he will be immerged with Brahman or will become one with Brahman. What is immergence? Realization of Brahman is immergence with Brahman.

True Self of man is Brahman. Brahman, by His greatness, manifests as all forms and qualities. When man will realise that state, at that time he can say that he is Brahman.

Water is composed of Hydrogen and Oxygen. Water has also different states such as vapour and ice. Ice and vapour are also H_2O. In different conditions, H_2O manifests as ice, water and vapour. When forms are different, qualities are also different. The properties of water are different from the properties of vapour. Ice is different from water and vapour. But essentially, they are all H_2O. Brahman has become man. Human qualities are seen in man. When one will acquire knowledge and attain Brahma-bhava, he can say that he is

Brahman. There is a Mahavakya. "Tattvamasi which means, Thou art That."

If you are not Brahman, how could you know that there is Brahman? If you are a human being only, how can you speak about or think of Brahman?

In a drama, if a landlord plays the role of a servant, he will act like a servant. The landlord's powers will not be seen in him in course of acting. After the end of the drama, he is the landlord. Even during the drama, he never ceased to be a landlord. When man elevates himself to the state of Brahman, he will realise that he had assumed the form of man, but he was Brahman then and is Brahman always.

Man craves for happiness, peace and bliss. For this, he must acquire the related knowledge and enhance his qualification. In absence of this, bondages and sufferings are inevitable. We see around us that a person with less knowledge always gets a subordinate position. He is administered by a person with higher knowledge. We humans know several ways to control the animals. Very often, we ill-treat them, exploit them, and force them to toil for us. Whatever we throw away, they eat. When man's knowledge will increase, he can experience more powers in him. According to situations, he will utilize the powers. Ultimately, he will feel that he is none other than the Supreme Brahman. This realization of formlessness will come even if he is in a human form.

The example of the role play in a drama is cited in the foregoing paragraph. The landlord who is playing the role of a servant, if asked about his identity, he will reply that he is the landlord only if he has not forgotten his identity during his role play. Otherwise he will say that he is a servant.

You have forgotten your Self, being in the human garb. When you will realise your True Self, you will know that you are the Supreme Brahman who has manifested as innumerable forms and qualities and now you are in human form. Remember, your human form is temporary, but you are the eternal Brahman who is all-powerful and formless. With your limited powers, how can you say that you are the Supreme Brahman? Man must acquire more and more knowledge to acquire more and more powers. All your sufferings will go away. With increased knowledge, you can know what to do and what not. You can know what your duty is and how to perform the same deftly and with righteousness to reach the goal. Man can thus know the truth one after another, more and more to ultimately realise the Supreme Truth.

When you are told repeatedly that you are the Supreme Brahman, when the scriptures and sages reiterate this truth, why are you delaying in responding to this? Why are you not getting prepared to realise your True Self? Due to the darkness of ignorance you are suffering. Why can't you light up a candle of knowledge to dispel the darkness surrounding you?

It is already told to you that Brahman is beyond knowledge. Knowledge is only up to 'Om' level. Beyond 'Om' there is no knowledge, but *bhava* only. In other words, there is a power that cannot be comprehended by knowledge. It means, knowledge will not reach there. Knowledge will have no role to play. He is Brahman. He is Supreme Existence. It is wrong to believe that you can attain Him by your knowledge. By knowledge, you can only know about Him. But by *bhava* and *Mahabhava*, you can be one with Him.

*****

Self-Knowledge

[The greatest spiritual challenge before man is to know his Self. Man is ever curious to know his True Self. Being intelligent, he knows that he is not the body; there is someone else which is inside the body with whom he is in contact always and he is inquisitive to know about this 'someone else'. Once man becomes inquisitive to know his Self, his spiritual journey starts. There are many scriptures which elaborately explain the different streams of spiritual philosophy, through meaningful Sanskrit verses and emphasize on different practices to understand Self. But Divya Darshan presents Self-Knowledge in a simple language and easily comprehensible style.

To achieve this goal Sadguru Sri Sri Arjun is not asking us to do japa every day; or go to temple; or visit religious places or go to secluded places for meditation. He is only asking us to understand and do with awareness whatever we are doing; to know that whatever we are doing in our day-to-day life is for our Self and to realise our Self only. He is only asking us to practice and blossom the inherent divine qualities like renunciation, restraint, spiritual practice, service, truth, love and forgiveness. To tell truth, to believe, to serve others, to sacrifice and to love are all divine qualities.

Additionally, one should do deep thinking (chintana) and contemplation (manana) to understand the greatness and manifestation of Brahman. Then hopefully after some time, by His grace one may realise the True Self. One has to go through the grind to know and experience the True Self. Sadguru's advices and prescriptions are definite pointers in that direction.

Sadguru had never used a difficult word during his discourses. But during translation, a few not-so-commonly used words might have crept in. As far as possible, attempt has been made to keep the simple and uncomplicated flavour of the original language of the discourse.]

Who am I?

[6]We always utter the word 'I' but we do not know who and what 'I' is. Man has been repetitively using this single lettered and simple 'I' since time immemorial and shall keep on uttering this in future too. Names like Ishwar, Brahman and Atman are assigned only to explain this mysterious 'I'. But truly 'I' has no name, form or quality. By His latent powers, He manifests as various names, forms and qualities. The sages have realised 'I' and according to them God is formless as well as attributeless. He is all-pervasive. Everything else exists because He exists. In order to express Himself, He manifests as different names, forms and qualities. This means, whatever we come across or experience, visible or invisible, are all His manifestations. He manifests as the Creation. His self-identity is represented by 'I'. Even though we all utter 'I', we are neither able to understand nor explain it. 'I' has no name, form or quality. In such a case, how can 'I' be explained or described? The sages described 'I' as 'unmanifest'. In other words, 'I' represents that unmanifest and inexpressible existence. One may be in any situation, circumstance or thought; it is only He who manifests as such i.e. as everything. In the Creation there are countless manifestations. He cannot be explained by names, forms or qualities. He is at the background of

---

[6]*Odia Divyadhara Vol 4 Page 21*

everything and manifests as all names, forms and qualities. Therefore, He cannot be described or pointed out by anything created after him and by him. He, being the Supreme, cannot be explained by citing any example picked up from His Creation. There is no language to speak of Him. All languages are subsequent developments only. Hence, He is inexpressible. A spiritual mendicant can only experience Him within but cannot express anything about Him. Realisation of 'I' is of topmost priority in this human life. On realisation of 'I' only, man can get rid of all sufferings. We always speak of 'I' but we never evince interest to know who that 'I' is. What can be a greater shame? He, who knows himself, can know everything else. Having taken human birth if man cannot know his True Self, it is to be understood that his life is wasted. Man is always ready or interested to know the external objects, spin out judgements over every happening, poke his nose in all affairs around him but rarely takes interest to know 'Self'. Therefore, he is not able to get rid of sufferings. On realisation of 'I', nothing remains to be known; nothing remains to be attained. Once he realises 'I', he would get rid of all sufferings although he would not be able to express what 'I' is. Although 'I' is inexplicable, it is experienceable. If we do not know what clay is, we shall have doubts about various earthen pots of different designs, shapes, sizes and colours. Once we know the basic material that is given various forms, we shall fully understand all forms made of that substance without any doubt. Similarly, we all see the soil, plant, stone, birds, animals and humans etc. but we are not able to know the material cause or the efficient cause of different forms, different shapes and attributes. If we ask an earthen pot about its true identity, most likely it will reply, "I am a pot". It is true that it is, for the time being, in the form of a pot but on further questioning, the pot may finally say, "I am clay (earth)."

If we ask someone about his identity at that time he says, "I am so and so". But he does not understand the word 'I'. In other words, man does not really understand, "Who am I?"

'I' does not mean any name, form or quality. Even after the physical body is destroyed the subtle body also says 'I'. In other words, the subtle body even without a physical body identifies itself as 'I'. When a subtle body enters another body and speaks through that physical body, it uses the word 'I' and identifies himself with his earlier name which he had while he was in his physical body. 'I' does not mean any name, form, mind, intellect or conscience. 'I' is different from all these. It is indicated by the term 'Atman' or 'Brahman'.

When man will realise 'I', he would experience that 'I' is present everywhere. That is why everyone is using the word 'I'. This means that the 'I' in me is present in all beings and therefore each is identifying as 'I'. It shows that my 'Self' is same as that of all others. The 'one' is there in all. The forms are many and varied but the 'True Self' is one, one undivided existence. Therefore, everybody is expressing himself by 'I'-sense. 'I'-sense is present everywhere in all beings. Therefore 'I' has no specific form. It is formless but it takes all forms. In all names there is one who identifies as 'I'. So 'I' has no specific name. Thus 'I' is different from all names, forms and attributes; it expresses through different names, forms and attributes.

The real 'I' is all pervasive. Just to explain the term, 'I', the names such as Brahman, Atman and Ishwar are assigned. The purpose of human life is to realise 'I' which is True Self of one and all. True Self is also different from 'I'. 'I' is a term for expression only. Nothing can be told about that all-pervasive existence. Since 'I' is there everywhere and in all beings, if somebody scolds another person, why should one get upset or feel insulted? Both are one and the same 'I'. This means one is scolding oneself only. When I scold myself, shall I feel hurt or insulted? Since we do not know the underlying essence, we think everything is different from one another. And that is why we feel hurt or insulted. The truth is that due to ignorance about True Self, all perversions are experienced by us. Therefore, Divya Darshan says, it is a matter of regret and shame not to know Self; not to try to know Self.

Let us think for a while which one is worse in the following two situations. First, someone scolds me and therefore I feel upset or insulted. Second, I do not know the Self. Ponder over this well and deeply. Certainly the second situation of not knowing the Self is worse. Due to ignorance about Self the unwanted effects like sorrow, shame, pride, anger, greed and jealousy etc. raise their ugly hoods. All these reactions shall vanish on knowing the Self.

Divya Darshan emphasizes on jnana. Divya Darshan preaches that everyone should aim at self-knowledge which is the panacea to all ills and illusions. Where is the scope of any fear when one is present everywhere and in all beings?

Suppose someone pays respect to me. I am already there in him; who pays respect and to whom? 'I' is there in one who scolds. 'I' is there in one who receives the scolding. Hence it is the play of the Self.

Once one knows gold, one can know all ornaments made of gold. Likewise, when Self is known, everything can be known. Atman is a naming word. But while expressing we say 'I'. Where there is doubt, there is fear. Where there is fear, there is suffering. They are all linked with each other.

Everyone is afraid of death. Why does fear of death come? We are afraid because we do not know what death is.

Once we know what death is, we shall not have any fear for death. If Truth is not realised, doubts will be there. He, who knows Self, knows all. Self is there in all beings everywhere and does everything. Therefore, it is the first and foremost duty of everyone to know the Self. All scriptures explain the Self. 'I' is unmanifest and inexpressible. As mentioned in the foregoing paragraph, whatever is expressed or described about 'I' is limited and finite. He can be realised only by spiritual practice, inquisitiveness and self-surrender. One should be eager to know one's Self. It is the best spiritual practice to have the curiosity and inquisitiveness day and night to know one's Self. The sages and seers after self-realisation could say "I am Brahman." They also say, "Thou art That" which means "You are Brahman."

Who is that existence that is nameless, formless and without attributes? Who reveals His identity as 'I'? 'I' is merely a word to express oneself. But the Self is different from 'I'. Self-realisation is the true goal of everyone.

*****

[7]We mistakenly identify ourselves by our names and appearances. But we do not know our true identity, nor are we interested to know. Appearance does not speak about the personality of a person. One's conduct is the only credential. He, who has realised the Truth, will not undergo any rebirth. On realization of Truth, the realiser becomes simple, and full of love and empathy. The scriptures lay so much emphasis on realization of Truth. Only Truth is eternal and the

---

[7]*Odia Divyadhara Vol17 Page 30*

basis of all. Acquisition of self-knowledge amounts to realization of Truth. Divya Darshan therefore lays stress on acquiring self-knowledge, whatever situation one may be placed in. Self-realization should be the goal of everyone. All other things except Self are illusory and transitory. To reach a temple at the other side of the river, you are crossing the river by a boat, but if you do not know about the deity in the temple, nor you are interested to know, your crossing the river is merely a wasteful exercise.

We are stuck up with some rituals or outward worship instead of trying to know who God is and what his greatness is. Divya Darshan says, "Whatever religion or sect you may belong to, liberation is impossible without self-knowledge." He, who is making efforts to acquire self-knowledge, will attain everything and will reach the goal. Nothing will remain to be earned or achieved. With divine grace, he will surmount all obstructions and reach the goal. But without knowing the right path and the goal, his movement will be very erratic and uncertain even after performing all the rituals and sacrifices. Divya Darshan says, he, who wills, will attain Him early, if not in this birth, in the next one or two births. It may so happen that he will realise his Self even within a second by Guru's Grace.

Guru is creating all-favourable environment for you for realization of True Self. Divya Darshan intends imparting you all knowledge but you are so unfortunate that even if God Himself comes to you, you are not prepared to recognize Him. In a couple of classes earlier, I (Sadguru Sri Sri Arjun) have indirectly told you that God is ever by your side. But you are not able to recognize Him because you do not know who God is. You are so unfortunate! Guru has nothing to give you anymore. God is never separate from you. How can Guru hand over God to you? Guru can give you the knowledge to recognize God who is always everywhere and in everything. Even if Guru gives you that knowledge, you are not interested to know. This happens due to your mindset. Therefore, you are suffering and will continue to suffer. With strong inquisitiveness, you can realise Him in this birth. Otherwise, several births may be taken by you. When I think of you, I am unable to sleep even. I always think how my disciples will receive true knowledge and get rid of sufferings but you are not coming to me.

The sages do their duties with utmost sincerity. But you are not performing your duties. During my lifetime, can any of you come up and attain liberation? Divya Darshan has come for you all, to fulfil the will of God by observing the Law of Eternity. Divya Darshan is meant for you all. In order to impart Divya Darshan, I have brought to you the essence of all spiritual knowledge and am presenting the same in a well-planned manner. I am imparting to you all essential knowledge of Satya Loka. If you do not accept this, you cannot get liberation so easily. Divya Darshan is replete with the essential spiritual knowledge for a harmonious and peaceful social living with truth, love and righteousness that will lead you to liberation. This is for the entire mankind and not only for a specific group or sect. You can realise the validity of my sayings once the level of your knowledge goes up. Let me repeat that I have come to impart this knowledge to the entire mankind irrespective of caste, creed and culture.

Your progress is slow. With your present level of knowledge, you are not able to understand what I say. If Divya Darshan is not accepted here, Guru will expound this somewhere else. Guru will relinquish his present body to be reborn in any other country for establishing Divya Darshan.

It is to be remembered that a realiser does not die. He assumes a physical body and leaves the same according to will. There are so many mysterious things here. I am not telling you all those because you may not believe.

You all must be wakeful in order to attain self-knowledge. Then only you will be liberated. My best wishes are always with you.

*****

[8]We, the people of present generation are well-qualified and consider ourselves quite knowledgeable. But whatever we know is quite insignificant. If man does not know Brahman, his knowledge is incomplete. Only after realising Brahman, nothing remains to be known. Therefore, everyone must conduct spiritual practice to realise Brahman. This is the first and foremost duty of man. This is his Dharma. Now the question is-Why we should know about God?

How were we all born? Who has made all these arrangements for our survival? Things have been created before for our smooth living and adequate knowledge has also been given to us for using those things. He, who has infused life into us, has also made all provisions for us so that we can live in happiness, peace, bliss and freedom. If we do not try to know Him, what else shall we know? It is essential for everyone to know Him. We have got this rare and fair form. The very purpose is to realise God. Our relationship with God is for ages. It is beginningless and eternal. Whatever knowledge is present in us by which we can live in peace and happiness and are able to do so many things are all possible because of Him. All knowledge belongs to God. The truth is that God Himself manifests as knowledge in every being. Since people do not have love and respect, they are neither able to understand God nor His role functions. The more you know about God, the more you shall be benefited. To get rid of sufferings, you should try to know its remedies. Without knowing what this suffering is, how it has come, how it would go, you would

[8] *Odia Divyadhara Vol 10 Page 1*

continue to suffer due to ignorance. Many persons, to get rid of sufferings, take the shelter of personal godheads. But it must be remembered that except God (Brahman), none can help you in this regard. None else can alleviate your sufferings except the Supreme God. He is all-powerful. None of the personal godheads can save you as they possess limited and specific powers. All scriptures assert that you should take shelter of the Supreme God from whom you have come. The entire Creation rests upon Him and is sustained by Him. He is the Supreme Lord Param-Brahman to whom everyone should pray for shelter. A person who is suffering does not know whom to worship to get rid of sufferings. He, therefore, worships blindly and does not get the desired result. Now in our society, this kind of blind worship is on the rise. It should be remembered that the personal godheads are there to obey the instructions of the Supreme Lord. They sincerely discharge their duties as ordained by the Supreme. Man does not understand the limitations of the personal godheads. In the puranas it is mentioned that there are always conflicts between the Devas and the Danavas. They are hostile to each other. The Devas possess sattvic qualities whereas the Danavas possess tamasic qualities. Since man stands in between the Devas and Danavas, he possesses tamasic as well as sattvic qualities. Normally he is in rajas. Hence it is quite clear that the Devas would not like someone with tamasic qualities. The persons who possess sattvic qualities would be liked by the Devas. Such men would get blessings and help from the Devas. The persons with tamasic qualities would not get the blessings from the Devas. Since man is primarily of rajasic qualities, the qualities like greed, attachment, desire, anger, pride and jealousy are normally seen in him. Sattvic men however possess noble qualities like compassion, piety, service, and many other virtues.

Now the question is whether we should hold on to the tamasic qualities or we should possess sattvic qualities full of divine virtues to get blessings from the Devas? What does our conscience dictate? Should we not go upwards? Should we slide downwards and invite more and more sufferings? Therefore, the sages have all along been advising us to inculcate sattvic qualities and get blessings from the divine powers. By outward worship, we get truly little. We reap the results of our own actions. But if we inculcate the divine qualities, we shall get more than what we get from outward worship; we get more and more of happiness, peace and bliss.

It is a matter of regret that although people have been worshipping various gods and goddesses for thousands of years, they possess truly little knowledge about the divine powers. Without knowing about the divine powers, what benefit can we get by only outward or superficial worship? The sages have mentioned so many things about the divine powers in the scriptures, but people do not evince interest in them. The divine powers are subtle. They always serve the Creation. In other words, they have been following the Law of Eternity and thereby obeying the commands of the Supreme. They are keen to carry out their specific responsibilities. But the common men by doing some outward worship consider themselves great and feel complacent. One must acquire spiritual knowledge in order to know not only the divine powers, but also the Supreme Lord. Real peace and happiness is there in spiritual knowledge. By acquiring spiritual knowledge, one will have desireless devotion towards the Almighty. Then only one will be able to get God's blessings and shall get rid of all sufferings. In course of time with acquisition of knowledge, one shall become a rishi and attain immortality. Just as a primary class student shall become a postgraduate and thereafter can become a Ph.D. one day, similarly a person who starts acquiring spiritual knowledge can get himself evolved to higher planes. Now a common man can become a sage if he acquires spiritual knowledge. A father knows that he was a child one day, but a child does not know that he would become a father one day. Every sage was a common man years before. It is certain that when someone acquires true knowledge, he can put an end to all his attachments and desires, get peace and bliss, and can get rid of all kinds of sufferings. In the olden days, the sages were living for thousands of years. They were also leading peaceful life. But today's man, despite his material prosperity and modern facilities, is not able to live beyond 60 to 70 years. The modern man is more beset with stresses and strains, doubts and apprehensions undergoing different kinds of sufferings. Spiritual knowledge alone can save us from disaster and bring us peace and happiness. Every conscientious person should think over this. This degeneration can be attributed to decline of spiritual knowledge in the society. Many are under the impression that a person who seeks spiritual knowledge has to leave his house, stay away from samsaric matters and must go to forest to make practices. Fact is that spiritual knowledge can be acquired anywhere even while leading a samsaric life. Only we should have a right attitude to acquire spiritual knowledge. It is to be remembered that unless man possesses the knowledge about how to earn peace and happiness, he cannot get peace and happiness wherever he may be. That is called heaven where there is peace and bliss. Hell is where there is misery and discontentment.

In the scriptures a lot of explanations have been given regarding jiva, Atman, Prakriti and Paramatman. Man is not able to understand the differences as well as unitariness of these terms. The sages realised that God is all-pervasive and all-powerful. Bhakta Prahlad's firm conviction about God's all-pervasiveness may be recollected here. But we are not certain about the existence of Atman inside us. We do not believe this statement also. The knowledge regarding the existence of Atman inside us is called spiritual knowledge i.e. self-knowledge. He, who is present eternally everywhere is also there inside us as Atman. When He is inside us, He is called Atman or Self. We are able to do everything because of Atman. Knowledge about Atman is called self-knowledge. Real peace comes only after realizing Atman. That realization of Atman is called *Moksa* or liberation. Man is suffering because he does not know his 'Self'. On the path to self-realization, man would crave for peace and bliss, and ultimately he would realise God. That state is liberated state. In other words, he, who would make efforts for realizing God, would attain peace, bliss and liberation. God expresses Himself as happiness, peace and bliss. Where God expresses Himself, there peace and bliss rule. God is the reservoir of all bliss and all wealth. He, who would realise God, shall possess all divine powers and divine glories.

First, we have to understand who God is. Who has been named as such? Scriptures have exhaustively described about God. Divya Darshan has been preaching, without using any scriptural jargon, about God in a very simple manner which is intelligible to the common man even. It does not matter whether he is a sanyasi or a householder. Spiritual knowledge contains everything. People are not able to understand and appreciate this. Out of ignorance they are wandering here and there to get peace and happiness. In their efforts to find peace and happiness, the ignorant men get some solace from temporary pleasure. But at a subsequent stage that temporary pleasure turns out to be their sufferings. It is to be remembered that no material knowledge can bring us real peace and bliss. Only spiritual knowledge can.

Self-knowledge is imparted by Sadguru. Everyone should approach Sadguru for self-knowledge. By self-knowledge, everyone can get rid of fear, anxiety and all sorts of sufferings. This is what Divya Darshan preaches.

*****

[9]Man is the best Creation of the Creator. After innumerable births, one has got human birth. Man is endowed with the power to know the past as well as future. Other creatures cannot know this. Both the demoniac qualities and divine virtues are present in man.

"God is inside me." This can be known only by possessing divine virtues. Man's predominant quality is rajas which is a combination of sattva and tamas. Usually man is rajasic in nature. He experiences both weal and woe. People of sattvic quality believe in the existence of God. There are human beings with animal instincts. There are also persons with demoniac qualities. There are persons with divine qualities. They are divine beings in the form of humans. Man gets elevated to sattvic quality after several human births. After possessing divine qualities, he gets convinced that God is there in all beings and believes in the all-pervasiveness of God.

Every human being must know that this human birth is only for knowing God. Only man can acquire true knowledge. By knowledge man can know so many things. By knowledge also he can know the existence of God in everyone's heart. When he realises that God is in his heart, he can attain God-realization. By acquiring knowledge, man can discriminate between good and bad. If he undertakes good works, he gets good results and becomes happy. According to Divya Darshan, man has the right to action. But the results are at the disposal of God. There is no doubt about the fact that man gets suitable results according to his actions. It is essential to know that

---

[9]*Odia Divyadhara Vol 19 Page 45*

Atman does not enjoy any fruits of action. Atman remains unattached from all actions. Due to jiva feelings or his sense of doership, man reaps the results of his own actions. When man comes to know that he is being activated by God, and controlled by God, he will be eligible to get God's blessings. Since man is not able to realise the greatness of God, he suffers. If he rises above jiva feelings, he will start getting happiness. Even if God is there in the man, due to ignorance he behaves at times no better than animals. At times, he betrays demoniac qualities. God, remaining inside, makes all sorts of arrangements for him to give him peace and happiness. Due to limited knowledge, man is not able to understand God's greatness.

During the childhood, some persons are able to recollect the happenings in their past birth. As they grow old, they forget all about it. One earns bliss when one realises the all-pervasiveness of Atman. The relationship between Atman and jiva are like that of light and shade. Jiva is searching for God outside but God is very much there inside. He is pure and uncontaminated even remaining inside. "I have been rewarded with human birth only to realise the Atman within." As man is not aware of this goal, he goes off track and gets entrapped in the cycle of birth and death.

Because there is Atman or Pure-Consciousness within, you are able to contemplate; experience and realise. When you are asleep, who wakes you up? He wakes you up. After you know His presence inside, you can also know His presence outside.

Those who realise Self, realise everything and get liberated. He is dearest to all. Everything becomes possible because of Him. But we are incurring sins by not evincing interest to know Him.

Atman is Peace-Absolute and Bliss-Absolute. He, who knows like this gets peace and becomes blissful. He, who knows that Atman is

Freedom-Absolute, attains freedom. "Try to know Atman and surrender to Him." This is what Divya Darshan repeatedly emphasizes on.

To realise Atman, pray for more knowledge and power which He will give. But all our activities are directed towards fulfilling our desires. We lead selfish life. One must be desireless to realise Him. We ask for wealth and properties. We ask for children. But we have never put strong faith on Him.

The sages teach us to undertake desireless karma. A mother takes care of her children, takes lots of pain and makes lots of sacrifices. She does everything for the children without any motive or desire. Our desires make us narrow and self-centred.

Following the instructions of Sadguru is essential. Guru's grace comes by that. Without His grace, Truth cannot be realised. Realizing Truth or observing Truth amounts to following Guru's instructions. We suffer because we do things that are not in conformity with Guru's instructions. God is there as the Truth and Law of Eternity. He, who will conduct himself in compliance with this Law, will receive His grace and attain Him. Once one attains Him, nothing remains to be known or attained. Hence everyone should surrender to Truth.

*****

[10]It is quite natural for anybody to consider himself knowledgeable even with scant knowledge. When man realises Brahman, nothing remains to be known. The common man thinks that only the knowledge pertaining to the mundane world is important and therefore the same should be acquired. He does not

---

[10]*Odia Divyadhara Vol 6 Page 6*

evince interest in acquiring spiritual knowledge, considering the same as different, extra and optional. He does not know the value of God. Therefore, many people do not attach importance to God. If one acquires spiritual knowledge, then only one would come to know about the importance and greatness of God. Why is it necessary to know God? We shall discuss below.

By whom are we born? Who has provided everything? Who has made all pre-arrangements for our survival? By whom are we able to maintain our lives?

Someone is there definitely who has made all arrangements for us. He has given us knowledge to maintain our bodies, live in society with peace and happiness. For happiness, peace, bliss and freedom whatever is required are all provided for by God. There is not even a slightest flaw or omission in God's arrangements. The ignorant man does not understand the role of God. That is why he suffers. If he could understand the perfect arrangements of God, he would have been totally benefited. The sages had realised God and that is why they call Him benevolent. Many people, without knowing the greatness of God, estrange themselves from God and land themselves in sorrows and sufferings.

The sages say that man has got the most intimate relationship with God although man does not know. True, everybody has intimate relationship with his parents but that is for one birth only. Our relationship with Guru is for innumerable births. Whatever knowledge we have in order to survive and to live in harmony in the society is all His contribution only. But since we do not possess that level of knowledge by which we can understand His contributions, we are suffering. If we acquire more and more knowledge about God, we can be benefited more and more. Without adequate knowledge, we are not able to know the perfect arrangements and provisions made by God as a result of which we are not able to enjoy things he has given us. We suffer ultimately. The more we know God, the more we get benefited. The more we know, the more we can acquire, possess and enjoy. God has made all provisions for all of us to live in peace and happiness and ultimately to go back to Him.

Due to lack of understanding about God's systematic plans and arrangements man is not able to utilise them as a result of which man suffers instead of living peacefully. By cursing sufferings, sufferings shall not go away. We must find suitable remedies for a cure from our maladies. To get rid of sufferings some people seek the help of personal godheads. Some seek help from the spirits. The personal godheads possess limited powers, but God is all-powerful. The scriptures exhort, "He, who has given you birth, also sustains. Take His shelter in order that you may get rid of sufferings. By Him, all movables and immovables in this world are sustained."

The sages who realised Brahman exhort mankind to take shelter of Brahman to get rid of sufferings. But we are not paying heed to their instructions. We are simply imitating others and practising some rituals in a mechanical manner. It should be remembered that the personal godheads are just like departmental heads of a large organisation who wield specific powers delegated to them by the Supreme Brahman for maintaining the Creation. They do only the allotted jobs.

In the mythologies we observe that there are so many instances of fights between the Devas and the demons. Knowledge is divided in three segments according to the three qualities such as sattva, rajas and tamas. Knowledge expresses itself through these three qualities and they create all variations.

- Sattva- It represents the qualities of goodness, knowledge and calmness; these are all noble qualities, or the qualities of the Devas.
- Rajas- It represents human qualities such as activity, passion and unrest; these are admixture of good and bad.
- Tamas- It represents darkness, inertia and delusion; these are demoniac qualities and also animal qualities.

Good qualities are divine qualities such as love, renunciation, service, righteousness etc. The opposite qualities are greed, infatuation, anger, jealousy etc. Man is in the middle state. Therefore, the qualities of the Devas and the demons are seen in him in varying proportions. Now-a-days, there is predominance of tamasic practices because of which man is undergoing more and more sufferings. If man would just upgrade himself to sattvic qualities, Satya yug would prevail and man can live in happiness, peace and bliss.

The demons are the traditional enemies of the Devas. Hence Devas do not like the demons. If man possesses demoniac qualities and worships personal godheads, he will not get blessings from them. Devas are of sattvic qualities; they would not accept our tamasic offerings; they take nectar and not the common diets which we humans take. They do not accept the food we offer to them. That is why we are not getting blessings from them. We always get the fruits of our actions. If we possess divine qualities, we can easily have access to Devas and get their blessings. If our conduct is not in commensurate with divine qualities, we shall not be accepted by them. The sages had possessed and were utilising the divine qualities. Therefore, things happened as they wished. Devas are always supportive to the sages. In fine, it can be said that if man would possess divine qualities, he would get rid of all sufferings.

That is why the sages have all along been advising us to acquire divine qualities and spiritual knowledge by which we can get rid of all sufferings, tensions and unrest. The various ways and means, tricks and techniques for getting rid of sufferings and living in peace and bliss are there in spiritual knowledge. Due to want of spiritual knowledge man is suffering. The more he acquires spiritual knowledge, the more he gets rid of sufferings and enjoys peace and bliss. Spiritual knowledge is imparted in various stages keeping in view the receptivity of the recipient or his standard of knowledge. The last lesson of spiritual knowledge is one of self-experience. A father knows that he was a child one day. But the child does not know that he would become a father one day. Persons with lower level of knowledge cannot comprehend higher knowledge. Divya Darshan says, "The power by which one can realise Truth is knowledge." Truth cannot be realised without knowledge power. So far as spiritual knowledge is concerned, the present mankind is in its infancy. A child neither understands himself nor the world. Man considers himself as quite knowledgeable. Since he is deluded, it does not occur to him that something higher remains to be learnt.

We have heard that people of olden days were living longer, even for thousand years but in the present age, the average life span is 60 to 70 years. This indicates that man does not know how to live longer. Man suffers from several diseases mainly due to irregular food habits and thereby his life span gets shortened. Social harmony is also awfully lacking. Man is not able to live in peace and happiness as feeling of respect for each other is missing. There is groupism everywhere leading to continual fights among themselves. Family life also gets worsened due to absence of divine qualities. We create more and more enemies by quarrelling with each other. Due to want of spiritual knowledge, we do not know what our goal is. If the final goal is borne in mind, life can be made simple and disciplined. We shall not go astray. Many people think that they are to leave samsara and go to forests or mountain caves to acquire spiritual knowledge but that is not correct. For acquiring knowledge only inquisitiveness is essential. He, who would try to know, would know. He, who possesses inquisitiveness for true knowledge and divine virtues, would earn happiness, peace and bliss. This is called heaven.

In the scriptures many concepts like Jiva, Prakriti, and Atman are described. These are all the different stages of manifestation of the unitary and all-powerful Supreme Existence. This Creation is pervaded by Atman. Atman is there inside and outside. The knowledge pertaining to Atman is called spiritual knowledge. If a man acquires knowledge to ensure his survival by maintaining his body, social living by inculcating divine qualities, he can ultimately realise God. This shows that there is intimate relationship between God and bliss. In other words, where there is peace and bliss, there is God.

Devarshi Narada approached and implored Guru Sanat Kumar to let him know the reason for not getting peace though he had mastered all scriptures and kept regular contact with God.

Guru Sanat Kumar replied, "You are yet to acquire Self-Knowledge. Without Self-Knowledge peace is not possible."

Self-Knowledge is knowledge about the Self. One must try to acquire this knowledge which is true knowledge. Then only peace and bliss shall prevail.

*****

[11]Man can attain God through this human body whereas other living species cannot. Having earned lot of virtues in the past births,

---

[11]*Odia Divyadhara Vol 19 Page 49*

man has got this rarest form. Therefore, man should live his life consciously and carefully. Some people believe that after death nothing remains. They discard the theory of rebirth. It should be remembered that man is born due to his past actions. Future will also be determined by his present actions. A virtuous man gets a very congenial and suitable environment after his death to further his quest of self-realization. On the other hand, a sinner is reborn after his death as a lower or demoniac creature. This is the law of nature which is of universal application.

Every moment, we are passing through vices and virtues. Man must deliberately try to increase his virtues and shun the sins. Everyone wants to go up and not down. A man will not like to be reborn as an animal or a demon. He should therefore choose his actions very consciously. If man is conscious of virtue and vice, he will try to avoid vice. This means, any whimsical style of living with pleasure seeking temperament will surely bring us sufferings here and hereafter.

Unknowingly we kill so many tiny creatures during our routine work like cooking, ploughing and even walking. The scriptures prescribe Panchayajna or five kinds of sacrifices to atone for the sins thus committed. Out of the five sacrifices or yajna, Brahman yajna is the most important yajna. It is also known as jnana yajna or rishi yajna. Man can get rid of all sins and sufferings. The other sacrifices are bhuta yajna, atithi yajna, pitru yajna, and deva yajna.

When we sacrifice a part of our food for the sake of birds and animals, it becomes bhuta yajna. Serving the guests who may come to our house without prior notice is atithi yajna. We can earn virtues by making sacrifices for the parents and Devas, and by sincerely obeying their instructions. Many people do not know the importance of these sacrifices. These sacrifices should be our way of life because of which our vices will get reduced and virtues will increase. We will get blessings from our parents and also Devas by which we will get peace and happiness. Since we are unmindful about vices and virtues, there is every chance that we may be committing many sins in our day to day lives. How sure we are that we would get human birth next time? If our vices outweigh our virtues how shall we be reborn as humans or as better humans? Are we not suffering now for our past vices? How to get rid of sufferings? There are many religions with different ways and opinions. People of all religions are praying for peace and happiness. They are praying to get rid of sufferings. There are so many temples, mosques, and churches. Different forms of worship and prayer are there. Many religious activities are performed on a regular basis. But, where is peace? Why sufferings are still there? Some people believe that God will forgive us and shall release us from any amount of sins. But why there has ben no solution so far?

There is Law of Karma. As you sow, so you reap. Every action has got equal and opposite reaction. Good work will get us good result. Bad work will give us bad results.

We should repent for our past mistakes and vow not to repeat the same. We must take to righteous path and earn virtues instead of vices. Then only we will be happy. Our sufferings will go away. It is clear from this that we cannot easily escape from our sins by asking God to forgive us. If God will simply forgive us, will not sins be on the rise? Is there any certainty that people will become good after God forgives them? What about habitual criminals? Will not they be encouraged to increase the intensity and frequency of their crimes?

We do not know whether we are committing more vices or earning more virtues in our day to day lives. We just make our living. We just want to enjoy our lives. If things go on in this process for ages together also, we will not know for sure if we have been free from sins.

We all acquire knowledge. We consider ourselves very knowledgeable. This is our ignorance or effects of Maya. Maya will give us sufferings and will obstruct the way to higher knowledge. The children also assert that they know more than their parents. The children cannot know where their mistakes lie. Only an elderly person can point out the mistakes. The children can know their own mistakes when they grow up. The sages and wise men know more than we know. They can find out where we go wrong but we ourselves cannot know our own mistakes.

From the scriptures also we get right knowledge. But we should not only read but live up to the scriptural prescriptions. After proper understanding of the scriptures we get knowledge, truth and righteousness. Without having any knowledge about what right is and what wrong is, one will be susceptible to do wrong things. Some wrong doings are corrected when we grow in age and gather experience. Some new mistakes or wrongdoings also affect us. Unless Truth is realised completely, it is sure that flaws will remain in our activities throughout. A student's mistakes are pointed out by the teacher as he possesses higher knowledge. Similarly if we approach sages or Sadguru for right knowledge, they can mend our ways by imparting knowledge. By simply worshipping or imploring in a holy place, one may not get the right knowledge. The Deva whom we worship cannot breach the Law of Karma. We are bound to reap good results for our good actions and bad results for our bad actions. Therefore, we must consciously choose our actions so that we will not commit sins to suffer as a result.

Today's man has distanced himself from right knowledge or true knowledge as he does not evince interest in knowledge. It is seen that people construct new temples in the names of some new gods and goddesses of their imagination, and start worshipping them. But who can save us from our wrongdoings or sins committed by us knowingly or unknowingly? Some people ultimately become atheists when their desires remain unfulfilled. God of our imagination cannot save us. God cannot give us a chocolate even. We are not interested to know about the real God. The Vedas and Upanishads teach us who God is. He is different from the God of our imagination.

In other words, the God who is made by us (by our imagination) cannot protect us. He, who has made us, can protect us. The Almighty, who is all-pervasive and all-powerful, can do everything. He remains as Pure-Consciousness everywhere. He manifests as everything in the Creation. He is there as our knowledge and strength. God of our imagination cannot give us cooked food. But by our acquired knowledge, we can prepare food for hundreds. It is not necessary to ask for anything from God. He has already provided everything. He has also given knowledge to use the materials. He, who knows Him, will get more and more.

But we are after the God of our imagination. How will sufferings go away? Scriptures say that Brahman is Peace-Absolute, Bliss-Absolute and Freedom-Absolute. He has fulfilled all our needs. He has created everything for our well-being. We are created by Him. We survive due to Him. We do everything after getting all energies from Him. We plan and execute everything by the knowledge He has endowed on us. Everything is becoming possible only because of Him. Man is not able to understand Him. Without knowing about Him, man expects a lot of things from Him. How will man get? He has been providing all essential things to us. For example, before a baby is born, there is provision of milk at the disposal of the mother. For everything He creates, He makes all prior arrangements for the sustenance of the creatures. If man can know about His greatness, he will be eager to realise God. It is beyond his imagination what he will get after attaining or realizing God.

To get rid of sufferings one must take the shelter of God. The more one knows about Him, the more peaceful and blissful he becomes. But God of our imagination cannot give us anything. Therefore, the atheists are rather more knowledgeable than the blind believers. The atheists do not believe in the man-created Gods. However, the atheists stop at this point and do not try to understand and appreciate the scriptural instructions as laid down in the Vedas and the Upanishads regarding Brahman and His greatness. It is all right if they do not indulge in idol worship. But they should not restrict themselves to that much only. There are still higher things to know about the existence of Brahman i.e. Reality.

In absence of adequate knowledge, most of our actions become faulty. We do not try to know how to do things in the right manner that will give us good results. Apologizing to God after committing wrongs after wrongs will not help. Remember that the Law of Karma is effectual and operates impartially.

Lord Buddha says that when there is suffering, there is a cause of suffering. Suffering which has come must go. In other words, there will be cessation of suffering also. There is also a cause for the suffering to go away. The moment the man will realise the truth behind suffering, he will get rid of sufferings. If we do not try to know the cause of sufferings, how will sufferings go away? One must try to know where the fault remains. He must try to find out ways and means to come out of sufferings. Instead of that, he relies more upon some divine miracles to happen. To get rid of sufferings, we should know the Law of Eternity and observe the same. There are ways to get rid of sufferings. Man must acquire more and more virtues and refrain from committing sins. If we are of tamasic nature, we should make efforts to become rajasic and further from rajasic to sattvic. Normally men are of rajasic nature. They tell truth and also take recourse to falsehood. In other words, man possesses both demoniac qualities and divine qualities. In other words, man stands in between Devas and demons. We must consciously try to move towards sattva. When man will possess divine qualities, he will not suffer. Divine qualities will bring peace and happiness. By possessing asuric qualities, which means all sorts of negative qualities like greed, anger, malice, and deceptiveness, one cannot live peacefully. Shrimad Bhagavad-Gita lays stress on divine qualities. The kingdom of nature is replete with divine qualities. There are many divine qualities. Some of these qualities are discussed below. They are-Renunciation, restraint, spiritual practice, service, truth, love and forgiveness. The Creation is sustained by the divine qualities. If a mother will not love and serve her babies, they will not survive. We are all brought up by divine qualities. Similarly, father also serves us. We get service from many others like soldiers, engineers, doctors, nurses, teachers, farmers etc., in the society and we are benefited. We are served by the plants and animals also. The tigress also takes care of her cubs. Divine qualities are the underlying principles of the Creation otherwise there would have been no Creation.

Some people think that if they tell the truth, they cannot survive. But they expect others to tell truth. They expect to be loved by others. If we are benefited by service, love, and truth etc., others will also be benefited by us if we possess those qualities. For example, during our travel when we ask others about the correct route in a junction, and if he gives us a wrong direction, will we not be in trouble? If the doctor prescribes a wrong medicine out of greed or anger, will the same not harm us? Similarly, if a bus changes its route without prior notice, will not many people be inconvenienced? If our children cheat us, wife does not tell the truth and if the earning member of the family instead of going to his work place goes for gambling, can there be peace in the family? Food is prepared and kept ready by the mother relying on the fact that the children will come back from school or husband will come back from work place at a particular time. We live in peace when everything occurs in an orderly manner. Even the thieves also observe some truth. They faithfully distribute their booties among themselves according to the agreed plan. The gang breaks away when there is a breach of trust. Man is not able to realise the importance of truth even though he lives by truth. Where there is deviation, there is suffering. We want the court to decide on the truth. When there is a breach of justice, we pray to the Court for restoration of justice. Any misunderstanding means not understanding the truth properly. This shows how important it is to observe the truth sincerely and honestly. Otherwise we cannot live in peace and happiness.

Likewise, love and forgiveness are also important and essential divine qualities. We forgive the child for his mistakes. Had we not forgiven him, he would not have survived. There are many instances of intolerance of the demons killing their children. Forgiveness is a divine quality which the demons do not have. We have committed so many mistakes, but our parents have forgiven us due to their divine qualities. When we quarrel among ourselves, someone mediates and calms us down due to the quality of forgiveness. The animal kingdom remains protected by divine qualities. Divine qualities are the gifts to us from the Creator. Everyone is gifted with divine qualities. Divine qualities are quietly present in the kingdom of nature. But we are not aware that we are surviving because of the divine qualities. He, who possesses divine qualities, enjoys peace and happiness. But due to ignorance, we go on begging before God for something or other. God must be smiling at us, having already given us the divine qualities since our birth for our survival, peace, bliss, and freedom. If we want to be blissful, we must possess the divine quality of love. We must love others so that we shall get love from others. Then only we shall remain happy. Without this quality how can God give us bliss? Bliss is to be experienced by us in us. It is not a gross matter which can be purchased or borrowed from others. Our latent quality of love will bring us peace and bliss. On the other hand, if we are malicious, arrogant, and violent, how can we get peace and bliss? Similarly, if we serve others, we will be served by others. If we serve one, we will be served by many. Once we ignite divine qualities in us, from all sides it will come back to us multiplied. Whatever we need, everything can be achieved by divine qualities which are present in the kingdom of nature. But due to ignorance we do not develop our divine qualities from within as a result of which we suffer in many ways and ultimately, we pray God to save us.

Many people think that by acquiring wealth, they will be recognized and honoured in the society. But how many people will love us after getting money or some material objects from us? Our money will get exhausted. Then what? But if we are of loving nature, thousands will love us. In other words, divine qualities are our greatest assets. This Earth can be a heaven if everyone realises the value of divine qualities and consciously try to develop the same from within. If people utilize these divine qualities, Kali Yug will go away yielding place to Satya Yug. By spending money we cannot acquire divine qualities. Can love and forgiveness be purchased? This is how the sages were enjoying peace, bliss, and freedom. Material wealth is temporary which may be lost or stolen. Anybody who possesses divine qualities is supported by the Devas. They are nearer and ready to help us. But since we do not know the secrets of divine qualities, we are not getting their help. Many persons break down under the pressure of wants. They do not arouse divine qualities in them. They do not take interest in acquiring true knowledge either. Man must develop divine qualities to get rid of sufferings. Therefore, the sages wear smiling faces whereas people in general look dejected. In fine, it can be said that none can help us to enjoy peace, bliss and freedom unless we ourselves try to know and practice the Laws of the Creator by which the whole Creation is being governed.

*****

[12]It is an admitted fact that every action has got equal and opposite reaction. This is the Law of Eternity. Good deeds yield good results. Even God cannot negate or nullify this. Likewise, bad deeds are followed by baneful results. Results are always linked to all types of actions in this Creation. This Law is applicable to all including matters, plants and animals, humans and even up to Ishwar. Results are certain. One should not disbelieve this. Our good or bad intentions, good or bad actions, beliefs or disbeliefs are bound to come back to us as good or bad results. But it is unpredictable when the results would come. A series of changes do take place in the kingdom of nature and ultimately the results therefrom affect us. Therefore, Divya Darshan emphasises on good deeds. Good deeds bring us peace, bliss and ultimately freedom on self-realisation. Hence Divya Darshan lays stress on "Divine thoughts, divine expressions and divine actions." If we habitually and consciously continue with good things of life, everything good shall come back to us from every side.

Therefore, to be a good person, one must have good thoughts, good action, good conduct and good expression. We are not conscious of these good aspects of a good life. All actions yield

---

[12]*Odia Divyadhara Vol 8 Page 17*

results; nothing goes waste. We must remain careful about this. Attaining goodness would lead to attainment of God. No extra effort is required for attainment of God. Therefore, without wasting a moment, we should know what goodness is and consciously cling to goodness. This means, we should arouse inquisitiveness to know what goodness is. This would pave the way to God-realisation. Since we are not trying to know what goodness is, we are not able to lead our life well and realise God. That is why we suffer. Man wants to live in peace and happiness. But the basis of it is goodness. If we do not know what goodness is and do not apply goodness in our day to day life, how can we get peace and happiness? Practising goodness shall make one good. Many people are making spiritual efforts to attain God but due to ignorance about this simple technique, they are not able to achieve success. The sages and realisers know this and that is why they have been imparting true knowledge. If we try to acquire true knowledge, we can know what goodness is. Jagadguru Shankaracharya also laid emphasis on knowledge. Buddhist philosophy also lays emphasis on knowledge. God is good. God expresses Himself as goodness. The basis of goodness is Brahman, Atman, Dharma, Truth and Justice. Specific powers of God are called personal godheads. Aggregate of all these is Sat-Chit-Ananda. It is further explained that what we call 'Sat' is not Brahman. That Existence was there before. After realising that Existence who is Consciousness-Absolute, the sages have termed the same as 'Sat'. 'Sat' expresses himself as 'Chit'. After realising that Existence termed 'Sat', the sages also named him as 'Chit'. 'Chit' is Bliss-Absolute. After realising this, we ascribe the term 'Ananda' to Him. Hence, the terms 'Sat', 'Chit' and 'Ananda' are the terms ascribed to Him at a subsequent stage i.e. after realising His Existence. This means, He is different from 'Sat' or 'Chit' or 'Ananda'. 'Sat' means, what was there, what is and what shall remain. By the term 'Sat' the sages simply point out that Existence named as Param-Brahman. He cannot be pointed out by means of any language. Hence the realisers concluded by saying 'Neti Neti'. Only to explain that unmanifest Existence, He is termed as Sat- Swarup, Chit-Swarup and Ananda-Swarup. The sages have adopted various means to explain or describe the unmanifest Existence. The term 'Sat' only points out His Existence. Hence it is said in scriptures that Brahman is neither 'Sat' nor 'Asat'.

That unmanifest Existence is called Param-Brahman. The source, from where we have all come is called Brahman. Different stages of His manifestation are named as Ishwar, personal godheads, different animals, plants and matters. The Vedas cannot point out Him. Only his manifestations and greatness are explained in the Vedas. Simply by knowing some terminology one cannot realise Him. Very few people realise True Self. True Self is far from the scriptural narratives or wise men's articulations. To realise the unmanifest Existence is called real siddhi. There is no language to express.

After realising Brahman, Sadguru Sri Sri Arjun took about 5 years to realise Param-Brahman. Only His manifested states can be talked about but not the True Self which is far beyond.

The greatness of Brahman

[13]Vedanta Darshan extols the unity of jiva and Brahman. But to explain things, dualistic approach is to be resorted to and therefore it has been said that, the jiva is a part and parcel of Brahman. But with increase in knowledge one can appreciate that the jiva is none

[13] *Odia Divyadhara Vol 7 Page 7*

other than Brahman. Since we have not reached that level, we consider ourselves as different from Brahman.

It has been mentioned in the scriptures that Brahman is Happiness-Absolute, Peace-Absolute and Bliss-Absolute. True, we do not consider ourselves as Brahman. But it is a fact that we constantly seek happiness, peace and bliss. This clearly indicates that we instinctively seek Brahman i.e. True Self.

When we suffer, at that time we try to wriggle out of sufferings and try to get ever-flowing happiness, peace and bliss. Since we are in physical forms, the sufferings pertaining to the physical bodies come at periodic intervals. There is a subtle body inside the physical body. The subtle body does not have the feelings of hunger and thirst. Jiva is a combination of 17 tattva with different qualities. The qualities a jiva possesses correspond to his form. Like form, like qualities. Like qualities, like forms. Although man undertakes his works in order that he may get peace and happiness, he very often lands up in sufferings due to inadequate knowledge about the sources of peace and happiness. Suffering is not our true nature. Our true nature is Peace-Absolute and Bliss-Absolute. We are suffering since we have forgotten the True Self. The sages have taught us that by knowing God, we can get peace and happiness. So, they have imparted various instructions on how to know God. They have taught us to believe in God, to have devotion and ultimately to surrender to God. Unless we take shelter of God, we can never get peace and happiness. By knowing God only, man can get rid of all sufferings. The sages have prescribed different stages of knowledge for different recipients so that man would become inquisitive to know more and more about God. Hence spiritual knowledge ranges from primary stage to the highest state. God is pure and taintless. Many types of social functions and rituals are there so that the common man can connect himself to God through all these. Different kinds of worship and rituals are there in different religious places to take man Godward. God is good. If man keeps contact with 'Good', he will become good. There are many ways to become 'good'. In fact, goodness is God. Everywhere there is the presence of goodness. God is helping us through goodness. Since we do not know His importance or greatness, we do not believe Him. Good qualities are also known as divine whereas bad qualities are demoniac. By good qualities only everything exists. By goodness, we not only maintain our bodies, we also get peace and happiness.

Wherever there is goodness', Lord Vishnu is there. Wherever Lord Vishnu is there, Goddess Laxmi is bound to be there. In other words, wherever there is goodness, both Laxmi and Vishnu reside there. It is futile to hope for good things of life by means of demoniac qualities. Since we are not conscious of all these techniques, we disbelieve God and lead reckless life. We become atheists.

After the Creation, three aspects are functional such as creation, sustenance and dissolution. For this, Brahman manifests as Brahma, Vishnu and Maheswar, the female consorts of whom are Goddess Saraswati, Goddess Laxmi and Goddess Kali respectively.

After we take birth, we take food for our survival. Mother Laxmi plays her role in this regard. Whatever ingredients are necessary for survival are all given to us by Mother Laxmi. The more we know about her powers, the more we would be benefited. Laxmi Shakti is everywhere around us but due to paucity of knowledge we are not able to know her powers. Hence if anything is to be begged of God, it is knowledge and only knowledge. By knowledge, we can understand the significance of everything and would be able to get benefited from the same. Man is always placed on the lap of the Mother energy. He can do everything by Her Power. The scientists after understanding the energy can do wonderful things. The power is there inside us and all around us. Mother Goddess represents knowledge power that helps us to understand and utilise things. The knowledge power guides us throughout in the form of mother, father, teachers and various books etc. When we contemplate on something at times, we get the answers from within. That means, Goddess Saraswati, the knowledge power is inside us also. For creation of different forms and qualities some knowledge is involved. For transformation or dissolution also the knowledge power is involved called Maheswar whose female consort is Kali. With limited knowledge an ordinary man cannot understand these things. We should understand that Brahman has manifested as all the above powers and have been creating, sustaining and transforming things perfectly well for further evolution to perfection. Tears would come out when one realises the role of Brahman, more so when he remembers Him and His all-inclusive contributions towards the Creation. The sages had realised this and that is why they were living blissfully. But the ignorant men due to lack of knowledge and lack of interest in God know little and therefore they suffer. Spiritual knowledge starts from faith and ends up with self-realisation. He, who knows about His existence, contribution and True Self, would be blessed more and more and shall ultimately attain liberation. The gist of Chhandogya Upanishad is- "The more the knowledge, the more one advances. The more one advances, the more one unveils and enjoys."

Every man, after knowing that Brahman is Peace-Absolute, Bliss-Absolute and Freedom-Absolute, can peacefully and blissfully live and realise the True Self. This is the duty and Dharma of every individual.

*****

[14]The sages and seers having realised Atman, have stated that "Self can be realised by self". It is a matter of self-realisation. By mere reading and getting scriptures by heart, Atman cannot be realised. Even though Atman is there inside everybody, man is not able to realise it. All the matters and the five gross elements are manifested forms of Atman. Atman also manifests as conscience, ego, mind and senses. Therefore, Atman cannot be known by senses, mind and intellect. By conscience (Viveka) only some glimpses of Atman can be experienced. Scriptures as well as the sages reiterate the existence, all-pervasiveness and omnipotence of Atman. Many of you believe in the existence of Atman. By believing in the existence of Brahman or Atman, and knowing about His greatness, there would be changes in our conduct and behaviour. Everything is created from Atman and ultimately gets merged with Atman. This man would one day regain his completeness or perfection. This is what the realised sages affirm. Seed becomes a tree and again returns to its original form of a seed. Similar is the water cycle. The water in the ocean gets converted to vapour and forms cloud. It rains and ultimately mingles with the ocean. Man will one day realise that he is none other than Atman. That is called self-realisation. But Atman is different from all names, forms and qualities that constitute the Creation. From all these multiplicities, we get some indication about the existence of a Creator. Many people claim, after reading and understanding some points from the scriptures, that they know Atman. The sages say, "Atman can be known and cannot be known." This statement conveys a deep meaning. He, who is simple and humble and has a strong inclination to know Atman, can realise Atman by the grace of Atman. By mere reading and listening, self-realisation is not possible. A good amount of spiritual efforts, strong inquisitiveness and eagerness is required to realise Atman. He, who prays Him only for

---

[14] *Odia Divyadhara Vol 7 Page 12*

fulfilment of desires, cannot realise Him. Our thoughts and actions are reflected as His blessings. Like thoughts, like results. Since people are steeped in desires, they are unable to attain Atman or Brahman. Brahman expresses Himself as and through the Laws. The Laws are ever operative. With all eagerness when someone tries to know the truth and keeps himself always conscious of his goal, he will be able to realise Him ultimately. All our thoughts and actions come back to us as reward or blessings. Whole day for 24 hours, one should try to contemplate on Atman. Whatever work is done, everything is for attaining Atman. This thought must be borne in mind always. Once Atman is realised, the realiser can feel that he is there in everybody and everywhere. When the Sun is reflected on various water pots, it appears as many due to reflection. Even if the electric energy is one, it works in different appliances for different purposes. Even if Brahman is one, He manifests as many due to different names, forms and qualities He assumes.

The Atman is One and indivisible. He is there in everyone. Atman is a subject of self-experience. It cannot be seen by our gross eyes. We are suffering. Suffering has no gross form. But after experiencing suffering a name has been ascribed to it. He is the only basis of everything else. He is also the medium. He is the effects also. Aggregation of smallest of particles like atoms and molecules forms planets and stars. Every atom is an abode of Atman. Every cell of the body is an abode of Atman. That is why everything exists. There are three types of rays such as Alpha, Beta and Gamma which are emitted by the atoms. Their subtleness is such that they can move or pass through any other matters. Atman being present even inside the atoms, it is almost impossible to comprehend the subtlety of Atman.

There are many colours in the space. Air contains many gases with many atoms and molecules. There would be nothing called air if the gases and the atoms are removed. All stars and planets are created from out of space. A common man does not understand the intricacies of the Creation. Space is subtler than air. Atman is also there in the space. How tiniest Atman is, cannot be expressed. Space is everywhere and contains everything. Atman is all-pervasive like space which is inside and also outside. Realising all these, the sages asserted that Atman exists everywhere in the Creation, even inside space. It is the subtlest existence. Hence it is present in all beings and matters. What we call void is also full, full of Atman. Because man is not able to realise the greatness of Brahman, he is suffering. Once he would realise that he is the Atman-Absolute, he would be free from sufferings. Shrimad Bhagavad-Gita says, Atman cannot be burnt by fire, cannot be wetted by water, cannot be dried by air and cannot be cut by sword. The reason is that there is Atman in water, fire, air and earth. In that case, how can Atman be destroyed? Atman or Brahman manifests in various forms and qualities. Atman is all in all. Hence it is said that Atman can be realised by Atman only. Therefore, we must know first who Atman is. Then only we should make spiritual efforts to realise Him and get rid of all sufferings.

*****

[15]This Creation is a manifestation of Brahman. We see gross objects because those are perceivable by our senses. Our senses cannot experience the vast subtle kingdom. The substances a man is composed of, are all present outside also. Energy or knowledge is present everywhere in this Creation. That energy has taken the form of all physical forms including the human form. Consciousness is present in all matters and all beings somewhere active and

---

[15]*Odia Divyadhara Vol 15 Page 23*

somewhere inert or static. Before manifesting as gross forms, the Creator has manifested as many subtle stages by modifications and combinations in a well-organized manner consistently and coherently in conformity with the Law of Eternity.

Five great elements such as earth, water, fire, air and ether are gross. Knowledge is involved in the process of creation, operation and transmutation. In other words, the entire Creation is a manifestation of knowledge. Our senses can perceive truly little from the entire Creation. Around 90% of the things in this Creation are invisible. Man cannot see Devas, ghosts and different spirits. Out of the five gross elements, air and ether are also invisible. The gross world constitutes only one quarter whereas the subtle world constitutes three quarters. By means of knowledge, we can experience so many things including the subtle. By knowledge, we can say whether it is a plant or animal, earth or water. By intellect, the fourth state of matter can be realised. The super-sensual state begins from the fourth state of matter. Buddhitattva is Mahatattva. It is to be understood that the fourth state of matter has ultimately taken gross forms. But man is unable to see the fourth state of the matter since it is beyond the receptivity of senses. In the fourth state, due to the orbiting of the electrons, different rays radiate out. These gross forms or the visible universe of varying objects are made of the rays. To realise the fourth state, intellect is not enough. Conscience is necessary to comprehend the fourth state.

Buddhitattva or Mahatattva emanates from 'Om' or conscience. Intellect comes thereafter. Mind comes next. By whom and why the fourth state of matter gets organized or regulated? This subject comes under the ambit of conscience which is beyond intellect, mind or senses.

Had there been no tri-qualities, all these forms and qualities would not have been there. The knowledge about the tri-qualities can be had only in conscience level. Beyond conscience there is Atman or Self. Since Atman is there everywhere and in everything, it is to be understood that everything of this Creation is in the Self. It must be understood that everything has emanated from the tri-qualities. It cannot be said which quality of the tri-qualities (sattva, rajas and tamas) came first. The scriptures explain that sattva is of conscience level. Rajas is of intellect level. Tamas is of mind level. Thereafter gross forms were created. After gross forms, what will happen? The answer is - there was Creation; there shall be transformation or dissolution. All will ultimately get dissolved in the source from which they emanated. At the time of dissolution or deluge, tamas will get merged with rajas; rajas will get merged with sattva. Beyond sattva there is a unique state which is beyond all qualities. This state is that of liberation.

As told earlier, on the disequilibrium of the tri-qualities, the Creation begins. For creation, consciousness is an essential pre-condition. In other words, we experience the forms and qualities which are but different stages of consciousness. Consciousness remains everywhere as knowledge. Consciousness and knowledge are one and the same. While the term consciousness is also used in respect of the insentient objects and lower animals, it is equally applicable to the humans. The term, 'knowledge' is mostly used in respect of explaining and understanding things.

When electrons revolve, at that time three rays namely, Alpha, Beta and Gamma are radiated. X-ray is not visible to our eyes, but it can penetrate through our bones. Gamma ray is so powerful that it can even penetrate a six inch thick lead plate. These rays are all invisible. The Creation is based on tri-qualities. One must be conscientious to understand the Creation. Until man frees himself from the influence of tri-qualities, he cannot be free.

Tantra science deals with the fourth state of matter. Tantra works at that level. It is a subject matter of conscience level. I (Sadguru Sri Sri Arjun) bless you all to transcend mind and intellect and be in the state of conscience to move forward towards the goal.

*****

[16]The gross Creation has come from the subtle. The gross ultimately merge with the subtle. The subtle things are more expansive than the gross. The wise have explained about Brahman's manifestation by saying that He willed to be many. If a man does not know the subtle, he cannot be subtle. He will remain confined to the gross. The gross undergo changes. Therefore, those are temporary or passing phases. But the Truth is changeless. Not realizing the Truth is Maya. Since you are in illusion, you generally consider the gross as truth. You get yourselves attached to the gross without knowing the background which is the subtlemost Existence. Therefore, you suffer just like fear overwhelms you after seeing a rope but misconstruing the same as a snake. Although there is no snake, the idea of snake gets superimposed on the rope. People shout and cry for nothing.

*****

[17]Whether man can attain Brahman by simply contemplating on Him? The answer is an emphatic 'yes'. Coal becomes diamond after thousands of years. Water becomes ice and ice becomes water. Some changes occur fast and some changes are time taking.

---

[16]*Odia Divyadhara Vol 20 Page 36*
[17] *Odia Divyadhara Vol 15 Page 30*

Those, who have realised Brahman, try to explain about Brahman. Brahman is a naming word. That means there is a state attaining which the realisers have named it as Brahman. What you realise or experience, you are that. That knowledge or realization always remains in you. He, who does not know what bliss is, cannot be blissful by simply going through some books. A student of class V cannot understand the subject matter, or the courses taught to class IX students. This is because the student of class V has not gone up to that standard. If he understands, it must be accepted that he has the standard of a class IX student. It means, whatever we can understand now, our standard is that much, and we are that. If we do not understand the subject matter of higher classes, we are not that because we have not attained that level of knowledge.

Gold cannot be iron. Iron cannot be gold. They cannot be blended. Gold can be blended with gold only. Iron can be blended with iron. It is because the atomic compositions of gold and iron are different.

Man has come from Brahman passing through various stages. Man's form is different. That is why man considers himself as jiva. If man can come out of the jiva mindset by upgrading his knowledge and thoughts, he will be able to realise Brahman. Because we wear human forms, we identify ourselves with our respective bodies. We live with jiva feelings and die also with jiva feelings. The jiva feelings are carried over to the next birth. In the process of manifestation, there are gradations of knowledge from one form to another. By acquisition of true knowledge, jiva feelings can be replaced by divine feelings. Hence, a person who has so far been considering himself as a jiva can also experience in him a divine being after gaining knowledge by spiritual practices. In other words, when a jiva transcends his mind, intellect and the tri-qualities, he can attain the highest level which is Brahman. It must be remembered that thoughts of Brahman manifest as infinite forms and qualities in this Creation. All manifested things undergo continuous changes to ultimately go back to the state of Brahman from which everything has emanated.

Once a person reaches a higher level, the thoughts of the higher level will be expressed through him. His conduct will also change. It means, the different manifested stages of Brahman appear as thoughts. Forms and qualities are based on bhava. Example- Vapour, water and ice are different forms or stages of water. In different stages, qualities also differ. Thus, Brahman manifests in different forms such as man, animal, bird, water, fire and air etc. All these manifested stages are subject to changes. A brick cannot mix with soil. Brick has a different shape and colour. If a brick is broken to pieces and crushed to dust, then only, it can mix with the soil. Jiva in order to get united with Brahman must relinquish his negative qualities, acquire true knowledge and inculcate divine virtues to move to the highest state.

Your thought is the indicator of your level. Higher the level better is the quality of thought. You are the thoughts. Guard yourself against any negative thoughts. If your thoughts keep on moving to higher level, you will one day attain Brahman. This body is only an instrument or a covering through which thoughts play. If thoughts are different, we are different. In a dream state, thoughts change but not the body. Our thoughts are the driving force behind all our actions. If you remember somebody or something, your thoughts immediately reach there.

The Devas stay in bhava state. Without any physical body also, thoughts are exchanged there. The activities of the sages are all subject matter of bhava state. Ordinary people cannot understand them. Body gets top priority for the ordinary man. Those who are in bhava state do not keep much link with the physical body. They do not die. They remain forever. In this physical world, we come across different types of bhava. The thoughts or feelings (bhava) between husband and wife, lover and beloved, father and son, friend and friend, animals and animals, birds and birds, the devotee and God etc. are all divine. Bhava plays in subtle state independent of the physical body. Atman is eternally everywhere and in everything. Atman experiences everything because it is there as everything, such as, man, animal and tree etc. The process of union of thoughts of one with those of the other is always on. This is called self-love. When self realises the greatness and powers of Self, that is called Atmananda. He, who knows this, knows no death. You are always living with Atman inseparably. You love Atman and Atman loves you. There is love that rules everywhere.

Divya Darshan says, "You are all immortal and ever free." You are eternally Brahman in a transitory human garb. But you consider yourself as jiva. You are in bondage because of your thoughts and qualities. Free yourself from those thoughts and qualities. "I am that Atman. There is none second to me. I manifest as the Creation." This thought is *Moksa* or liberation.

Divya Darshan says, "True, you never welcome sufferings. Only your ignorance brings them to you. You are absolutely divine. Therefore, pursue divine knowledge, desire only divinity and engross yourself in divine thoughts, and then only, divine bliss will be bestowed upon you."

"You are divine; divinity is your goal; divinity is your base; divine is your life and divine is your True Self."

*****

[18]Brahman is beyond the Creation. He can only be experienced. He is inexpressible. According to the physical science, everything is made of atoms and molecules; they are invisible. But when they get combined or condensed, the gross Creation becomes visible. Likewise, the gross Creation is a manifestation of Brahman. This means that we are always seeing the gross forms of Brahman. But, due to want of knowledge, we are not able to realise Him who appears as all these gross forms. To see the subtle our ordinary eyes cannot help. Knowledge-eye or divine-eye is essential for the purpose. Jagat constitutes the subtle and gross forms which are manifestations of Brahman. Brahman is saguna when forms and qualities appear. He is nirguna when He is beyond the forms or qualities. The saguna and nirguna are the two aspects of Brahman who is unitary and undivided whole. He is formless but manifests as forms. He, who realises both the aspects, realises Brahman. That means, his individual entity gets lost in Brahman. We should feel restive for not being able to have any inkling of the all-pervasive conscious existence which manifests as gross forms and corresponding qualities in them. Due to want of true knowledge, we imagine God in a specific form and try to find Him out.

There is an all-powerful and all-pervasive Existence which cannot be described but can only be realised. He is known as Brahman or Atman. These are just naming words. Different stages of His manifestations are named as devas, man, animal, plant, earth, water, fire, air and ether etc. The inexhaustible range of His manifestations is due to His greatness or potency. Sapta swarg and sapta patal (fourteen divisions) are but the manifestations of that infinite Existence. The Eternal Being always remains in Satya Loka. But the

---

[18]*Odia Divyadhara Vol 15 Page 40*

common people remaining in the surroundings of forms and qualities argue over the existence of God. It leads them nowhere. Brahman is there much beyond their imaginations.

There are many scriptural texts including the Vedas, the Upanishads, six systems of philosophy, Shrimad Bhagavad-Gita and many puranas. To read all scriptures, one may take at least 50 years. People come across different names of different characters, compare one character with the other and carry varied opinions instead of understanding the unitary essence. To explain the greatness of God, lot of examples are cited in the Vedic texts and puranas.

Broadly speaking, Brahman has two aspects. One side is invisible, and the other side is visible. We can see the branches but not the root. The sages have explained the whole matter by dividing it into four quarters. Three quarters are invisible, and one quarter is visible. He, who realises Brahman becomes Brahman and attains everything including immortality. Brahman when manifests as a form, remains in the form and at that time, He is known as Atman. This means, Brahman is there in all beings as Atman or Self. Every cell or every atom is a form. Atman is subtler than the subtlest. Therefore, Atman is everywhere in all forms and qualities. It is mentioned in the Shrimad Bhagavad-Gita that Atman cannot be cut by a sword; cannot be wetted by water; cannot be burnt by fire and cannot be dried up by air. It is like the space which is there in air, fire, water and earth. Space is neither burnt by lightning, nor gets hit by thunder stroke. Space cannot be wetted by water nor shredded by any weapon.

A dead body undergoes change due to putrefaction. This means there is energy inside the dead body also which is at work to activate or create bacteria in it. It is due to Atman who is present in the body. Due to the presence of Atman, one can see, hear, speak, think and act. But due to opaqueness, people do not understand and appreciate the presence of this great power, Atman within. One must be transparent or pure to realise Atman. Opaqueness is due to our ignorance and impurities within.

When Guru imparts true knowledge to the disciples, it is to be understood that Mother Saraswati, the presiding goddess of knowledge is blessing us with knowledge. When Guru speaks about good individual living as well as harmonious social living, at that time, Mother Laxmi, the presiding goddess of wealth is blessing us. When Guru speaks about Atman, it means, Atman expresses through Guru. The disciple, who follows Guru's instructions, will become Guru one day. By divine blessings, one can realise Atman. Be it creation or transformation, truth is everywhere. Truth is the process, and truth is the product. When transformation takes place from one truth to another, it is truth that enables the process. Hydrogen is truth. Oxygen is truth. When they mix, water is formed which is also truth. The proportion in which they mix is also truth. The circumstance which includes required temperature or pressure etc. is also truth. Brahman expresses Himself as truth. He is Truth-Absolute.

*****

[19]Advaita siddhanta is the final and highest spiritual knowledge. But while starting spiritual knowledge one must start from dualism. Some spiritual aspirants get stuck up here, and consider this level of knowledge as final. But, dualism is only a passing phase of spiritual knowledge. It initially helps and inspires the aspirants to move

---

[19]*Odia Divyadhara Vol 17 Page 25*

deeper into the spiritual science. Suffering cannot be eradicated fully if one continues to remain in dualism.

Man suffers from various diseases because of improper care of the body. Passing through different stages of life, he finally undergoes decay and death. This is the Law of Eternity. Divya Darshan terms these changes as temporal truths. Until one realises the Supreme Truth, all these changes will bring sufferings throughout life.

According to the Advaita siddhanta, the eternal and unitary Brahman manifests as everything in the Creation. His manifested states are but His *Lila*. It is also known as Maya. By His greatness, creation, sustenance and dissolution are going on uninterruptedly. Divya Darshan explains this through its Theory of Change or Theory of Transformation. We are all parts of Brahman. We suffer because we misconstrue ourselves as jiva and therefore, we are in Maya that arises due to manifold and varied manifestations of Brahman. Due to ignorance, our thinking is influenced by the changes we come across in and around us. Ignorance means limited knowledge or fragmented knowledge. It is not total absence of knowledge. Due to darkness, we misconstrue a rope as a snake and get frightened. But when light comes, we see the rope and realise that it is not a snake. Ignorance is compared with darkness. When an aspirant will attain enlightenment, he will realise that he is the Supreme Brahman. By acquiring true knowledge, the aspirant reaches the highest level of realization.

In dream state, we experience so many things and consider them as true. After we wake up, all those objects seen in dream state vanish forthwith. Likewise, on the advent of true knowledge, the world of matters which are changeable will be considered as unreal. Ignorance of man is so deep that he considers the unreal as real. He seeks happiness but ends up with sufferings. Knowledge about Brahman is true knowledge. Therefore, man must take shelter of knowledge to realise Brahman and get rid of sufferings. Brahman is same as Atman. The all-pervasive Existence inside some form or body is called Atman. There are innumerable forms such as bricks, earth, tree, the Sun, the Moon, atom, molecule, air, fire and water etc. In the human body since Atman is there, all activities like digestion, blood circulation and respiration are going on. The growth and decay of the body take place due to the presence of Atman inside. When man attains the highest level of knowledge, he realises Atman. It is said that man has taken birth 84 lakh times. All the bodies in the previous births were inhabited and supported by Atman. In the present birth also, Atman resides inside. In the future births also, Atman will be there. In fine, our existence is not possible without Atman. But man has forgotten his Atman. He misconstrues himself for the body. Body is only a medium or instrument for the Atman to express itself. In all the forms or bodies Atman is one and the same. Apparent diversities are because of the differences in the bodies which are mere coverings. This is Advaita. Unless man acquires highest knowledge, Advaita or monism cannot be appreciated and accepted.

A jiva has not come from nothingness. He has come from a previous state. We see fruits and flowers. They have not come from nothingness. There was a bud. Before that there was a plant. Before that there was a seed. Like this, everything has emanated from Brahman and gets finally dissolved in Brahman. This is a great cycle of the Creation that moves on incessantly. Man is a dot in the cycle. Man has got all the capabilities to contemplate deeper into the subject and ultimately rediscover himself as Brahman or Atman. At different stages of the plant, its branches and leaves, flowers and fruits appear. But every part is a manifested state of the seed itself.

I am the eternal Atman. I have taken a form which is transient. Body, senses, mind and intellect are all my manifestations. My life is my *Lila*. I play different roles in this life. Brahman or Atman is the only reality. Everything else is evanescent and hence unreal. Everything else is Maya or mere illusion. In a drama, people hurl so many accusations at the villain. Their anger is against the character and not against the actor who plays the role of villain. Therefore, the wise do not feel perturbed if anybody scolds them or ill-treats them in any manner. Self-knowledge means self-realization. This is awakening or enlightenment.

Guru is trying to wake you up from deep slumber. You are trying to open your eyes but again falling asleep. When you are asleep, you are not aware that there was rain throughout the night. Similarly, you are not able to know the divine blessings being showered upon you. You are not conscious about God or Guru. All your attention is diverted so much towards mundane matters that you do not find time to remember God or Guru. You are in deep illusion. Guru is trying to wake you up in time so that you should not miss the train. But you are falling asleep again and again. How many times Guru will wake you up? Cast off your laziness and wake up to make the most in this life itself.

*****

[20]There are four steps of Brahman as mentioned in the scriptures. Those four steps are- gross, subtle, Causal and Supra-Causal. In the scriptures there is also mention about the 14 worlds. These 14 worlds correspond to the four steps. Accordingly, we have got gross

---

[20]*Odia Divyadhara Vol 8 Page 9*

body, subtle body, Causal body and Supra-Causal body. The Causal body is said to be Sat-Chit-Ananda.

To explain the Supra-Causal state, the sages explain by saying that Brahman willed to be many. The thought to become many is consciousness. In other words, it is consciousness that illumines everything. It always expresses itself and manifests as many by its inherent power. When we are awake, we do express ourselves in some way or other. We do not know the why and what of it. To will is a characteristic sign of waking state. Everything manifests because of the Will. The Will of Brahman should not be likened to our individual desires. That Will is called Chit-Shakti or Consciousness power. Will is always backed by Consciousness power. Chit-Shakti is Consciousness and Consciousness expresses itself as Will. Brahman is Chit-Swarup or Consciousness-Absolute. Therefore, Will is a spontaneous expression of Consciousness. By Consciousness, everything gets activated and regulated. When we are asleep, we cannot think; nor can we do anything. But Brahman is ever awake. He is the cause of our waking as well as sleep states. He, who is ever awake, has no death. Everything manifests according to His Will. We can experience everything like pleasure and pain, the Sun and the Moon etc. We experience all these after they are all created and after we are all created. Brahman is therefore called as the cause of cause, which means Supra-Causal. Everything like gross, subtle and Causal is manifestation of the Supra-Causal state. The Supra-Causal is the basis of all. He is the Consciousness-Absolute. Chit-Shakti is His first manifestation. Due to Consciousness, we have got our gross bodies. Due to Consciousness we grow. It is Consciousness that regulates death also.

He is there in everything as Consciousness. Due to Consciousness, creation, sustenance and dissolution are possible. Due to Supra-

Causal Existence, everything gets manifested. To explain this grand manifestation the sages briefly said, "Brahman willed to be many. "Creation, sustenance and dissolution take place by His Will. He, who realises Brahman as ever wakeful Pure Consciousness, becomes wakeful and immortal.

*****

[21]Brahman manifests in the following states such as - body consciousness or waking state, dream state, sleep state and Transcendental state of Consciousness i.e. Turiya Consciousness.

Sleep state is a state of bliss. By Yoga, one attains this state. By knowledge path also one attains this state of samadhi. The Transcendental Consciousness, also known as Turiya Consciousness, is present everywhere and always. This Consciousness also resides in waking state, dream state and sleep state. By the Will of Turiya Consciousness, everything has been created. All changes such as creation, sustenance and dissolution take place due to Turiya Consciousness. Thus His Lila goes on eternally. In the state of samadhi, there do not remain any fears or anxieties, pride or prejudice. In Turiya Consciousness, everything gets dissolved into emptiness, i.e. void or shunya. When this state is realised, one gets equal vision that extends to one and all. That is why God is said to be all-pervasive. This state of Consciousness is Nitya Loka.

Divya Darshan explains this Supreme Truth in four steps.

---

[21] *Odia Divyadhara Vol 8 Page 12*

- Temporal Truth
- Partial Truth
- Truth
- Supreme Truth

Body consciousness or waking state is called temporal truth. Dream state is called partial truth. Sleep state is Truth which is Brahman. Turiya state is the Supreme Truth (Param-Brahman).

Divya Darshan says that Consciousness was there before the five gross elements came into being. Temporal truth and partial truth get dissolved in course of time but Truth is eternal. Hence Jagadguru Shankaracharya said that Brahman is Truth (Real); the Jagat is unreal. Truth is indestructible, unchangeable, formless, eternal and all-pervasive. This Supreme Consciousness manifests as jiva and all other forms and qualities.

How could the sages name Him as Brahman? It is evident that they realised that state of Consciousness. Unless you experience certain thing, how can you name it? The sages had experienced different states of Consciousness and therefore named Him as Brahman, Param-Brahman etc.

Brahman is Pure Consciousness. Consciousness always expresses itself. Consciousness is energy. Energy is Consciousness. The rishis had realised this Truth after reaching the transcendental state. All knowledge ends there. Only Self-Consciousness remains. By Chit-Shakti Energy gets manifested to various forms with different qualities. In other words, Brahman Himself is both Chit (Consciousness) and Shakti (Energy). Energy, in consonance with the Law of Eternity, has very systematically evolved as the world of matters. Before manifestation, Brahman was there. He exists eternally. There is no duality there, but He manifests as many. Then dualities come to play. In the non-dual state, He is called Param-

Brahman when there is none except Him. He is also called unqualified Brahman. That state is unmanifest and inexpressible. This formless unmanifest state is the Supreme Truth. His manifested states are all truths but some are temporal and some partial. This unmanifest state has to be realised to realise Param-Brahman. There is no name, no form or quality. This state transcends everything else. Senses, mind and intellect cannot reach there.

In the manifested state, He is clay, He is potter and He is the pot. He is gold, He is goldsmith and He is the ornament. He is the Creator, He is nature, He creates and He causes deluge. Births and deaths are going on but He is unaffected and unmoved. He is eternal and ever blissful.

Remaining as Consciousness He creates by his Self-glory. This means Consciousness continues its play in this manner. This is His greatness. Whatever we imagine or contemplate is all His greatness. How great is His greatness! Wherefrom and when He begins? Everything is inexpressible. His greatness is Chit-Shakti (Bhava). Being established in the Self is Mahabhava which is state of thoughtlessness. That is why it is inexpressible.

We have taken human births. In these bodies, demoniac qualities are also seen. Why can't divine qualities be developed within? Inside the gross body, there is subtle body. Inside subtle body, there is causal body. In other words, inside the gross body, there are subtle bodies as well as causal body. Gross body is visible but the other two bodies such as subtle body and causal body are not visible.

He, who has no form and no quality, is only the Supreme Truth. We ascribe different names to different things which are only the manifested states of the Supreme Truth. "I am the Creator; I am Prakriti. I create, I also cause the deluge. In the physical state, deaths and births do take place always. But I am immutable and unmoved, unperturbed and immortal." This is what the realisers of the Supreme Truth experience.

The centre is void which is inexpressible and unmanifest. Based on the centre, whatever have manifested are all expressible. Centre is unqualified and formless Brahman. This Centre is all-pervasive. This means there is no circumference to limit Him. This is His unimaginable greatness. As discussed earlier, the Pure Consciousness is full of energy. That energy manifests itself from one form to another by Chit-Shakti. In other words, the Chit Purusha became energy that assumed various forms of matter. The unmanifest state is called Param-Brahman. The manifestation started from Brahman. That unmanifest got manifested. Whatever is manifested is truth but not the Supreme Truth. The highest state of knowledge is beyond body, mind and intellect. This is known as super-sensual state.

Pure Consciousness expresses itself by its intrinsic energy. Therefore Pure Consciousness is but energy. Energy is consciousness. Consciousness and energy are one and the same.

The unmanifest gets manifested. The manifested again goes back to unmanifest state. That is how He manifests Himself. To say that He does not manifest is also His manifestation.

The mansion of Truth is such that some reach and stay there. They fully know the ins and outs of it. Some have gone up to its outer corridor. Some have gone near the gate of the mansion. Whoever has seen or experienced that mansion from his own stand point, describes it accordingly.

Whatever you experience, you are that. When you experience sufferings, you are that or you are the sufferer. When you experience bliss, you are that. Whatever you think of, you are that. When you experience that you are neither happy nor unhappy, in other words, you are beyond happiness and unhappiness, you are that. He, who experiences greed, is greedy. He, who renounces, is a renouncer. One expresses oneself as greed or renunciation.

The first stage of self-manifestation is bhava or thought. How can Self which is unmanifest, be explained! Any expression through any language is an afterthought which is different from what you are in reality. That is why it is said that nirguna (without attributes) became saguna (with attributes). Nirguna manifests as saguna. There remains nirguna in saguna. It is said that whatever you think of, you are that. Whatever is unmanifest, you are that. Whatever all are manifested, you are that. You have ascribed different names to the manifested things. Those were all there inside you. You are all these. You have manifested as the Creation. If you think that you are the Creation, you are that. If you think that you are different from all these, you are different. When you consider yourself nothing, you are nothing or 'Neti Neti'.

In the gross body, the subtle body and the causal body are present with all their qualities. Whatever thoughts come out through the gross body, by whom those are experienced? It is not experienced by the gross body. The subtle body and the causal body inside the gross body experience everything.

He is that or becomes that at that time, whatever he thinks of. He, who thinks and also experiences that, becomes that at that time. If you think of divinity, you are divine. If you think of the demon, you are a demon at that time. He, who speaks, or thinks or experiences, is the subtle body, or the causal body or you may call the same as Atman.

Whatever a man knows how is it that he becomes that?

We are those thoughts that are generated in us. We use our physical bodies to speak out. According to the thoughts one entertains, one is classified as demon, human or Deva.

Inside the physical body there remains subtle body and inside the subtle body, there remains causal body. In other words, inside this physical body there are two other bodies, namely, subtle body and causal body. Beyond these three bodies there is one more state which is known as Supra-Causal.

What is True Self? What is thought? There are different kinds of thoughts sometimes more and sometimes less. Those thoughts are different from time to time. One experiences one's thoughts. Hence the experiencer is different from the thoughts. Viewed from a different plane of consciousness, whatever I thought, whatever I knew that I thought, I am none other than those thoughts. In a state of thoughtlessness, I remain eternally as only Pure Consciousness which is inexpressible.

Thoughts are expressed and names are also given to the subjects or objects. The experience of all thoughts suggests names to the objects and subjects.

Something is sour or sweet (of different qualities). All these thoughts are in the state of Shakti. Shakti is converted to matter. Shakti, in other words, assumes innumerable forms. Forms are experienced (by Consciousness) as such and they are named afterwards. The sages had realised these happenings and that is why they said, "Brahman willed to be many."

Thoughts are different from the thinker. Thoughts and names are subsequent to the thinker, or the experiencer of the thoughts. He, who thinks, is different from what he thinks. That is why, Rishi Yajnavalkya had said, 'Neti Neti'.

Thought or bhava is the first manifestation. Various contemplations follow thereafter. Prior to thoughts, you were there and after thoughts, you remain. Again some thoughts may come and gradually they fade away. But the experience is present throughout. What really you are cannot be expressed. Any thought of it or any language to express is only subsequent to what you are. Hence you are different from all these names and forms. These names and forms are only subsequent manifestations.

Hence it is said that Nirguna (attributeless) Brahman became many with attributes. The attributeless Brahman is always present in the manifested forms and attributes/qualities. In other words, you are the unmanifest who is inexpressible and hence unexplainable. You are also the manifested forms and qualities.

If you understand the greatness of Brahman you can get bliss. You will start loving Him. You will surrender to Him and be one with Him. He is so beautiful and so blissful. There is no language to express. All manifestations are but His greatness. Simultaneously remaining unmanifest is also His greatness. Here we are able to speak about Him and there we are not able to speak of Him and His greatness. Both the situations are also His greatness. He is tinier than the tiniest. He is bigger than the biggest. There are no words to express Him. This is also His greatness. Whatever we come across are all His manifestations or atma-prakash. This visible Creation is but a sample of His greatness. His greatness includes His Lila, glory and true nature. Feeling of self-surrender comes on knowing His greatness. Every splinter of His Greatness is truth. His greatness eternally radiates through His Consciousness. In fact, His greatness is Consciousness; Consciousness is His greatness. He remains as eternal

Consciousness and also manifests as infinite matters and the material world. This is also His greatness. His Play goes on due to Consciousness. Whatever we think of or contemplate is all His greatness. His greatness is His glory. How great is His greatness? This is unthinkable and hence inexpressible. Greatness, bhava and true knowledge taken together are Mahabhava which is self-realisation. Nothing else, no other thought even is present in Mahabhava.

We all suffer but we never try to find out the cause of sufferings. If one would contemplate on this, one would find some ways to get rid of sufferings. According to the highest spiritual knowledge as depicted in the scriptures, there is nothing like happiness or suffering. Those are all mental creations or different states of mind only. According to Vedanta, you are the Self-Absolute. Self is eternal; it remains unperturbed and unaffected by the changes in nature. Due to ignorance, man has forgotten the True Self. He considers himself to be the body and mind. He considers himself as the jiva. Therefore, the qualities pertaining to a jiva find expressions in him. He gets affected by all external happenings as well as by his mental reactions.

Normally, whatever all is visible, we call it as Creation. There are so many invisible things like qualities which play predominant roles but we are not able to see them. Both the visible and invisible things are controlled and manipulated by the invisible energy. We are not able to see energy but we are able to experience it by knowledge. According to the physical science, the matters get transformed to energy and energy gets transformed to matters. Total Energy is constant i.e. without any loss or erosion. Energy is Shakti which is eternal and all-pervasive. The more one acquires energy, the more one would become energetic or powerful. Everything is possible by Shakti. Shakti appears as the Creation; it is in the Creation; it is also in the background and foreground of the Creation. It is the Pure Consciousness which is full of energy. The Primordial Energy is also Consciousness. Pure Consciousness and Shakti are one and the same. It is called Chit-Shakti. Energy prompted and propelled by consciousness gets converted to various forms and qualities. Different qualities are seen in different forms. Everything is perfectly engineered by the Creator for the sustenance as well as the well-being of the Creation. That is why we find the Creation already enriched so systematically and caringly with everything we need. On realizing this truth, the sages reiterate from time to time that God has Himself manifested as the Universe. He is the only eternal essence of everything we come across. True, the Creation is changeful, but God is the changeless eternal entity. A great deal of spiritual practices, under the guidance of a spiritual master or Sadguru, is essential for realizing God. Without Guru's Grace, none can attain Brahman, the Supreme.

The Chit-Purusha is Shakti. Shakti takes different forms. Therefore, it is said that the entire Creation is a manifestation of Consciousness. Atma Chetana is Brahman. He manifests as waking, dream and sleep consciousness. Self-realization is therefore essential to realise this. Brahman has become gross as well as subtle. The subtle is there inside the gross. When we see water or fire, we can also experience the qualities present in them. We experience the flowingness of water. We also experience the burning power of the fire.

Brahman manifests Himself in four steps. The first step is the gross Creation (Visible to the senses). The second is from Tan-matra (sound, touch, sight, taste and smell) to 'Om' (which can be experienced by intellect). The third is 'Om' a glimpse of which can be had by conscience (Vivek). The fourth and the highest state is Param-Brahman.

About Shakti: The sages affirm that Shakti is Brahman. Common people cannot understand this. The sages have described about the greatness of Shakti. But Shakti is indescribable. It requires intense spiritual practices to realise what Shakti is. To explain Shakti, the sages have divided it into Para and Apara. Shakti itself does not have any forms or attributes. Rishi Yajnavalkya concluded by saying "Neti Neti" which means not this much, not like this. Because the sages realised Brahman by Consciousness, they call him as Consciousness-Absolute. It should be remembered that names are ascribed only after realization of the infinite, eternal and unitary Existence which is all-pervasive.

Consciousness, forms and qualities involve dualities but Shakti is independent and non-dual. Divya Darshan presents Shakti in the following way. "There is someone that manifests as this Jagat (Universe). Existence of Shakti appears as the universe. But Shakti is indescribable because it is the one and undivided total Existence that is the Supreme Truth."

The principle by which self-manifestation, from one truth to another or from one to many, happens is known as the Law of Eternity. Shakti is neither masculine nor feminine. It manifests as both male and female, Purusha and Prakriti. In other words, both male and female aspects are present in everything we come across in this Creation.

Therefore, to realise everything as Brahman is true love and to love God is to love all. One has to know the purpose of one's birth so as to attain the highest realization by spiritual efforts. Efforts to know the self is sadhana. Everything you do in your day to day life is meant for sadhana but it does not happen as your pursuits are mostly whimsical and purposeless. That is why you remain bound although the True Self is eternally free and immortal. Ignorance is the cause of sufferings. Ignorance can be dispelled only by the light of knowledge and divine virtues. Therefore, welcome knowledge and realise the True Self.

*****

First we have to assess our needs. Thereafter, we should try for fulfilment. The truth is that there remains completeness but due to ignorance, we are not aware of the same. That is why we are in wants. The jiva, being bound in a particular form, is not able to realise his intrinsic completeness. Therefore limited knowledge is expressed in him. He is ever in wants due to his endless desires.

When jiva will know what Maya is, what God is, what knowledge is or what ignorance is, he will be in a position to act and react suitably and shall adjust himself appropriately. One must know and overcome the six enemies such as desire, anger, greed, infatuation, pride and jealousy. There are also divine qualities like renunciation, restraint, spiritual practice, service, truth, love and forgiveness which bring peace and happiness. Knowledge is essential for this. With the advent of true knowledge, ego will gradually fade away. People are not interested to acquire knowledge, but at the same time they wish for peace and happiness. How will it be possible?

He, who will know what Maya is, can get rid of Maya. He, who will know what ignorance is, will get rid of ignorance. He, who will know who God is and how He exists, will know God. Since you are getting some indications, you take interest to know more and more about Him. After unfolding layers after layers, you will attain perfection.

When you are not interested to know about Him, that means, you are an infant only.

A carpenter makes a cot. He measures all sides correctly and makes various pieces of the cot according to requirement. But due to lack of knowledge we are not able to assemble it. By trial and error, we try to assemble the same. We fail to do so at times. But finally we are able to assemble the same properly. That means, when we understand the carpenter's plans and designs perfectly well, at that time our knowledge about the cot is complete.

Not evincing interest to know is a demoniac quality. Trying to know more and more is a divine quality. Atman expresses itself through divine qualities. It is not that we do not know anything. We definitely know something due to which we survive.

Our only aim should be to make sincere efforts to realise the Eternal Truth behind the changeful Creation. The sages, having realised Him, have named Him as Brahman. Since we are not able to realise Him, we disbelieve His Existence.

Physical science deals with Apara Shakti which is lower energy. But the sages had realised Para Shakti which is higher energy. Para Shakti manifests as Apara Shakti. Para Shakti controls the Apara Shakti. Para Shakti resides in Apara Shakti. The rishis had realised this. The visible universe is nothing but manifestation of the higher energy i.e. Para Shakti. Matters do not have permanent existence. Matters come and go but Para Shakti remains forever unaffected and unchanged. Para Shakti is all-pervasive. Everything is possible for Para Shakti. Para Shakti is Conscious Energy. Not knowing this higher energy is ignorance only. This higher energy has no name, no quality and no form. It does not have any epithet. It is indescribable.

You are that Chit-Shakti. You are expressing yourself in infinite ways as infinite forms, qualities and names. He, who realises himself as Chit-Shakti, has no decay or death. Understanding something is power. We understand things by consciousness. By consciousness when we understand something, it is called knowledge. Knowledge and consciousness are one and the same. Consciousness remains at the root and everything happens due to consciousness. By the power of consciousness, Atman can take the form of jiva. By this power, jiva can go back to Atman. Waking state is controlled by dream state; dream state is controlled by sleep state and sleep state is controlled by Turiya Consciousness. Turiya Consciousness manifests as sleep, dream and waking consciousness and is constantly present in sleep, dream and waking states. Names have been ascribed to different stages of manifestation such as seed and tree. These two names are essentially the unitary Consciousness. The seed becomes the tree and tree becomes the seed in course of time. Seed, tree, mountain, ocean, birds, animals and various stars and planets, earth, water, air, fire and sky and innumerable such names are given to different stages of manifestation. Atman already exists as the 'Self' in jiva. The jiva can become Atman just as Atman has become jiva. The greatness and potency of Atman is such that it can take different forms. Brahman eternally exists as the Supra-Causal factor. Once one realises the Supra-Causal Existence, one can know Brahman.

Seeing others in Self and Self in others is equal vision. This means, there is nothing for him other than Atman (Self). Loving Atman culminates as real union or 'Yoga'. Since Atman is undivided whole, it amounts to 'loving the Self'. This state cannot be expressed. Silence is the only answer. By knowledge, when you realise that due to Him, you exist, at that time you will love Him. Bhava is the first manifestation of Self-Consciousness. There remains bhava in jnana.

Pure Consciousness is Brahman, Prajnanam Brahman. He, who takes shelter of knowledge, ultimately realises Brahman.

A truth in order to come out as truth, the help of another truth is essential. In other words, it is truth that enables another truth to express itself as truth. Truth (Existence) expresses itself as Knowledge and Bliss. This Creation is a form of Knowledge and Bliss. Consciousness cannot be called a quality but Bliss can be called a quality. Bliss is a state of Consciousness. Chit-Shakti manifests as various forms and qualities. We experience bliss after seeing different forms. He, who expresses Himselft as Consciousness, is inexpressible Existence. Unless man realises Consciousness, he cannot realise bliss.

Existence (Truth), Consciousness (Knowledge), and Bliss (Ananda) represent Para Shakti. Due to ignorance, man is not able to realise this. Truth (Sat) and Bliss (Ananda) can be realised by Knowledge (Chit). But by sense organs, we can only see wood, stones and the likes.

Chit-Shakti signifies the primal cause of manifestation of Brahman. Chit-Shakti has no attributes such as small or big, form, colour or quality. That means when Shakti becomes functional, we experience the same by our senses and intellect.

There exist infinite things in this universe with infinite possibilities. Not like this, not this much, many more remain still. Nobody can realise Him. When that knowledge rises within, He will appear from within. Since there is no language, it is said that without Guru's Grace, realization of Brahman is not possible. This situation of Guru-disciple relationship is Guru's blessings only.

Guru's Grace: Brahman manifests as everything according to His Laws, some for short time and some for long time. For the maintenance of the things and also for their upbringing, divine qualities are essential. For anything to come to light and to be functional, His grace is involved. Brahman has become Guru. Brahman and Guru are one and the same. Guru's grace is essential for self-development. Everywhere His love for all creatures is quite evident. A person with sattvic quality can feel His grace and love. Until one comes to possess sattvic quality, one cannot understand the greatness of Gurushakti.

Avyakta is what cannot be expressed or explained. Avyakta means unmanifest. He is Param-Brahman. Everything manifested is different from Avyakta. He is beyond everything else, beyond the sensory world. To describe Him, Rishi Yajnavalkya said, 'Neti neti'. He manifests Himself by Chit-Shakti. Chit is Brahman who is none other than Energy and Consciousness. Chit manifests as air, fire, water and earth. Chit has to be realised first, thereafter Param-Brahman. But Param-Brahman is neither Chit nor Achit. He is inexpressible.

According to Divya Darshan, everything is Truth. One truth comes out from another truth. Thus every truth owes its origin to the Supreme Truth. Falsity is also a form of truth. Because there is truth, the question of falsity arises. Truth remains always in some form or other.

Chit-Shakti equally pervades everywhere. By our limited or fragmented knowledge, we experience the manifested things and consider them as less conscious, more conscious or unconscious. Everywhere the same power remains latent, be it an atom or a celestial body, be it an insect or an elephant. Chit-Shakti manifests as qualities and also as innumerable forms. Atma-Chetana or Self-Consciousness is all-inclusive that experiences or witnesses everything whatsoever. Be it an ocean or a river, everywhere there is water. Somewhere there is motion and somewhere it is motionless. Somewhere there are whirlpools and somewhere water is steady. Similarly in this Creation, Consciousness pervades everywhere with motion and motionlessness. This all-pervasive Consciousness manifests as Devas who in turn manifest as innumerable creatures and things. Thus the unitary and undivided Atma-Chetana who is formless appears divided as innumerable forms in this Creation of multiplicities.

Everything is a manifestation of Brahman. Everything gets merged in Brahman. In between, we come across different forms. Every form contains and represents some qualities. They all ultimately merge in the attributeless Brahman.

Brahman is Chit-Swarup. Chit is potentially Chit-Shakti that manifests as all forms and qualities. In other words, every form or quality is a state of Consciousness. Consciousness has taken forms and assumed different qualities. Consciousness remains in them all. The world of qualities and forms is Apara Shakti. Consciousness (Sense) has another state which is called Para.

As discussed in the foregoing paragraph, Brahman is Chit-Swarup. In other words, Truth remains as Consciousness. Consciousness is the glory and greatness of Brahman. After knowing His greatness, we call Him Truth-Absolute. Due to His greatness, we experience Consciousness by Consciousness. In other words, Brahman is there as Consciousness in all beings. Consciousness is there behind every act of creation, sustenance and dissolution (transformation). By the Vedas, Brahman is called Chit–Shakti. Consciousness pervades all, remains in different states in different forms and qualities. The very basis of forms and qualities is Consciousness. We experience things by Consciousness. All our experiences are but Consciousness. What we experience and call as void is also Consciousness. Void is a state of Consciousness. Man is another state of Consciousness.

Atma-Chetana or Transcendental Consciousness is Para. Sleep, dream and waking consciousness are all apara. It is Para that controls and regulates all other three states of consciousness (apara).

By bhava, His greatness can be realised. By Mahabhava, true nature can be realised.

Consciousness is called knowledge when we explain or understand things. Knowledge becomes functional due to senses, mind and intellect. In other words, knowledge expresses itself as senses, mind and intellect. Senses, mind and intellect are different states of knowledge. Consciousness is knowledge; knowledge is Consciousness.

A dead body cannot speak. The sense (energy) that is essential for speaking is conspicuously absent in a dead body. But dead body or a dead matter is also a form of energy. Energy is present in the dead body for which it exists and gradually decomposes. In this process, consciousness is involved in breaking the inertia of rest and triggering decomposition.

Shakti evolves itself as consciousness. The first expression of Consciousness is bhava. Shakti is beyond thought. It cannot be expressed. Shakti is Param-Brahman. Shakti contains all, even bhava. Brahman with attributes is a state of Consciousness. Shakti is 'Neti neti'. 'Neti neti' is a superior state of Consciousness which the rishis had realised. All scriptures have described up to bhava state and not beyond, for That is inexpressible.

Everything (all qualities and forms) has come out of Consciousness. Consciousness is Truth. Consciousness is unchangeable. Consciousness experiences the Shakti. What we call world of matters is Energy only, one and undivided Energy. Where are matters then? I have given you some glimpses about Satya Loka. I shall tell about Nitya Loka afterwards.

In the state of Samadhi, no thought is present. There is nothing other than Consciousness. The thought that "I am the Consciousness" will also be not there. There remains only Consciousness which is Pure Consciousness.

Chit-Shakti is bhava. Bhava as the causal factor expresses itself as knowledge as well as the Creation.

One becomes happy to see a beautiful form. Who has assumed the form? Who is experiencing happiness? It is He, the witness consciousness who has taken the beautiful form and also is the enjoyer.

It is Consciousness that causes all changes. Wherever there is consciousness, there is change. Because of consciousness, we are able to work, speak and write. Brahman is present everywhere as consciousness. Without consciousness, no change can occur. Consciousness appears as subtle as well as gross. That is why we come across so many forms and qualities.

Chit-Shakti expresses itself as the changeful universe. In other words, changes appear as the Creation full of forms and qualities. The Creation is experienced by the Chit-Shakti itself. Due to changes that occur incessantly i.e. from moment to moment, there is illusion (Maya). Not understanding changes is Maya. Due to changes, we could become conscious beings, realise Brahman and affirm that He is Infinite Existence.

By the light of consciousness, we can experience both light and darkness. Both the seer and the seen (such as- The Sun, The Moon, The Earth, vegetable kingdom, animal kingdom, mineral kingdom, air, water and fire etc.) are the manifestations of Consciousness. He is the disciple and He is the Guru. He is the self-consciousness who appears as your body.

He is also there as divine qualities in you and has been protecting you. By developing divine qualities in you, you can realise Him.

Turiya Consciousness or Atma-Chetana also remains in sleep consciousness, dream consciousness and waking consciousness. Atma-Chetana pervades all and as such it is present in all beings, the sentient and the insentient. One attains equal vision on realizing the Consciousness as the Being and all becomings.

Whatever you experience, by what you experience, He, who experiences, is only Consciousness. That Consciousness is 'I'; that Consciousness is 'you'. That Consciousness has taken the form of body (consciousness) and sees itself (consciousness) by Consciousness. He Himself is the cause of all changes.

Before you could understand it, your body was there. Before the body, there was nature. Before nature, there was Consciousness. The Sun radiates heat and light. Due to that light we could see both the Earth and the Sun. But the light (rays) remains unseen. When it gets reflected on any object or particles, we feel having seen the light (rays).

Chit-Shakti is the dynamic state of Shakti. Consciousness manifests as forms and qualities, strength and intellect. The principle by which Consciousness manifests itself is known as the Law of Eternity. Brahman is Truth-Absolute. By Chit, He manifests as different truths. By Chit, one experiences Bliss. In other words, we experience Him by Him. This means, the experiencer is He Himself.

He is different from intellect and intellectual expressions. He is 'Neti Neti' which means 'not like this, not this much'. He is His boundary. He is thus infinite. Experiencing the unitary thought is 'bhava'. Thoughtlessness is Mahabhava.

Brahman illumines Himself, regulates Himself and identifies Himself. Everything is His manifestation. Brahman pervades everywhere as Consciousness. His Existence, greatness and manifestation are to be realised to realise His True Nature.

It is by Consciousness that all changes do occur. We call it knowledge when we understand something or explain something by the help of consciousness. In course of acquiring knowledge, one meets with Truth. Truth manifests from one truth to another by means of another truth; e.g. Water is a truth. Ice is a truth. Temperature is another truth that is necessary to transform water into ice. In other words, the process or principle involved is also truth. Water becomes vapour. Vapour makes the cloud. Thereafter it rains and flows as rivers to merge in the ocean. This is water cycle. This is the Eternal Law or the Law of Eternity. In other words, manifestation of Brahman happens by the Law of Eternity. In other words, the law by which one truth manifests as another truth is known as the Law of Eternity.

The Supreme Truth manifests as various forms (Truth). Different names are ascribed to different forms. Every form exists and gets protected due to the Supreme Truth. Contemplating on the True Self or staying connected with the True Self is real worship.

Who can disown consciousness? Pure Consciousness is Brahman. He is called by various names. By mundane knowledge, we can know about forms and qualities. He, who reaches the highest state of knowledge, reaches bhava state which is beyond knowledge. He, who reaches bhava state, can realise Brahman.

*****

[22]Shakti is there everywhere. To displace something, force is required; even to express something, force is required. Force and energy are one and the same. The energy is all-pervasive. It expresses itself as force in different circumstances. Every moment Brahman expresses Himself. We call the same as consciousness or energy. Brahman who is Energy-Absolute also manifests as energy. He expresses Himself as various qualities, and also remains without any quality. To go back to the previous state is also His manifestation. To tell that He is not expressing Himself is also His manifestation. In other words, Brahman is always expressive. Whatever we feel or perceive are nothing other than Brahman. Brahman pervades throughout this Creation and beyond. But due to ignorance we are not able to understand that we are Brahman. We are not able to understand the thoughts that manifest as all these in the Creation.

Whatever beautiful picture you draw, it is full. An ugly picture you draw is also full. Everything is Purna (full). Brahman is full. He, who realises Brahman's all-pervasiveness, can say, "I am Brahman." This is known as self-realisation. In other words, whatever we see as different things are all different states of the unitary Brahman. Brahman manifests as one and all. This realisation is called equal vision. The real equal vision comes only after self-realisation.

Whether it is fire or water, everything is Brahman. Even after attaining equal vision, the realiser can also know the differences or gradations in the Creation which are all but the manifestation of the

---

[22]*Odia Divyadhara Vol 8 Page 14*

unitary and infinite Brahman. Brahman manifests as heat as well as cold. At His Will, He takes different forms and assumes different qualities. Everything is Brahman. Therefore, the sages, who have reached the peak, can do anything they want. They are independent. Hence the sages can do as they will. It is difficult to know a true realiser. We are in specific forms. But the realised souls exist in all forms. Only a realiser can know another realiser. Not believing in God or any sage is also a form of mind. Since a realised soul is in all forms, he can say that whatever manifests or happens are all manifestations of Brahman; everything is His manifestation. He expresses as all these. "I am there everywhere as Atman." This realisation is siddhi. A realiser does not expressly say that he is Brahman. When such circumstance arises, he may say that he is Brahman. "I am the Brahman". He, who realises that, can do anything. He can create and dissolve the whole world even. It depends upon circumstances. In the Shrimad Bhagavad-Gita Lord Krishna had said, "I am the Sun, the Moon, mountain, river and sea." Lord Krishna speaks and Arjun listens. Lord Krishna is in total form. Total form controls the specific form which is listening. The realiser understands and appreciates all forms since he has realised the total form, whereas people in general are in different forms. One specific form cannot understand another specific form or the total form. When we are creating a certain thing, it means, we are creating a specific form. This means, one is confined to a specific form. Hence, one cannot understand a true realiser. The realiser understands all specific forms as the manifestations of the total form that is Brahman. Hence the realiser lives happily. "I am everything. I am the Self-Absolute." Having realised thus, he has no suffering; he has no fear. There is no feeling of duality. In the nirguna state he is silent. In the saguna state he is aware that he has assumed all forms and qualities. When the sages apparently suffer, that is also a form. Whatever we all come across, perceive or experience are all

His forms. He manifests according to the need of different situations at different times. "I am there as suffering, I am lamenting and I am also enjoying peace and happiness. But I, being the Self-Absolute, am always pure and unperturbed, formless and taintless." He, who understands the play as well as the nirguna state i.e. the True Self, is a true realiser. But we are so much engrossed in His Lila that we are not able to reach to the Self. Due to our ignorance, we say that the sages or realisers are smiling and crying etc.

Suppose I cook different types of dishes. These are different forms. I add poison to it. This is another form. It is to be understood that I am nectar and I am also poison. Further, I am neither nectar nor poison. I am Self-Absolute. He, who realises Atman, becomes Self-Absolute.

*****

[23]Self-restraint plays an especially important role in spiritual practice. It is the first and foremost pre-requisite for Yoga. Without self-restraint, spiritual progress is not possible. The spiritual mendicants should talk less. They should talk only the minimum required. By talking more not only energy is spent, one may also tell some lies and exaggerated things or make controversial statements. Talkative persons may also speak ill of others. People also start their talks well but end up in quarrels. Most of the people do not have control over their tongues. Due to all these, mind becomes restless which is unbecoming of any spiritual aspirant.

Controlled food habit is another requirement for spiritual practice. At times, we get tempted to eat more of some tasty food. By doing so, we invite problems for ourselves. Therefore, it is always advisable to have restrained food habits according to need, and not

---

[23]*Odia Divyadhara Vol 14 Page 42*

more than that. Controlled tongue and controlled diet are two basic pre-requisites for Yoga. By restraint, one gets more and more power to do things easily which he was not able to do earlier. In the day to day life, restraint is necessary in all matters. While reading books also, we should read only good books which will guide us on the right path. Books with undesirable contents must be avoided. Throughout our life if we get ourselves habituated to spiritual enquiries, we will get more knowledge on the Supreme Brahman. At the time of death also, spiritual thoughts will overwhelm us. Next birth will be determined by our last thoughts before death.

Even if realization of Brahman does not happen in this birth, in the next birth, favourable surroundings will be available for further spiritual progress. It must be remembered that a person without spiritual thoughts, may not get proper environment in the next birth to be back on spiritual track. Births after births may be wasted like this without any spiritual progress.

Therefore, instead of thinking of sensual pleasure day and night, and thereby misleading our children, we should take to spiritual practice and always keep in mind the goal of life. Controlled senses are our good friends. They can be our enemies if left unbridled.

Our tongue is so useful. It tells us whether something is eatable or not. Nose also helps us in discriminating if something is fresh or stale. Without eyes, we may fall into ditches. By using our hands, we can do so many things; we work, and we earn. Hence the senses are immensely helpful to us. The senses are protecting us. They are the divine gifts to us. On the other hand, if the senses are left unbridled and become demoniac due to tamasic qualities, they bring us untold sufferings. They destroy us. If we have bad food habits (tamasic) the senses get habituated to it and nurture demoniac tendencies. They, instead of protecting us, become the cause of our destruction.

Therefore, we should take appropriate food that befits Devas. On the other hand, if we take tamasic food and intoxicants befitting the demons, we invite our destruction. In other words, we should take sattvic food. Senses are provided to us as our benefactors. With their help, we survive and do everything including attainment of goal. The wise men keep senses under their control and are never goaded away by their dictates. Therefore, they move faster to their goal. All spiritual aspirants must properly nurture their senses to reach the goal of self-realization.

*****

[24]God is Sat-Chit-Ananda. He is the life and vital energy of all. He is all-pervasive and dwells in every heart. He, who attains the Supreme, gets rid of all sufferings. The sages had realised Him and tried to share their experiences which are available to us in form of scriptures and Shrimad Bhagavad-Gita.

If we do not know about electricity, how can we utilize the same and get benefits from out of it? If we do not know about God's greatness and His role function, how will we have respect towards Him? We do not know anything about God. Whatever we think that we know is very insignificant. Therefore, most of us do not believe in God. The sages had known and experienced God. We try to know something by going through some scriptures. We just read but do not contemplate on that. Therefore, we do not have true devotion towards God. When we do not believe in Him, how can we feel that we are being protected by Him or we are getting any benefit from Him? Still at times, we expect so many things from Him. We offer some fruits and eatables in forms of Prasad (a sweet or any vegetarian eatable which is distributed to people after worshipping

---

[24]*Odia Divyadhara Vol 12 Page 35*

God as a blessing of God) and try to propitiate some deities with the sole motive of getting something in return from them. We also pray and praise them to make them happy. But it is not possible to get anything from the deity in this process because we do not know anything about the deity. We grope in darkness and reach nowhere except hitting ourselves against walls and pillars. We are suffering because of our ignorance about God. We must realise God in order to get rid of sufferings. First, we must know about Him.

Whatever we come across in this visible universe, everything has some characteristics. To describe something, we use various adjectives like white, black, big, small, long, short, soft, hard, heavy and light etc. We describe things as we observe. We observe things by our senses, mind and intellect.

While explaining the spiritual knowledge in preliminary stages we normally use the terms like God and Brahman interchangeably. But God and Brahman do not connote same state. The devotees believe in God and they imagine that God has a certain form and He holds different weapons in his hands. According to the bhava of the devotee, reflection occurs and accordingly the devotee ascribes forms to the God. But the background power or the causal force that radiates bhava and its subsequent reflections is known as Brahman who is all-pervasive and formless. The God, which the devotees talk about, pertains generally to the gross universe. But people possess very little idea about the subtle universe. In this world, we enter into different types of relationship with different individuals and normally we introduce them as our friend, brother, sister, uncle, aunt, father and mother etc. We also sometimes speak about their achievements and qualifications during introduction. Now the question is how we shall introduce Brahman. Brahman is the primordial cause of the gross as well as the subtle universe. In other words, He is the basis of one and all. Therefore, how is it possible to describe Him by picking up some examples from the gross world? Can the gross matters help to explain the subtle-most existence? Only the realised souls can speak something about Him. Therefore, it is exceedingly difficult and almost impossible for us to establish contact with someone, who is unknown to us. How shall we get His blessings? Even if we have been receiving His blessings since our birth, we are unable to know that whatever we possess are only due to His blessings. Even if we feel that we are not getting His blessings, we do not try to know how to get the same. Rather we choose to remain indifferent about God.

He, who does not know about the personal godheads, cannot know Brahman. Most of us have been worshipping different personal godheads but without knowing about them. He, who does not have knowledge about the subtle forms, normally worships gross forms. Everyone is ignorant since birth itself. But as a person gathers knowledge, at a later stage he refrains from worshipping gross forms of different deities. It is futile to expect anything from the deities without knowing them. We are shrouded by so much ignorance that we do not have adequate knowledge to detect our own mistakes. Due to ignorance, a baby puts his finger into fire. He does not know that his finger will be burnt. Like this, an ignorant man does not know what impropriety is, what injustice is or what *Adharma* is. He goes on committing mistakes after mistakes without any intent to rectify. That much of knowledge is not there in him.

Man has been worshipping for years but without any positive result. If we do not know whom we are worshipping, we shall not get anything. Even if somebody gets something by worshipping gross forms, he does not know who has given it to him. Whether the specific deity has given him, or he has got it due to some other reasons? It is to be remembered that one deity is not vested with all powers. Each deity possesses specific power. We cannot expect anything outside the purview of the deity we have been worshipping.

Brahman is one. He is Supreme. He possesses all powers. His different powers are named after different personal godheads. For example, Goddess Laxmi gives wealth, and Saraswati gives knowledge. Laxmi cannot give knowledge. Similarly, Brahma can only create but the power of sustenance is with Vishnu. Similarly, Vishnu has no power to create. But people do not understand this. They worship a specific deity and seek fulfilment of all their desires. In other words, they worship some deity and put forth a long list of varied issues and items before the deity expecting quick fulfilment. Most of the items in the list do not come under the purview of the particular deity.

Different Devas oversee allotted departments. They merely carry out the instructions of Brahman. They are not independent. They have little discretion. Unless sanction comes from Brahman, Devas cannot dispense anything. Devas are there to perform the allotted duties, not more, not less. But our subsequent beliefs and disbeliefs depend upon what we have received and what not.

It is well known that we reap the results of our actions. Therefore, it is a misnomer to believe that someone has given us something from heaven. Without action, there is no result. If we act properly, good results shall accrue to us. There is no doubt about it.

One more point is relevant here. It is mentioned in the puranas that there is always fight between the Devas and Asuras. Devas possess sattvic qualities whereas the Asuras possess tamasic qualities. Both are hostile to each other. Man possesses rajasic qualities mostly. It is due to difference in level of knowledge. Those who possess least knowledge are of tamasic qualities. They are *Asuras* (demons). Humans are above this level. They possess rajasic qualities. He, who possesses still more knowledge, possesses sattvic qualities. Due to this quality, he can discriminate between Dharma and *Adharma*, right and wrong, justice and injustice, truth and falsehood etc. He believes more in God. But the persons of tamasic qualities are just opposite. As told earlier, man belongs to the rajasic category. Rajasic quality is an admixture of tamasic and sattvic qualities. This means, man possesses all the three qualities. Man possesses the qualities of *Asuras* (demons) and Devas as well.

In the Shrimad Bhagavad-Gita, Lord Srikrishna says to Arjun, "I am within you and you are within me." This means, man is a part of the undivided whole. Only the knowledgeable persons can grasp the underlying monistic spirit amidst all apparently dualistic narrations presented in the Gita. Shrimad Bhagavad-Gita contains the gist of the Vedas and the Upanishads. He, who will make an analytical study of Gita, can get everything. Gita deals with Karma Yoga, Bhakti Yoga and Jnana Yoga. Gita is packed with knowledge be it on karma, bhakti or jnana. For doing a job properly, knowledge is essential. Bhakti is also jnana so far as one must know what bhakti is and how to do bhakti. Gita imparts essential knowledge on all aspects such as how to do karma, how to do bhakti and how to attain *Moksa*. Gita is relevant for all categories of persons in the society. Karma, bhakti and jnana are but the three phases of jnana only.

Divya Darshan divides life into three phases; to survive; to harmoniously live in the society in peace and happiness; to attain liberation or *Mukti*. Divya Darshan also preaches, 'Right Thought', 'Right Expression' and 'Right Action'. Divya Darshan further adds, "If you want to live, be dutiful; if you want peace and happiness, possess divine virtues; if you want freedom, acquire self-knowledge." The above expressions signify karma, bhakti and jnana respectively. While explaining things in phases, the concepts of karma, bhakti and jnana come sequentially. But the basis of everything is knowledge.

Man is dipped in ignorance and has forgotten Self. Ignorance does not mean total absence of knowledge. It means limited or fragmented knowledge. He, who does not have the sense of discriminating between good and bad, right and wrong, is ignorant. Even if an animal possesses some knowledge, it is called ignorant.

Knowledge is essential for maintaining physical body for doing one's duties, performing Dharma and living harmoniously in a society with peace and happiness, ultimately to attain liberation. Thus, knowledge plays a predominant role since birth to death and still beyond, till *Moksa* is attained.

But due to paucity of knowledge, man is not able to understand what all his duties are and the ways to perform his Dharma. Too much of indulgence with matters in this mundane world brings him sufferings. He is not able to understand where he has come from and what is the purpose of his living? That there is an all-powerful existence called God is beyond his comprehension and belief. He remains totally engrossed in the worldly affairs.

In the Shrimad Bhagavad-Gita, Lord Srikrishna, in order to dispel the ignorance of Arjun, very tactically presents the subject beginning with karma and ending up with jnana. "Should I wage war against my own brothers and relations?" This question baffled Arjun on the war field. His famous bow named Gandiva slipped down from his hands as there was shivering all over his body. Arjun wanted to escape from the terrible scene to avert the horrible consequences. At that moment of misperception, Arjun considered even a begging bowl preferable to a glamorous throne and a grand empire. Lord Srikrishna could appropriately diagnose the malady of Arjun who was beset with doubt and despondency due to his ego-generated sense of doership. Lord Srikrishna advised Arjun to relinquish the sense of doership, not to eye the fruits of action but to surrender all karma to God.

He further tried to convince Arjun about the mortality of the physical body and immortality of Atman within and without. None, be it living or dead, should be grieved for. He exhorted Arjun to rise to the occasion, casting off his faint-heartedness, to uncompromisingly fight for the establishment of Dharma. And that is the very purpose of God's occasional incarnation. "Whether you fight or not, all will be destroyed; it is God's Will. Consider yourself merely as an instrument, raise your weapon and fight with the enemies. I have already killed them. If you fight, victory is certainly yours. You will be famed for your heroic deeds. On the other hand, if you choose to escape from your duties, your image will be tarnished as people will view it as an act of cowardice or an unheroic deed."

Further, Lord Srikrishna also imparted true knowledge to Arjun in order to remove all his misconceptions on life and explained about the unitariness and supremacy of the all-powerful Brahman.

Darkness of ignorance is dispelled by lighting the candle of knowledge. There is nothing purer or cleaner than jnana. It eliminates all illusions. A person with inquisitiveness gains true knowledge that enables him to walk with an equanimous mind on the righteous path to attain liberation. He who realises the Supreme Brahman becomes Brahman. Brahman is the Supreme cause of whatever is manifested or remains unmanifest. He is the essence of everything that we see or do not see. He is the cause of this Creation.

He maintains; He dissolves. He is the ultimate refuge of everyone. He resides as Atman in all beings. He, who surrenders to Him, attains the Supreme Brahman. He responds to all prayers and saves the devotees from ignorance, sins, sufferings and rebirths. He is beginningless and endless. He is the beginning of all. Lord Srikrishna demonstrated His wondrous Cosmic Form to Arjun. Arjun stood puzzled. He prayed to the Lord to come back to His original human form. Convinced, Arjun surrendered to the Lord and finally rose to fight.

While imparting knowledge on various aspects, Lord Srikrishna said, "I am the cause or basis of everything that happens in this Creation. Without surrendering to me, there is no other option for you. I have manifested as one and all. I am the end-all and be-all of everybody."

It may be clarified here that while trying to explain monism, one must necessarily take recourse to dualism at the initial stages. One must first describe the greatness of God who is the cause of creation, preservation and dissolution. The sages had explained the spiritual knowledge to convince the people in several ways so that the aspirant will surrender to God. In the Shrimad Bhagavad-Gita, emphasis is laid on self-surrender as everything is done and regulated by God. The spiritual aspirant will first understand and appreciate the existence of God and greatness of God. God is doing everything. Scriptures are also divided into three parts such as karma, bhakti and jnana to explain the subject to various categories of recipients. But the basis of everything is jnana. The practices relating to some rituals in the initial stages are mainly intended for purifying and restraining the mind. By taking to righteous path, the spiritual practitioner's chitta gets cleaned and his negative qualities such as falsehood, anger, greed and jealousy etc. gradually vanish.

Finally, he will surrender to God completely. An unclean mind cannot surrender to God. He, who does not know anything about God, cannot surrender to God. He, who surrenders to God, finds his sufferings waning away to the extent of 75%. He will attain bliss on God-realization.

Without knowing about God, self-realization is impossible. Lord said, "Leaving aside all faiths and religious activities, surrender unto me; I will save thee from all sins." Self-surrender is the culminating point of all karma, bhakti and jnana. In this sacred scripture, Lord Srikrishna imparted the Supreme Knowledge to Arjun which is applicable to the whole of humanity. Shrimad Bhagavad-Gita is divided into eighteen chapters containing 700 slokas. It contains the essence of the Vedas and the Upanishads.

Right knowledge is essential to dispel the misperceptions born out of ignorance. It leads one from attachment to detachment, passion to dispassion and from the conflicting mind to the serenity of inner Self. Finally, the seeker and the sought, the seer and the seen, the knower and the knowable become one undivided whole. There remains neither dualism nor monism, neither adjective nor epithet, neither manifest nor unmanifest. Only Consciousness exists transcending Time or Space.

But unfortunately, even after worshipping God for years together, we have neither been able to cleanse our minds nor possess adequate knowledge about God. When shall we attain bliss and freedom?

We all suffer. But we do not try to find its cause and remedy. It is to be remembered that as long as man has not acquired true knowledge by reading scriptures and approaching spiritual masters, he cannot get rid of sufferings. The sages have taken so much pain to handover to us so many scriptures explaining clearly how to get rid of sufferings, but we do not pay attention to all those. At least, everyone should study Shrimad Bhagavad-Gita that contains the essential knowledge in a very compact and precise manner. Gita unfolds the secret knowledge layer after layer and presents the essentials required for everybody.

Surrendering to God is not that easy. Who is God and whether He can protect us? Why should someone surrender to somebody unless he knows the capability of the person to whom he surrenders? "Has He got more strength and power than what I have?" One must know this before deciding to surrender. Any amount of instructions from others will not make us surrender to God. For surrendering, a certain level of knowledge about God's greatness is a pre-requisite.

How man should live, what should he do for harmoniously remaining in the society with peace and happiness, and how to make spiritual efforts to realise the Supreme Brahman? Answers to all these questions are very clearly dealt with in the Gita. Hence Gita is a store-house of knowledge. He, who understands the import of Shrimad Bhagavad-Gita, will overcome the cycle of birth and death. The truth that is expressed in the Gita is for all time and is applicable to everyone. It is necessary for those who want to lead a disciplined life on the righteous path ultimately to attain self-realization. Most of us are not aware of this goal of life.

Everybody should read Gita regularly. Whatever is written in Gita, are all applicable to one and all. Never think that it is a private conversation between Lord Srikrishna and Arjun. Gita is for all of us indeed.

*****

[25]In the olden days, the ignorant men and women were not allowed to read the Vedas. That is because with limited knowledge people may misunderstand and misinterpret the essence of it. But the message of Shrimad Bhagavad-Gita as extolled by Lord Srikrishna is open to all. Through Shrimad Bhagavad-Gita, true knowledge has been imparted that can lead one to *Moksa*. Hence, knowledge of Gita is for everyone irrespective of caste and creed.

Shrimad Bhagavad-Gita reinforces the theory of monism or Advaita Philosophy in unequivocal terms. God's Lila is endless. His greatness is indescribable. Behind all these manifestations, remains the True Self which is inexpressible. The goal of every human life is realization of the True Self.

Some people feel complacent after knowing something about His Lila and Greatness. They remain in dualism. Self-realization remains a distant dream. The destination of all journeys is the Self which is immortal. By taking shelter of Sadguru, this goal of self-realization is achieved. True knowledge is nectar-like. It gives peace and bliss. When we are not interested to acquire true knowledge, it means we do not want to enjoy nectar. He, who attains God, attains all fortunes; he conquers death; he conquers time and attains all divine glories. Everyone has the right to realise God. Some of the persons get by heart some verses of the Shrimad Bhagavad-Gita and consider themselves to be very knowledgeable. But that does not mean God-realization.

According to Divya Darshan, whatever is done for realization of the Self is Sw*adharma*. Sw*adharma* is independent of caste or profession. Realization of the True Self is the true Dharma of the

---

[25] *Odia Divyadhara Vol 18 Page 50*

mankind irrespective of their different religious beliefs. Self-Knowledge must be acquired by one and all. On inculcating divine virtues, one will only do good to others; one cannot do any harm to others. Peace will prevail in the society. There will be no disrespect or deception to others. Everyone will have good relationship with the other. No one will break any rule. These qualities are expected from us as human beings, the best creation in this Creation.

It is said that those, who do not respect knowledge or Guru, should not be taught Shrimad Bhagavad-Gita. In order to get this nectar, it is essential to take shelter of Sadguru. By acquiring knowledge, one can understand the role of God. He will have faith and devotion towards Him. Guru imparts knowledge according to the standard of the recipient. Faith, devotion and love are the three stages of spirituality. Guru imparts knowledge to the disciples accordingly. He, who is in love with God, will easily surrender to Him. One begins with belief. Belief turns into faith and devotion. Bhakti turns into love which leads to self-surrender. In that state there shall be union between the two. In order to get all knowledge and powers from Guru, we must prepare ourselves accordingly. Guru is always ready to give but the disciple is not qualified enough to receive the same.

*****

[26]Birds are different from plants. Animals are different from birds. Man is different from animals. All these are controlled by nature. Arrangements are made by nature for the plant kingdom and the animal kingdom to survive. Plant kingdom primarily depends upon the mineral kingdom. The animal kingdom depends upon the plant

---

[26] *Odia Divyadhara Vol 17 Page 40*

kingdom. Everything in the Creation is inter-dependent. A creeper plant depends upon another tree to grow and rest. A tree gives shelter to birds and animals. Fishes remain in water. In other words, separate arrangements are made for different animals. Different animals take different type of foods. A man is a special creation. He is bestowed with more knowledge. Therefore, he must observe Dharma.

Divya Darshan discusses about man's Dharma in three steps.

- To maintain the body for survival is his first Dharma.
- To live in the society with peace and happiness is his second Dharma.
- The last but the most important Dharma is self-realization which is everyone's goal (i.e. to attain liberation or *Moksa*).

Whatever is essential to realise the True Self is sw*adharma*. For attainment of this goal, one must maintain his body and live peacefully and harmoniously in the society. In other words, Divya Darshan brings both individual life and community life under the ambit of spirituality.

Man survives; seeks peace and happiness. By doing so, knowingly or unknowingly he seeks his goal only. The ignorant men do not understand this truth. But the knowledgeable men pursue their goal by acquiring supreme knowledge. Without knowledge it is not possible to attain the goal of life. In absence of knowledge, man goes astray and suffers. Still many people do not know why they survive and why they take food. Behind all activities, there remains embedded a spiritual purpose. If man comes to know that all his actions should be goal-oriented, he can be simple and disciplined.

Without knowledge about his goal, he takes to zigzag route in a whimsical manner that leads him nowhere.

Observance of *swadharma*:

Many do not know how to observe *swadharma*. In the Shrimad Bhagavad-Gita, there is some discussion on *swadharma*. It is observed that many people misinterpret the term, *swadharma*. Some people interpret *swadharma* linking it to their occupations. *Swadharma* should be always linked to the goal of life. Everyone must know what should be done to earn virtues and attain the goal of life. In whatever situation one may be, if his karma is goal-oriented, he is doing Dharma. Purposeless karma brings sufferings. It is not the Dharma of a warrior to always wage war at any cost. Peace may not come that way. By waging war, if it indiscriminately destroys the natural kingdom and the whole of living beings, it is a demoniac act and not the *swadharma* of a true warrior. One should weigh the situations and circumstances and accordingly manage one's karma keeping in view attainment of the life's goal. One must carefully avoid sinful acts. Karma should not be done only for fulfilment of individual interest or for any selfish gain. It is learnt from the puranas that even the God-incarnates like Lord Ramachandra and Lord Srikrishna raised their bows for eliminating demons for the benefit of the entire mankind thereby establishing Dharma. In the Mahabharat, when all doors of peace were closed due to the arrogant attitude of the Kauravas, war became an inevitable option. Even Lord Srikrishna had to convince Arjun about his duty to plunge into war to ensure the welfare of humanity by establishing Dharma. Lord Srikrishna also became the charioteer of Arjun and guided him throughout that Great War. Even the great personalities, who were by the side of *Adharma*, were ruthlessly eliminated on the battlefield. It means, any act done for the establishment of Dharma is also Dharma.

If a butcher goes on butchering animals for earning livelihood and his children also take up the same considering it as their family occupation, then how will they attain self-development? He, who realises the purpose of his birth, can make progress on spiritual path. He should try to know what work should be undertaken to earn virtues. He should choose the right path to attain his goal.

Divya Darshan lays emphasis on divine qualities which form the basis of Dharma. By possessing divine qualities one can proceed faster towards one's destination. Holding on to divine qualities amounts to observing the Law of Eternity. Everyone should follow the Law of Eternity without any deviation. Knowledge is essential to know how the Law of Eternity operates in the kingdom of nature. By knowledge one can know the importance of truth and divine qualities and accordingly one's conduct gets purified. Due to want of knowledge, some people do not know about different food combinations because of which they lead an unhealthy life. If you flout basic norms regarding maintenance of the physical body, you are doing *Adharma* only. Ayurveda science deals with this subject regarding appropriate intake of food and water, fasting, medicinal use of some fruits, flowers, roots and leaves etc. very elaborately.

Spiritual practice becomes meaningful due to divine qualities. He, who conducts himself with divine qualities, is truly observing Dharma. Truth is an especially important aspect of divine qualities. He, who possesses divine qualities, comes to possess more powers in him and attains truth and divinity. Divine qualities bring peace and bliss. Demoniac qualities bring sufferings here and hereafter.

Divya Darshan lays emphasis on knowledge and divine qualities. Divya Darshan can establish peace in the whole world if everybody will take to knowledge and divine qualities. True Knowledge and divine qualities cost nothing but yield everything. Knowledge itself is a divine power. God creates, operates and transforms the Creation by knowledge. In other words, it is knowledge that manifests as the whole Creation. Knowledge is the very basis of our existence. True knowledge brings in divine qualities. Peace, bliss and freedom are the outcome of true knowledge and divine qualities. On the other hand, ignorant persons commit sins and that is why, they suffer. People are not able to understand the importance of Divya Darshan now. By resorting to violence, violence cannot be exterminated. The world we live in can become a heaven if we all practise divine qualities. Those, who are accepting and spreading this philosophy, are honouring and living up to God's wishes; they shall be blessed; they are divine messengers. Truth and peace shall prevail in the world sooner or later. Situations and surroundings have great impact on an individual. In this surrounding of materialistic air in the society, almost everyone gets entangled with materialistic desires and fulfilment thereof. The sages therefore teach us to be in touch with wise men or Guru and do satsang so that mind will turn Godward. When divine qualities will flourish in you, you will get stronger and therefore any outside impact of mundane matters will not be there on you. During spiritual practice, one must lead a simple and humble life. By doing so, one will muster up more power and will be able to surmount all obstacles coming on spiritual path. Others will not know that you are doing some spiritual Sadhana. Spiritual Sadhana is for acquiring more and more divine virtues. Divine qualities ultimately lead to God-realization. From the initial days of Sadhana, if a person comes to possess divine virtues, he will reach the goal faster. Divya Darshan says, "The more one knows the value of something, the more one gets inclined towards that." Since many people do not know the importance of divine qualities, they normally do not get inclined towards those qualities unless past samskara impels them. He, who possesses divine qualities, becomes a Deva.

A day will come when people will realise the importance of Divya Darshan. It will not be enough if you only become good. You must spread goodness around you.

People are very much worried about how to increase their wealth and secure their future. But very few seem to be worried about how to increase knowledge. By knowledge, we can realise truth which is invaluable. Any amount of material possession is insignificant and therefore cannot be compared with that. Material possessions may bring sufferings, but truth and knowledge will bring divine peace and bliss which is eternal. This is the goal of life. Spiritual practice to attain this goal is our *swadharma*.

*****

[27]While everyone craves for happiness, paradoxically, there is unrest everywhere and everyone is suffering. Everyone has a natural impulse to seek peace and happiness. But little does he know how to earn peace and happiness.

Man possesses some knowledge about how to live. But he does not possess adequate knowledge about how to remain strong, healthy, and disease-free. Further, man does not possess adequate knowledge about how to live harmoniously in the society with peace and happiness. As a result of this, he remains surrounded by problems.

---

[27] *Odia Divyadhara Vol 20 Page 42*

Divya Darshan expresses knowledge in three steps.

- Maintaining the body for a healthy living
- Harmoniously living in the society with peace and happiness.
- Acquiring spiritual knowledge for realization of the True Self.

These three steps, when combined, make complete knowledge. Different gradations of knowledge are seen on the way to complete knowledge. Scriptures speak about Karma Yoga, Bhakti Yoga and Jnana Yoga. These three taken together make complete Yoga. Divya Darshan as in the three steps discussed above, lays importance on Karma Yoga as well as bhakti with the aim of God-realization. Divya Darshan synchronizes karma, bhakti and jnana all at a time, taking knowledge as the base for attainment of the goal of self-realization. A famous quote of Divya Darshan is – "*Hrude bhaava, mukhe naam, haste Kaam*." This represents Divine Thoughts, Divine Expressions and Divine Actions.

A lazy person wants to earn more in a short time with little labour. He thinks that more money will bring him more peace and happiness. But this is a wrong idea. The richest man is not necessarily a happy man. Even if Devarshi Narada had acquired different streams of knowledge and had regular contact with Lord Vishnu, he was not getting peace. He had to accept Sanat Kumar as Guru to acquire Self-Knowledge for peace and bliss. Sri Ramakrishna, who was a great devotee, was even talking to Mother Kali. To acquire self-knowledge, he surrendered to a Guru named Totapuri. The great saint Sri Nigamananda Paramahansa even after seeing Goddess Taradevi had four spiritual masters.

Therefore, Divya Darshan says, "Why should you remain stuck up with such a low level of knowledge? You must acquire higher and higher knowledge and realise the True Self in this birth itself which is a great opportunity. Remember that you are Peace-Absolute and

Bliss-Absolute." You must acquire more and more knowledge about God. Without knowing about Him, you will not profit anything by simply chanting His name. He, who will try to know how to get peace and bliss, can ultimately reach God. Divya Darshan therefore strongly advocates and preaches, "Dispel your ignorance to get rid of all sins and sufferings."

Since we are facing towards darkness, we are suffering. In different situations, we are telling lies. But if our wife and children tell lies, we get angry. The reason is- we love truth. Telling more lies and less truth has been the order of the day. Man is not aware that he lives due to truth. Hence Divya Darshan asks everyone to turn towards light. The Vedas and Vedanta are the treasure of knowledge. The sages advise us to approach Sadguru. He, who contemplates on God, will get more and more knowledge about God. He, who wills, shall get the divine knowledge and power. Knowledge is divine and knowledge is light. He, who is knowledgeable, can do everything good to himself and also to others.

Being enveloped by ignorance, one considers oneself knowledgeable. He is not aware that higher levels of knowledge are there to be acquired. Once man reaches a particular level, he will have indication about the existence of still higher knowledge. Everyone should therefore take to knowledge and correct himself.

*****

[28]**Realisation of Self:** At the request of some of you, I (Sadguru Sri Sri Arjun) am going to give you some hints about what *Siddhi* is. It is an indescribable experience. Whatever may be spoken about *Siddhi*, it is difficult for the common men to understand. Since you are all curious about this subject, I will give you some indications of it.

[28] *Odia Divyadhara Vol 17 Page 4*

Realization of the Supreme Brahman is *Siddhi*. Ordinarily, the word *Siddhi* is used to connote some achievement or success in a specific pursuit linked to some desire. We are not going to discuss about that type of *Siddhi* which is temporary or partial. We do lot of work to attain a certain thing. We undergo so many difficulties to achieve something. We seek the help of our friends and relatives for getting success in our endeavour. But realization of Brahman by the grace of Sadguru is the highest form of *Siddhi*.

To get blessings from Devas, one must cleanse one's heart and possess divine qualities. In our social life also, normally everybody cannot go and meet a man of high position. Some qualification or position is essential to meet and mingle with him. Similarly, if we possess demoniac qualities, we may not be entertained by the Devas. It is mentioned in the puranas that the Devas and the demons were always divided into two warring camps. Therefore, it is essential for the spiritual aspirants to possess divine qualities in order to be eligible to get divine blessings.

We all seek peace and bliss. This means, everyone's journey is for a common destination. But as there is lack of sincerity in our efforts, it takes longer time to get peace and bliss. Several births are taken to get the Supreme Bliss on God-realization. But it is the birthright of everyone to attain bliss and remain permanently blissful. Sufferings must go away. Sufferings will permeate in no time and overwhelm us in absence of peace and bliss. Where there is bliss, there is no question of any suffering. We are not aware that God is Bliss-Absolute. Without knowing God, it is impossible to get peace and bliss. People adopt short-cut methods to get peace and happiness of temporary nature and remain satisfied with the same.

Man must seek permanent bliss and permanent freedom. For this God-realization is essential. Those fortunate few, who are listening to Guru's instructions, are acquiring more and more spiritual knowledge and getting more and more peace and happiness. One day or other, they will win the grace of God. Even when God takes human form, He forgets the True Self and gets entangled in the illusions of the worldly things. Therefore, Rama and Krishna also had to take shelter of Gurus namely Vashishtha and Sandipani respectively. Realization of True Self is *Siddhi*. For attaining *Siddhi*, the realisers have to make lot of spiritual efforts.

You need not be afraid of making spiritual efforts. You need not go to forest. You can carry on your spiritual efforts wherever you reside. Even in our daily routine life, whether in the paddy field or in any other work place, spiritual practices are possible by merely changing the attitude and approach towards work. One must know how to get peace and happiness and how to stay connected to it wherever one may be. This attitude to work will enable you to do the duties properly and move towards the goal of life.

"The dutiful alone owns life and is able to attain the Truth. Misery and fear remain far away from the dutiful. If Karma be your duty, accomplishment of the goal is inevitable." (Amritbindu-95)

"If you want to live, be dutiful. If you want peace and happiness, possess divine virtues. If you desire liberation, acquire self-knowledge." (Amritbindu-16)

Karma is what all you are doing in a routine course. But if karma is performed thoughtlessly, it leads us nowhere. It is meaningless to do any karma in a haphazard and half-hearted manner. Purposeless karma for karma sake is a sheer waste of time and labour.

Duty is 'what should be done'. That means, duty has to be synchronized with Dharma. In other words, there should not be any clash between duty and Dharma. Further, whatever duties you are performing, there must be truth, justice, righteousness and service motive in them. In other words, your duties should be purpose-oriented. It must take you forward towards your goal. Performance of duties is thus synchronized with observance of Dharma. When you perform your duties and thereby observe your Dharma simultaneously, you will be supported and blessed by God. You will get more strength and spirit to do big things that generally appear impossible. You will earn peace and happiness by performing duties in whatever field you may be working. Thus, all your duties also become your sadhana or spiritual practices. Action (*karma*), duty (*karttavya*) and spiritual practices (*sadhana*) get synchronized with observance of Dharma. Dharma will protect you and lead you forward to liberation or *Moksa*. You must make proper use of your knowledge and conscience to reach your goal faster. Therefore, Divya Darshan always emphasizes on acquisition of right knowledge by which you can abide by the Law of Eternity properly. Follow God's Will and not the whimsical dictates of your ignorance-generated ego.

"I must get peace and happiness. I must reach life's goal." That should be the attitude always. You must therefore speed up your spiritual practices so that you reach your goal in this birth itself. Do not get disheartened. Whenever any obstacle comes, we should pray to God to give us enough strength to surmount the same. Have strong faith on Guru. I (Sadguru Sri Sri Arjun) happened to meet a person who was very interested to learn spiritual knowledge. He asked me various questions. But he was not mentally prepared to take shelter of a Sadguru. Remember that as long as you have not taken shelter of a Sadguru, you will not be able to assimilate the knowledge properly. Unless you have love and respect towards Guru, you will not be able to retain the knowledge you have received from Him.

The conclusion is that if you do not welcome, love, acknowledge and accept knowledge, you will not be able to own that knowledge. You must therefore install Guru in your heart with love and respect. Be sure that He will give you knowledge since He is in your heart. Unless you have strong faith on Guru, you will never get peace and happiness. Without Guru your progress will be very slow. It may take several births for you to reach your goal. Therefore, surrender to Guru and attain your goal in this life span itself. It must be remembered that if you take more births, you will suffer more. Hence it is always advisable to hasten up and intensify your spiritual efforts.

I feel embarrassed to speak about myself particularly about *Siddhi.* I will give you some hints only. Everyone, be he a child or an adult, an old man or a sage, speaks about God. But the level of knowledge about God differs from person to person. A sage knows the most. For example, although everyone knows something about farming, an agricultural scientist knows more. You all know that Lord Buddha had got enlightenment. He attained *Maha Nirvana*. The Supreme Truth was realised. All sufferings vanished at once. It means, he got liberation from rebirths and sufferings. He did not take the name of any God like Brahma, Vishnu or Shiva. What he attained is the Supreme Truth. Supreme Truth is God. We have ascribed different names only. Lord Buddha thereafter preached to the mankind the ways to get rid of sufferings. He preached about truth and non-injury. You also know something about truth and non-injury which are very common subjects. You may be thinking what new or extra had Lord Buddha realised in his enlightenment?

Whatever we know by going through some scriptures, the enlightened person knows many times more. His knowledge is total and infinite. That is why we call him *Siddha* or the Enlightened. The

Enlightened person gets released from all bondages and becomes free. He crosses all delusions and illusions even though he resides in this material world. He experiences that he is eternal and therefore, he has neither birth nor death. He realises that the body is subject to decay and death but he is always there. He realises that he is Bliss-Absolute. There is no language to describe him. The experience of the enlightened soul cannot be expressed through any word. After lot of meditation and contemplation, that state of oneness is reached.

It took me 17 to 18 years to reach that stage; prior to that I was worshipping Mother Durga. By Her blessings I progressed on the spiritual path and I ultimately realised the Supreme Truth. Now I am not doing any worship. To whom shall I worship? She is in me and I am in Her. Whatever language I am using to express myself is nothing.

There are persons who have seen the forms of some Gods or Goddesses. When Yogi Sri Aurobindo was in jail, he had seen Lord Srikrishna. But he did not remain complacent with that. He knew that seeing the form of Lord Srikrishna was illusory. "The Truth is different from it. What is the Truth that appears as Lord Srikrishna?" This question haunted and hewed his mind. Yogi Sivananda had also seen Lord Srikrishna but he was not satisfied with that illusory form. Know that he, who realises the formless Supreme Truth, is an enlightened soul. Any form which is subject to decay and death is no real God. God or Brahman is eternal, all-powerful, and all-pervasive. He is Energy-Absolute and Consciousness-Absolute.

I was staying with my friend Sri Nilakantha Das, in his quarters C/4, HAL. It was evening of 14th April 1967. I was meditating. My prayer was not confined only to praising the Lord to propitiate Him. My prayer was to know the Truth. When I was praying sitting before the mother (Goddess Durga), tears were rolling out. Seeing her photo, I was thinking about the form of the Creatrix Mother. "Have you got only ten hands? If I say only ten hands, it will be an insult to you. If I say you have hundred or thousand hands, it will also be an insult to you. If I say millions also, it would be an underestimation. Your hands are infinite. Your heads are infinite. You cannot remain confined to any specific form." I went deeper and deeper and ultimately, I realised the Supreme Truth by knowing whom nothing remains to be known, by attaining which nothing more remains to be attained. It was all radiance, full of light on all sides. There was no specific direction from which light was coming; nor was there any source of that light. There was nothing other than light. It was all blissful. I was not able to know anything. Even I was not aware where I was. The jiva feeling vanished. My individual existence melted away. I had no feeling that I was sitting and meditating. I got merged with that Light. One becomes That. There remains nothing else; I realised; it is inexpressible. I closed my eyes. After that the Bliss I enjoyed is all inexpressible.

The knowledge, I am imparting to you all now, dawned upon me after returning from that state. What I told is just a tip of the iceberg. Many more remain unspoken. He, who reaches that state, can realise what it is. It is a matter of self-realization which cannot be explained to others. I hope that you will reach that state one day or other. If not in this birth, you will get in the next birth. You are all moving in that direction. I hope, you will progress faster and get rid of all sufferings. I wish to impart all my knowledge to the disciples. Those, who are interested, must remain fully dedicated to Guru and surrender to Guru.

I love my Gurus. By their blessings I have come to this stage. My first Guru is Socrates. Second Guru is Lord Jesus Christ, and third

Guru is Lord Buddha. Fourth Guru is Veda Vedanta (Scriptures). Fifth Guru is The Supreme Brahman. I had not seen them but since I had great love and respect towards them and I valued them most, I have got their blessings. Socrates was there before 2500 years or so. I was speaking about him and his philosophy to my disciples even though I had not come across any book on Socrates. It means, by Gurushakti I was able to speak about Socrates. He, who surrenders to Guru, Gurushakti will be expressed in him. The knowledge of Guru will find expression in the disciple.

Do never underestimate Guru. Have strong faith in Him. Surrender yourself to Him. You will be blessed. Without His blessings you may not be able to get peace and happiness; Love and respect knowledge. By knowledge you can choose the right way to get peace and happiness. God is Knowledge-Absolute. He is Consciousness-Absolute. He, who welcomes knowledge, welcomes Guru. He, who welcomes Guru, welcomes knowledge. By Gurushakti one can cross all bondages and reach the highest state. On this day, I bless you all. Let everyone attain that stage of enlightenment. There are many things to say. But I have restrained myself.

Remember, Guru does not mean any name or form. Guru means knowledge. By the blessings of Gurushakti, the disciple will become Guru one day. Let everyone get peace, bliss and enlightenment.

*****

Dharma in the Context of Spirituality

[Dharma is one of the most misunderstood words. It is translated as religion in English. Actually religion is not same as Dharma. Further people misunderstand Dharma as a set of rituals or practices. Dharma is also associated with temples, the idols, the priests and the rituals observed. Actually Dharma is not about observing some rituals; it is far beyond that. It is a way of life. Dharma when observed properly leads to self-realisation which is the goal of human life. In fact it is difficult to define Dharma and put a boundary on its meaning and implications. Dharma has been broadly defined as that which always upholds and protects everyone.

We think that doing charity, giving donation, extending social service, to visit temples and worship God, to sing Bhajan, to tell truth, to build schools and hospitals etc. are all Dharma, but these are not Dharma. These are only auxiliary requirements for observance of Dharma. These are all noble deeds one should do but these are not Dharma; these are all means to Dharma. By such acts our antahkaran (internal organs like mind, intellect, chitta and ego) shall get purified.

In the words of Sadguru Sri Sri Arjun, "Where there is Dharma, there is peace and bliss because Dharma protects us, sustains us and liberates us." Sadguru Sri Sri Arjun has explained in simple terms the true meaning of Dharma in the following discourses. But as one contemplates more and more one will move towards perfection faster]

[29]Man is the best creation of God. Food requirements, fear, sleep, and procreation are the basic nature of all animals. The man also possesses these four characteristics. What is extra in him is his inquisitiveness for knowledge and Dharma. The sages and seers have all along been exhorting mankind to know what Dharma is and how to observe the same. Dharma has been defined as that which always upholds and protects everyone. In some places, the ways to attain Dharma have been prescribed. The sages and seers knew what Dharma is and accordingly they were conducting themselves as a result of which they were getting peace and happiness. But today's man hardly understands the real import of Dharma. Due to ignorance, man is not able to observe Dharma properly. Hence man is getting less peace and more of sufferings. In the name of Dharma, man does perform lots of rituals but still peace remains a far cry. Instances of corrupt practices, falsehood, cheating, brutality and jealousy are on the increase. There are threats of war instead of call for peace. Sadguru Sri Sri Arjun says, "Where there is Dharma, there is peace and bliss because Dharma protects us, sustains us and liberates us."

Sadguru Sri Sri Arjun emphasises on, "Ignorance is the cause of sufferings". Ignorance about Truth and Dharma is the main reason for the disorder and disturbances. Self-realisation is true Dharma.

---

[29]*Odia Divyadhara Vol 1 Page 3*

What is Dharma?

It's not easy to speak about Dharma. It is a vast subject dealing with very subtle aspects. Many do not understand what Dharma is. Only sages and seers know the true import of Dharma. Many definitions of Dharma are advanced in the scriptures. Even if volumes of explanations are available in the scriptures, still the people at large fail to understand the true spirit and essence of Dharma due to ignorance and lack of interest.

We talk of Sanatan Dharma. But to whom the word Sanatan is ascribed, we do not know. The wise men interpret that whatever exists always and that which is beginningless and endless, is Sanatan Dharma. The eternal law that governs always is called the Law of Eternity. But the question is what exists always? What is that Law that is always operative? Since we do not know the basis of all these, we are not able to tell correctly about Dharma. We say that we are walking the path of Dharma but we make so many deviations. The truth is- "Wherever there is Dharma, there is peace; wherever there is Dharma, there is bliss; wherever there is Dharma, there is *Mukti* or Freedom."

Now the question is, when we do not get peace, bliss and freedom, then what type of Dharma are we observing? If we are not in peace and bliss, then how shall we get liberation (*Mukti*) or freedom? We must understand that *Mukti* is a state of mind where there is no fear, no suffering, no doubt and no anxiety. Since we are having all of these, it is quite evident that we are not moving towards liberation. Had we really progressed towards liberation, these negative symptoms would have waned away slowly. All these persisting negative symptoms expose not only our ignorance but also non-observance of actual Dharma.

We merely know that charity (to donate some amount or to extend some services), to worship God, to tell truth and to have devotion are all Dharma. But these are not Dharma. These are only auxiliary requirements for observance of Dharma. These are all means to Dharma. To make sacrifices, to dig wells and ponds are noble works which should be undertaken but these are means to Dharma only. Then the question is- what else Dharma is?

Generally, if somebody undertakes some pious works, we call him Dharmic. Even people who undertake different occupations treat their occupations as their Dharma or *karttavya*. In that case what shall we speak of a butcher? Is killing animals his duty or Dharma? Scriptures exhort us to practise non-injury. "Do not steal, do not tell lies, do not grab others' properties, do not think ill of others," thus instruct the scriptures. Hence whatever occupations we undertake may not be on the tracks of Dharma.

Dharma takes us on the path of self-purification or self–development, peace and bliss. Some people consider that their path of Dharma or their religion is the best. But after knowing the real meaning of Dharma, one would not say that any particular religion is superior and the other inferior. Dharma is always Dharma. Dharma is eternal.

We follow different traditions and practices on the pretexts of our religious obligations. But what exactly Dharma is, we do not know. There are some social laws which are followed due to local rules and practices. Our cultural activities, festivities and different types of social traditions are carried out in different manners according to local practices. These cannot be called eternal laws. These are only practices which are subject to change over a period of time. These practices are developed and being followed for a good and harmonious social living, but they are not eternal. Many traditions die down in course of time. The new generation may not have respect towards such age-old practices if those are unscientific, irrational or redundant. Slowly many old traditions fade into oblivion. Those social systems are man-made. When situations, circumstances or social priorities change, they also undergo suitable modifications or at times, conveniently bypassed.

But the Law of Eternity is observed always irrespective of time and place. The Sages of yesteryears knew what Sanatan Dharma or the eternal Dharma is. When we do not know what Sanatan Dharma is, how can we assert that we are observing Dharma?

Had we really known what Dharma is, we would not have suffered. We also do not know how to observe Dharma. The subject matter of Dharma, more often than not, remains confined to spiritual texts. Unless knowledge is acquired, Dharma cannot be understood in totality. In absence of knowledge, we construe the social laws, traditions and different racial or local practices for Dharma. We remain complacent with observing some rituals. There are some ethical practices or prescriptions developed in course of time for bringing discipline in the society. Courtesy, morality, good qualities such as respect, non-stealing and non-injury are considered to be parts of Dharma. These are all required for the well-being of human beings. These qualities create a healthy environment in the society to live in peace and happiness. But these are all auxiliary requirements for the observance of Dharma. We are ignorant about the essence or true nature of Dharma. To tell truth is Sanatan Dharma. To love others is Sanatan Dharma. Lord Jesus said, "Love thy neighbour as thyself." Buddha preached *ahimsa* or non-injury to others. By violent means this Creation shall be destroyed. By non-violence and love the Creation can flourish. Sense of love is also present everywhere even in lower creatures, insects and plants.

Love is divine. That love appears in different situations differently such as- love between husband and wife, love between father and son, love between mother and child, brother and sister etc. Had there been no love we would have always quarrelled with each other. This Creation would not have been there. Due to love a tigress takes care of her cubs. In case of human beings, after a child takes birth, his mother brings him up by taking lot of care. She educates the child, takes care for his well-being, and always thinks well of him. The animal kingdom would not have existed without love. For the animal kingdom to exist there are some divine qualities such as renunciation, service and love etc. These divine qualities are the divine provisions in the Law of Eternity that takes care of everyone in the Creation. When husband returns from his work place to residence, his wife keeps food ready, for she knows that her husband would come at a specified time. Any deviation from this truth would create disturbance and misunderstanding. Further without a spirit of sacrifice, no one can help another person. The divine qualities are already effective in the kingdom of nature as a result of which we see this orderly Creation. Deviations cause distortions and disturbances. In all sects or religions, importance is attached to the divine qualities. It is said that God becomes happy to see His children helping each other and sacrificing for each other. By divine qualities the Creation gets sweetened by peace, happiness and bliss. These divine qualities are the essential requirement for attaining the goal. In our society due to superstitions, we offer animal sacrifices to propitiate God. But the sages and scriptures had taught non-injury to animals. That means, we are doing *Adharma* in the name of Dharma due to want of proper knowledge about Dharma. By possessing divine qualities man can earn peace and happiness. By divine qualities he can move on the path of self-development and realise his true nature. The opposite qualities of divine qualities are demoniac qualities which impede the progress of man towards self-realisation as a result of which peace and happiness remain far away from him. In the name of Dharma, due to ignorance, we arouse the demoniac qualities in us. We are killing animals like goats, cows, buffaloes etc. Where is Dharma in these types of practices? Are we supposed to eat animals also? Whatever gives us peace and happiness and accelerates our journey towards self-development, and ultimately self-realisation is called Dharma. In other words, virtues lead us to self-development while the sins or vices drag us to sufferings. There is Dharma in virtues, *Adharma* in vices. We are bound to suffer because we are doing *Adharma* under the pretext of Dharma. Suffering is entwined with *Adharma*. Happiness is entwined with virtues. Because people do not know this, they steal on the one hand and donate big amounts to God on the other hand. They feel complacent after donating as they think that they are sacrificing for God.

God will be happy to see our devotion, and not the vulgar display of our wealth and properties. Some people take pride in carrying out different types of worships and getting themselves tortured by not taking any food or water even. To propitiate God there is no need at all to do any such penances. According to Ayurveda, the following four categories of people such as children, patients or weak persons, pregnant women and old persons should not undertake any fasting. But we do fast on different occasions and feel satisfied that we have performed our dharmic duties. This human body is a gift of God. It is our first and foremost duty to take care of the body. Then only we can do all the virtuous deeds. It is further mentioned in the scriptures that those who are healthy, they can fast once in a fortnight or twice in a month. If someone fasts, he should take plenty of water. There are many other injunctions in the scriptures on intake of food. One should not take non-veg food along with milk and ghee. One should not take meat and fish together. Blood will become impure if one takes food in such odd combinations. One should follow all scriptural guidelines which are meant for maintenance of the body. If we omit to take care of this fundamental duty, how shall we get peace and happiness?

The second requirement is that man must live harmoniously in society. There are certain principles to be followed for living in the society with peace and happiness. Those are all our social duties and responsibilities, but we neglect in this area also.

We should always be humble and respectful to others. If we are arrogant there will always be quarrel or heated arguments with others. How can we get peace possessing the qualities of selfishness, arrogance and jealousy etc.? Due to ignorance we suffer. Even due to jealousy, our sufferings get multiplied due to the growing happiness of our neighbours. At times, people go to temples only to pray for the ill of others. By any definition, this cannot be called devotion. Man must try to acquire knowledge and broaden his vision. Man should approach a Sadguru to learn different aspects of life such as duty, righteousness, truth and goal of life. One should at least read some scriptures that the sages have handed down to us. Man seeks peace and happiness. This would not come from cheating others. There are many virtuous ways to get happiness. We should learn those ways. Why man seeks peace and happiness? What is the purpose of this human birth? What is Dharma? What is the goal of life?

If a man does not know the answers to the above questions, it means, he does not know what Dharma is. Hence there would be lapses in observance of Dharma.

A person should ask himself, "Why is he taking food?" The common reply would be - "To survive."

Why is a man so keen to survive? If we do not know the answer, it is to be understood that we do not know what Dharma is. Dharma includes every dimension of our life. If we are not clear about the fundamental aspects of our lives, this means we do not know what Dharma is; we also do not observe Dharma. We simply follow some rituals or social practices blindly in the name of Dharma.

With such mindset, we are bound to suffer. Dharma only can lead us to peace and happiness. Observance of Dharma will lead to cessation of sins and sufferings. We commit different kinds of lapses in absence of knowledge about Dharma.

There are ways to get peace and happiness. There are also ways to get freedom or liberation.

Dharma explained:

- Whatever is done for maintenance of the body is Dharma.
- Whatever is done to live harmoniously in the society with peace and happiness is Dharma.
- Whatever is done to attain self-development and the goal of self-realisation or liberation is Dharma.

The law governing the above three points is known as the Law of Eternity. The food is different for different animals. Accordingly, their physical structures and systems are different. Nature has designed them accordingly. All these are governed by the Law of Eternity. The sages have envisioned this Law and exhorted mankind to observe the Law for maintenance of body, for happy and peaceful social living and ultimately for self-realisation. This Law is eternally operative. The same Law was applicable in the past to the animals and to the plant kingdom. Now also the same Law is applicable and in future too the same Law will be applicable. Everything is there in the kingdom of nature. We see the mineral kingdom, plant kingdom and the animal kingdom. This has been possible due to the Law of Eternity. Our existence, peace and happiness and ultimately liberation are all governed by the Law of Eternity. He, who consciously observes this Law, can speed up his journey to bliss and liberation. For that, first we must know what that Law of Eternity is. But due to ignorance, we are not able to know the indispensability of the Law of Eternity and are not keen to observe the same. We know a few things. That is why we are able to survive, maintain our bodies and live in the society with some peace and happiness. But we do not know how to get freedom. Overall, we do not have knowledge of Dharma. Whatever we know is very little and partial. With the scant and scattered knowledge that we have, we are under a wrong notion that we are observing Dharma.

We also do not evince interest to know more about Dharma. Divya Darshan says that if one does not acquire knowledge, one cannot know Dharma. By knowledge only one can distinguish between Dharma and *Adharma*. With the help of knowledge only we come to know what nectar is and what poison is. A small kid may swallow poison without slightest hesitation. He may also put his finger into the fire. An ignorant man is bound to commit various lapses at different stages of life. Therefore, knowledge must necessarily be acquired. For that only the sages and seers always keep on imparting knowledge. Knowledge is also available in scriptures. This means that knowledge is always there. The knowledge by which Law of Eternity can be understood properly is also available in scriptures. Because we have distanced ourselves from that knowledge, we remain ignorant about the same but still we nurture the feeling that we know everything. This is also due to ignorance. Although doing

Adharma, we claim due to misconception that we are doing Dharma. A child also at times says that he knows everything. But during examination, his teacher finds out his mistakes and therefore does not award full marks. The sages and seers impart knowledge on the Law of Eternity. But quite a few take interest in them. We are not even able to know what the Law of Eternity is although we owe our existence, sustenance etc. to it. The sages and seers want that everyone should understand this law and observe the same to attain bliss and freedom. To get some jobs, we have to acquire some qualification and undergo some training. That knowledge is only for our survival but that is not enough. The real knowledge enables us not only to maintain our bodies and live in the society peacefully but also to ultimately lead us to freedom. The Law about which we have discussed in the foregoing paragraph is also linked with knowledge.

Every person wants that he should protect his body, live in the society with peace and happiness, and ultimately attain freedom. In other words, he does not want to be subservient to anybody. He wants to be blissful. He shuns sufferings. He wants freedom from the shackles of rebirth and sufferings. He wants to be free from all bondages. He, who is inquisitive about this and makes efforts, shall ultimately attain bliss and freedom from sufferings, doubts, fear and desperation. By observing Dharma this state can be attained. This Dharma is the Eternal Dharma, i.e. the Law of Eternity.

Divya Darshan says, "To know the Law of Eternity is knowledge and to observe the same is Dharma. Dharma comes from knowledge and liberation comes from Dharma."

This is the process to attain self-realisation which brings with it bliss and freedom. All other knowledge, which is mainly for survival or living in society with status and position etc., is limited knowledge which would not carry us to our real goal.

Due to some knowledge and greater ignorance, we do a few things right, but we commit multiple lapses on a cumulative basis. Can we tell that we are on the path of righteousness and Dharma?

Right observance of Dharma would give us peace, bliss and ultimately freedom. It will take us forward on the path of self-development. If we are not able to achieve self-development, that means, we do not know what Dharma is and therefore we are not truly observing Dharma.

Many people try to appear as Dharmic persons by wearing special type of garments, performing different kinds of rituals, and wearing different patterns of sandalwood paste on their foreheads. But Dharma has nothing to do with the external coverings or make-ups. Divya Darshan says, "Knowing the Law of Eternity is knowledge; observance of the Law of Eternity is Dharma." He, who appreciates and assimilates this, is on the path of divinity and ultimately he will attain divinity.

Therefore, you must know what Dharma is. Try to learn from him who knows more than you. You may learn from your brother, parents, teachers or from spiritual texts. You may also approach a Sadguru. It is also our Dharma to learn what Dharma is. So far whatever we have learnt, are from some Guru or other sources as discussed above. If we know everything, why do we commit mistakes? That means, there is inadequacy of knowledge in us. We should consider ourselves fortunate that we are increasing our level of knowledge by asking questions to others who know more than us and who are able to guide us. We should not feel ashamed to inquire from others. If we know one truth after another, that means, we are acquiring more knowledge. In this process if we proceed, one day we can realise the Supreme Truth, i.e. God or Brahman. Approaching a Sadguru and acquiring true knowledge is a special opportunity in this life. Then life becomes purposeful. That means knowledge takes us to greater heights, promotes us, and elevates us to infinity, immortality, eternity and unity. Then why feel shy to acquire knowledge from the sages and seers, from the knowledgeable and wise persons? Due to ignorance we shy away from admitting our faults or lapses. We are not able to tell the truth, however qualified or educated we may be. We think without falsehood we cannot manage ourselves. Rather we make all out efforts to hide the truth. But it is seen at times that an innocent man goes to the police station and unhesitatingly confesses to the crime committed by him.

Man has been gifted with a rare and fair form. Only man can elevate himself to Godhood. It is said that 84 lakhs of births he had taken before taking human form. He is still in a processing stage awaiting completeness. There are different grades of men. There are persons who behave like demons and some others behave like lower creatures. They are yet to reach their real manhood. They are in the making. In other words, evolution is still on. Therefore man should lead his life carefully. If he commits more sins, there is likelihood that he may be deprived of human birth in future and be demoted to the levels of lower creatures. Hence man should remain away from sins and always try to tread on the path of righteousness. It is like the game of Ludo. There are ladders and snakes in it. One can rise with the help of ladder. On the other hand, there are snakes ready to swallow and cause downfall. Every moment we are passing through virtues and vices. Therefore, we should consciously make efforts to increase our virtuous deeds. We should never allow ourselves to get downgraded to animal or sub-human categories. Our virtues shall propel us to higher and more qualitative births while sins shall push us to the cauldrons of sufferings.

Scriptures describe five types of sacrifices (Pancha Yajna) which are –

- Bhuta Yajna - sacrifices for animals or lower creatures,
- Nru Yajna - sacrifices for humans
- Pitru Yajna - sacrifices for ancestors
- Deva Yajna - sacrifices for Devas

Jnana Yajna or Rishi Yajna or Brahman Yajna - Practice of True Knowledge.

Of all the above sacrifices, Jnana Yajna or Rishi Yajna is the best and highest form of Yajna that excels all other forms of sacrifices and gives eternal and unlimited result i.e. *Moksa* (Liberation or *Mukti*).

All religions guide mankind to peace and happiness. But people are not able to live in peace and happiness. Suffering is the rule rather than exception. Men clamour for peace but it becomes rarer. An angry man cannot get peace. A greedy man cannot get peace. In other words, unless one possesses divine qualities, peace shall be a far cry for him.

There is Law of Action. Whatever somebody does, the corresponding results also accrue to him. "Every action has got equal and opposite reaction," This Newtonian law of motion is also applicable to our own actions. If we undertake good actions, good results will ensue. If we do wrong things, the corresponding bad results will accrue and shall unfailingly come back to us. This Law of action is strictly enforced in the Law of Nature. Nobody can save us or give us any reprieve. We must be overly cautious while doing anything. The end result of sins is sufferings. Ignorance begets sins and sufferings; knowledge begets virtue and bliss. We are supposed to learn from our sufferings and refrain from sins. We must aim at increasing our virtues to get peace, happiness and ultimately freedom from all miseries.

Most of men are steeped in ignorance. They think that by taking shelter of any personal godhead, they can get rid of sufferings. But who is the dispenser of all fruits of actions? In the Shrimad Bhagavad-Gita, Lord Srikrishna says, "I am the dispenser of fruits. You have only the right to actions".

When the Supreme Power is the ultimate dispenser, how can any personal godhead deviate from the Law of Action and provide any relief or relaxation? So, everyone is bound to enjoy the fruits of his actions. Nobody else can intervene to dilute or manipulate the results. We should try to mend our ways and set right our actions so that we shall be happy with the ensuing good results. If we shall be repeating our lapses and approaching any powerful deity to forgive us, we would not be forgiven. In order to get rid of sufferings we are to find the right means for ourselves.

Many people do not believe in the existence of any such Supreme Power. Some other people believe in the Supreme Power, but they worship some deity of their own imagination. We are saddled with a host of desires. We pray God for fulfilment of our desires by performing different types of rituals and penances. The Gods created by our imaginations cannot protect us nor fulfil our desires. Because of this also, many people turn to become disbelievers (*naastika*). He is not God whom we imagine as such. The scriptures have tried to describe and give indication of Brahman in correct manner. Because we do not evince interest to know, we form our own ideas about God who is altogether different from Brahman described by the ancient scriptures as all-pervasive, all powerful and eternal existence. Gods of our imagination cannot give us anything since we only have created such Gods by our imagination. Whoever will try to know the

Brahman as realised by the sages and seers, can attain everything, all peace and happiness, bliss and freedom. God cannot give us cooked food and remove our hunger. God has given us knowledge and intelligence by which we can utilise the available resources and prepare food for ourselves and for others. God is there in all of us as our knowledge, our intelligence, our strength, our seeing power and hearing power etc. We need not beg of Him anything else. He has provided everything. Nothing extra is to be created. By acquiring knowledge, we can know His scheme of things and get benefited. We are getting His blessings always and every moment. Due to cataract of ignorance, we are unable to understand Him. He is there as the Chit-Shakti or Conscious Energy. He is our intellect. He manifests as everything in this Creation. Without Him, we cannot exist.

God is Bliss-Absolute. He, who knows Him as such, realises Him. God is Freedom-Absolute. He, who knows Him as such, liberates himself. Whatever we require, God has already provided everything to us before we asked for the same. We are not aware of the same. Nor do we evince interest to know. We find it easy to create a God of our imagination and seek his help in every matter. We have been surviving even without knowing God. This means that God has made everything for our survival even before we asked for the same. We are able to function because of His power. We are utilising the knowledge that He has bestowed upon us. But man is not able to realise this. He also does not know how much he can be benefited by Him! He is not able to understand that God has provided milk in the mother's breast before a baby is born. Before creation of anything, God has made all arrangements for its working and maintenance. If man acquires enough knowledge, he can get so many things from God. God has given us so many things before we were born and before we asked for the same. We cannot even imagine what all He can give us! This means, if we know Him and thereafter ask for something, we shall get.

But what are we doing? We are forgetting God. In the process, we are delinked from God. How can we get rid of sufferings? The more a man knows Him, the more peace and happiness he would get. In other words, we can get rid of sufferings.

Even the disbelievers are better than those who worship an imagined God, expecting benefits from Him. The disbelievers reject any idea of God created out of human imagination. Therefore, they hastily conclude that there is no God. But that there is an Absolute God or Brahman who is different from the imaginary Gods is yet to be understood and accepted by them.

If somebody knows the greatness of God or role of God, slowly he would believe in the existence of God. God is Knowledge-Absolute. He manifests as the Creation although He is formless.

But man thinks it easy to perform some rituals more often followed with befitting celebrations in a joyful and exuberant manner to propitiate God and to get something in return. Hence the need for knowledge is not felt.

Lord Buddha preached four noble truths thus.

- There is suffering (Dukkha arising due to birth, old age, disease and death). This is the first truth.
- There is a cause for the origin of suffering. This is the second truth.
- The third truth is the cessation of suffering. That means, suffering which has come must also go once the cause of the same is known.
- There is a path to cessation of suffering. Once man knows and moves on this path, his sufferings shall come to an end.

In other words, we are to analyse the reasons of sufferings and take appropriate measures for cessation of sufferings. But, instead of doing this, we approach different deities of our imagination for alleviation of our sufferings.

We should know God's scheme of things and his laws. We should follow the Law to stay blessed. We should possess sattvic qualities and shun tamasic qualities. We should possess divine qualities and remain away from demoniac qualities. We should thus tread on virtuous path to get peace and bliss. Falsehood, crookedness, arrogance, jealousy and anger etc. would bring in more unrest than peace.

All divine qualities are there in the kingdom of nature. The Creation is sustained by means of divine qualities such as-

- Renunciation
- Restraint
- Spiritual Practice (Efforts)
- Service
- Truth
- Love
- Forgiveness

God has bestowed all these divine qualities upon everyone including animals. The Creation survives due to divine qualities. If a mother would not take care of her baby, the baby cannot survive. It is the mother who brings up the baby. The father takes care of the family. Even a tigress feeds its cubs and protects them. This shows that the entire Creation is sustained due to divine qualities.

He, who possesses these divine qualities, is really *dharmic*. Therefore, man's Dharma is to conduct himself on the path of righteousness with divine qualities for attaining self-realisation.

Truth is also an important trait that upholds the Creation. We expect others to speak truth. But we ourselves take to falsehood. We feel that one cannot survive by telling truth and therefore falsehood must be resorted to for survival. But if truth prevails everywhere at all points, then we all shall be benefited. We have survived due to truth. Without truth man's survival would be a big question mark. When somebody comes back home, his wife has kept food ready because she knows that her husband will return at a specified time. The wife expects her husband to tell truth. The husband also expects his wife to tell truth. We all expect our children to tell truth. A gang of robbers also obey and honour truth in their dealings otherwise the gang shall break away. They distribute their booties among themselves truthfully. Man is suffering because he does not know truth to the extent he should know. There would be disturbances in the family and in society if truth is not honoured and followed. Disaster and disturbances are bound to occur wherever there are deviations from truth. Many violate truth and ultimately go to courts for justice. Like this, in every phase of our life and even day to day living we observe truth because of which things happen smoothly and systematically. Similarly love and forgiveness are also two especially important divine qualities. Those, who possess love and forgiveness, are elevated human beings. Even the demons possess some divine qualities. They take care of their family and children. A demon king takes care of his kingdom.

If someone wants peace and bliss, God will not give any such thing separately. Unless man possesses or develops the quality of love in him, he cannot get peace and bliss. A jealous, crooked, or revengeful person cannot get peace and bliss. Bliss is an outcome of love. Bliss is something which is intangible and can only be experienced. If somebody serves others, many people will come forward to serve him. If somebody is of loving nature, all will love him; love shall come back to him from all sides. Divine qualities are God's gift which are there everywhere in the kingdom of nature. We should apply those qualities and conduct ourselves accordingly for peace and happiness of self and society. A person, who possesses great amount of material wealth, cannot satisfy everybody. But a person with divine quality of love can satisfy one and all. Love is intangible and inexhaustible. Such a man would be loved by millions of people. Love is therefore a great divine asset. If men and women understand the value of love and start loving each other, the earth shall become a heaven. Human beings can do this by upholding and applying the divine virtues which are the free gifts of God. They cost nothing. Service, love and forgiveness cannot be purchased by money. Money is exhaustible and transient whereas divine qualities are inexhaustible and permanent. If some person possesses the quality of love, there would be manifold reciprocation of love, just unimaginable! God is there everywhere as love. His store house is here only. Due to ignorance we are not able to utilize the divine resources. The sages and seers utilized those resources and enjoyed divine bliss, eternal and unlimited.

God cannot mitigate our sufferings permanently. God cannot give us peace and happiness for all time to come. Let us therefore develop the divine virtues in ourselves. That is true Dharma and Dharma shall lead us to eternal freedom from all sins and sufferings, from the cycle of birth and death, and from the bondage of samsara.

*****

The Greatness and Existence of God

[This is a collection of divine discourses by Sadguru Sri Sri Arjun delivered mostly during 1981 to 1989 on the greatness and existence of God.. The discourses revolve around the one and only Brahman; how He manifests as everything in and around us. The essence of all the discourses is that God cannot be seen physically but can be experienced. With deep contemplation and sincere effort, a practitioner may be able to understand His manifestation and experience it in his day-to-day life. Sadguru Sri Sri Arjun has explained it in simple words. We have tried to maintain the simple and soothing flavour of the original discourse.]

(Consciousness is the cause of the Creation. Consciousness is present everywhere in all forms. It has no beginning and no end.)

[30]There are many people in the society who do not believe in God. That is because God does not expressly make His presence felt. They do not even know that He is present in them as the 'Self'. It is not necessary to search for God outside. One can realise Him inside one's own body. Atman can be realised only by knowledge. He remains as 'I' in us. He manifests Himself as various forms and qualities. He expresses Himself as knowledge and love. He, who realises Him as

[30] *Odia Divyadhara Vol 20 Page 12*

such, gets His blessings. His divine play (*Lila*) takes place by way of our different activities. Because of Him, we can do everything. He manifests as ether, air, fire, water and earth. He is there in all activities; He is the only actor; He moves from street to street as beggar; He steals and is lodged in jail. He blesses us as a pious man; He is Guru and He is also the disciple. Guru possesses complete knowledge and the disciple possesses less. That is also His manifestation. He is there in void; He is all-pervasive. Everything we come across is none other than He. He, who sees Him everywhere and in everything, gets His blessings.

Atman does not perish. It is immortal. Atman is there both in the gross body and the subtle body. After destruction of the gross body the subtle body remains in which Atman also exists. Till a jiva attains complete knowledge, it undergoes death and rebirth. But the ignorant man does not believe in the existence of Atman. Nobody can assert that he does not exist. Because He is there in us, we can speak, we can hear, and we can do so many things. But we are not able to understand what Atman is. If you know yourself, you can know others also. Atman can be realised by Atman after going beyond mind, intellect, and conscience. Atman is there in you as your mind, intellect, conscience, and Self. Atman is the Guru. Atman is the Guru of intellect and conscience. We can do everything, understand everything and experience so many things. When you will realise that Guru is there in you as your Atman, conscience and intellect, you will always get His blessings.

He, who realises that due to the grace of Sadguru he is able to know everything, will get Guru's blessings. Guru has given us Ishta Mantra which means that we are going to realise Atman by the grace of Guru. Those, who have not taken initiation, will not be able to realise Atman. Those, who have strong faith on Guru, will realise

Atman in this birth or in next one or two births. Those, who have taken initiation but have forgotten Guru, do not have faith on Guru. They have deviated from the right path. People, who consider Guru as the physical body, will not be benefited much. "Guru is always there in me as mind, intellect, and conscience." He, who understands like this, will get Sadguru's blessings.

*****

[31]We all talk of God, but we do not have clear idea about who God is and what his role is. Therefore, we do not pay that much respect to God. Many people imagine God as a superhuman being with some additional features or some divine weapons. But they cannot trace out such imaginary entity. They are ultimately caught in the whirlpool of belief and disbelief.

But God is formless and therefore invisible. When He wills, He can appear as forms and qualities. When our faith becomes strong, we can see Him according to our contemplation. The sages had realised Him and called Him by various names. It is a matter of self-experience. It is a fact that without experiencing something, no name can be attributed to that. The thought of some truth has been subsequently given a name. There are so many scriptures handed down to us by sages, but we do not evince interest to go through the scriptures. Many of us deny the existence of God. The power by which you are raising your hands and the power by which you can experience your own existence is God.

Changes are always going on in this Creation. The Creation itself is a product of changes. Any change that occurs is the effect of some cause or power. In scientific terms, inertia cannot be broken unless there is an external impressed force. Who is that background power

---

[31]*Odia Divyadhara Vol 17 Page 53*

that initiated the Creation and made it blossom? Nothing or no changes can happen without power or energy, asserts Divya Darshan. The sages have named that basic power as God or Para Shakti.

Energy manifests as matter. There is energy in matter. Matter is a form of energy. Matter is converted to energy. Energy and matter are one and the same. The energy pertaining to the visible universe of names and forms is called by the sages as *Apara Shakti*. Para Shakti has become *Apara Shakti* for the purpose of the Creation. Para Shakti is called Brahman, the Supreme. When He becomes *Apara Shakti*, multiple forms come into being with different qualities or properties infused. This is how water is different from fire, an animal is different from a man, and a tree is different from an animal. Here the Earth, holding the mountains and oceans, is nurturing the plants as well as animals. There, the Sun is emitting light and heat. An independent Shakti, known as Para Shakti, enables or activates all powers that are seen in the Sun as well as all other forms and qualities.

We are all born by that Shakti, we survive by that Shakti, we can speak by that Shakti, we can see and hear by that Shakti. Shakti manifests as different forms and qualities. But the ignorant man does not know the role played by Shakti. Not knowing Shakti is ignorance. He thinks, "I am hearing, I am seeing, I am doing everything etc. etc." If that is so, then why he is dying? Why can't he stop decay and death? Why a dead body lies motionless even with all his limbs intact? Where have all his powers gone?

The sages, having realised that omnipotent Existence, call Him Brahman. A yogi calls Him Atman. A devotee calls Him God.

Even with little knowledge, man considers himself very intelligent or wise. With limited or fragmented knowledge, a person cannot know where he has gone wrong. A child does not know his mistakes. As he grows up and his knowledge gets enhanced, he can know his mistakes committed earlier. A wise person, who knows the truth, knows what is wrong and what is right. The ignorant persons do not know the truth. They are far away from it. The sages are called enlightened souls because they have realised the truth. They can instantly sum up the entire heterogeneous Creation of innumerable names, forms and qualities into a unitary, homogeneous, all-powerful, infinite existence who is none other than Brahman. Changes in forms of creation, preservation and dissolution are always on in this Creation. Man is born; he lives for some years and then passes away. We come across various forms and qualities undergoing changes in this Creation, during our lifetime. For creation, there is some law, for preservation or maintenance, there is some law, and for dissolution also there is some law. True, all these three aspects take place in the kingdom of nature. But who is the king or ruler of the kingdom of nature?

The powers that regulate the above-mentioned three aspects such as creation, sustenance and dissolution are known as Brahma, Vishnu and Maheswar respectively. Brahman Himself manifested as Brahma, Vishnu and Maheswar.

To express this in a different way, it is said that the female consorts of the above three are known as MahaSaraswati, MahaLaxmi and MahaKali respectively. The primordial Energy is called Maheswari Shakti who manifests as MahaSaraswati, MahaLaxmi and MahaKali.

It is not enough if a seed becomes a seedling. Water, light, air and manure etc. are essential for a seedling to grow into a full-fledged plant. Therefore, the Creator has not only created this Creation but has made all arrangements for its sustenance and further development.

After birth, so many other things are required for a baby to survive. God has planned for secretion of milk in the mother's breast for the baby to live on it. Before creation of the animal kingdom, God has created the plant kingdom. The animal kingdom cannot survive without plants, its fruits and flowers. Before the plant kingdom, there were earth, water, fire, air and space. Not only food grains, but God had also perfectly designed in-built digestive system, blood circulation system and respiratory system etc. for every living being. Since man does not understand the provisions made by God, he goes on asking for something or other. Without knowledge, man can neither understand God's Creation nor His creativity. The more man knows about His Creation, the more will he be benefited. It is God who remaining as MahaSaraswati gives us knowledge. God also remains as our mother, father, teacher and Guru to give us knowledge. God remains as different powers in this Creation and all along He has been serving us in different forms. One will be at a loss if one contemplates on the role played by God for our well-being. He has given things to us before we asked for the same.

Due to technological development, man is now-a-days shying away from laborious works. He has become lazy. God is there in us as energy and has been providing us inspiration and strength. We must thank God that he has provided food, water and different materials for clothing and housing etc. We are getting love and care from our parents, brothers, sisters, friends and relatives. The sages understand and appreciate the benevolence of God and live happily.

"I am in God's kingdom which is complete in all respects. He has provided everything. He has given me a perfect body with the required limbs and sense organs. He resides in me. He has given me consciousness and power. I must remain obliged to God for everything He has given even before I asked for it. How can I describe His greatness?" This should be our contemplation. The sages had realised God's role and His greatness.

The more you contemplate on Him, the more you will be flooded with divine thoughts and feelings. Lots of past impulses and knowledge collected in your previous births are stored in you. Do not consider yourself as insignificant. Revive your knowledge from within and come forward to teach Divya Darshan to the mankind. Your main duty is to acquire more and more knowledge about God. Have love and devotion towards God. Surrender yourself to God. All sufferings will go away. Remember that you are pure, free and immortal; divine bliss is your birth right. You will one day realise that you are one with Him. This is the divine goal of life. My blessings are always with you all.

*****

[32]Divya Darshan takes recourse to jnana path. So far as self-knowledge is concerned there is no question of any caste, creed or religiosity. It is the Self that manifests as all. Everyone is none other than Self. To realise Self whatever knowledge is to be acquired and whatever laws are to be followed are known as Sanatan Dharma. It is the Law of Eternity. Divya Darshan dwells upon the Law of Eternity in a quite simple manner intelligible to the common men. Whatever the people of yesteryears were doing, we have been blindly following those things, but the intelligent and wise men should give a relook to those methods and practices. They should try to find out the essence or truth in the same and abandon the unnecessary and

---

[32] *Odia Divyadhara Vol 5 Page 40*

irrational things. It is to be remembered that God is everywhere. He is clean and pure. Due to paucity of knowledge we are not able to realise Him.

If '4' is added to '4', the correct answer is '8'. He, who does not know addition, cannot arrive at the answer. Similarly, even if God is there, due to our ignorance, we are not able to realise Him. It is said that God expresses Himself through the sages and seers. Even if He is present in all of us, He remains eclipsed due to the impurities in us.

Even if we know the answers, when somebody asks us we cannot recollect the same if we are in a disturbed mood. In such a state, we usually forget the answer. When we regain calmness, we start remembering. We get reflected on all sides. But we are not able to see the images because the surfaces on which there is incidence of light are not suitable for reflection. But when we stand in front of a mirror, the reflection is visible because mirror is a good reflector. Again, if the mirror is dirty, reflection will not be clear. Hence the reflector being the medium to reflect should be clean or pure. If our heart is clean and pure, God will be clearly reflected in our hearts. When our thoughts and conducts would be clean, we can realise the Atman within. Due to ignorance, different kinds of distorted thoughts swarm through our mind and therefore we forget God. We are not able to realise God although we owe our existence to God. We pray God for fulfilling all our requirements. He is the life of our life. He is the essence and propeller of our vital energy. We are not able to experience His presence. First, we must know that God resides inside us, in our hearts. Then only we can understand what His contributions are or what He does for all of us in this Creation. By knowing this, our conduct and behaviour would change. Others can also feel the changes in us.

If someone is violent and fighting with others, it means demoniac qualities are predominant in Him. If divine qualities are perceived in someone, he is a divine personality. He, in whom God expresses Himself, can tell everything i.e. past, present and future. Nothing remains as mystery for Him. He has the power to know or experience everything. He would be established in divine wisdom. The presence of divine qualities in him can be easily observed by others.

The scriptures say that God is Bliss-Absolute. It is true also. Those, in whom God clearly expresses Himself, enjoy divine bliss or Supreme bliss. But the ignorant men possess complexities and crookedness and many other demoniac qualities. Therefore, they suffer. The sages in their gospels and teachings speak of God's greatness and glories. From their teachings it can be known whether the sage is a true realiser or not. Many people recite various kinds of scriptures after getting those by heart. But it cannot be said for certain that they are true realisers. God expresses Himself in the person, who is simple, pure and possessed of divine qualities.

We hear from others that God is present in all beings. Intense yearning for realising Him is true worship. God expresses Himself through us as conscience. He, who obeys His rules, is a real worshipper. Lord Jesus used to say, "By calling me Lord, you cannot go to heaven. He, who would follow the rules or laws, can go to the kingdom heaven."

But we worship here and there in a very casual or wanton manner. Even if someone worships like this for ages, he cannot be pure and clean, nor can he realise the Self. Atman or God would express through him, who listens to his conscience and acts accordingly. By outward worship, God cannot be realised. If you serve a man, you may get something from him in return. But how a stone or wood would give you anything? Only the conscientious can know God.

Inward worship of Self is the real worship. Lifelong we have been doing the outward worship but we hardly get desired results. Whole life is spent in the process. If we encourage others for doing outward worship, it amounts to misleading them. Worship of Self is inward worship. Inward worship is far superior to outward worship. Those, who indulge in outward worship, may not give up the negative qualities from within. By inward worship, *chitta* gets cleansed up. In the outward worship, lot of importance is given on offering coconut, banana and incense etc. to God. Different procedures are followed for worshipping different godheads. On the other hand, in case of inward worship no material is required. Tears would come out while worshipping.

But in case of outward worship, lot of formalities are observed that are quite expensive. The thieves also go to temples and offer so many things. People treading on immoral or illegal paths also worship God for relief from sins. Temples, mosques and churches are on the rise. The devotees also grow in number. But paradoxically, instances of sins and sufferings, injustice and unrighteousness are also increasing.

If a person becomes pure, 50% of his sufferings shall vanish; by self-surrender, 75% of his sufferings shall vanish and by self-realisation 100% shall vanish.

*****

[33]Man wants happiness, peace and freedom. It is his basic instinct. He has passed through many stages before becoming a man. All the impulses and samskara, actions and tendencies collected in his previous births keep him imprisoned. When we do not know

---

[33]*Odia Divyadhara Vol 5 Page 45*

ourselves and think ourselves to be somebody else, are we not in bondage? A person who is chained cannot move as he wills. Our conditions are like those of a chained animal. An animal when tied cannot move far. We also remain in narrow surrounding like the chained animals. Chain or bondage does not mean only being confined to the four walls of a jail room, but whatever we want to become, or whatever we want to have, we are not able to get that. This means, we are chained. We are also not ready to believe that we are free and are under none other. "I am only the Self." Realisation of this is called 'Self-realisation'.

We must make efforts to realise our Self. The sages and seers impart knowledge on this subject. Those are known as Dharma (Law of Eternity) or spiritual conduct. True spirituality lies in good conduct.

The first step of spirituality is to believe that God is there. This comes under dualism (Dvaita). Going further the sages say, "You are the Self or Thou art That." This means, you are the Unitary Existence.; there is none other than you. This is monism or Advaita. The sages and seers had realised the Law of Eternity based on monism or Advaita.

It is true that to believe in God and observe His Laws is spiritual conduct. By doing so, man's basic and common urge for peace, bliss and freedom can be fulfilled. By taking recourse to spiritual conduct man gets peace and bliss ultimately to realise Him who expresses Himself as peace and bliss.

The sages know and observe the Law of Eternity. Anyone who follows the Law can get happiness, peace, bliss and freedom. The sages who realised monism ultimately, also passed through dualism initially. Since we do not know right type of spiritual conduct, we commit many mistakes in our day-to-day life and at times we end up with some superstitious beliefs. The law, the observance of which makes God realisation possible, is known as the Law of Eternity. Laws are there only to give us happiness, peace and bliss. We, even without knowing about God, are taught many good practices and good conduct by our parents and teachers. That is how our conduct gradually gets purified. We are taught to be obedient, humble and respectful towards others particularly to elders. When we start respecting our elders, we pay respect to God also. We would also have devotion and love towards God. When we offer namaskar or pay respect to others that means, we express our feeling of sraddha and love. We must teach this to our children also. Even if we have already offered namaskar to our elders, we must demonstrate this to our children by doing namaskar once again to our elders in the presence of children. Simply instructing the children to do namaskar is not the right way of teaching. We should bend ourselves with all humility while doing namaskar. At times we are to completely bend ourselves to touch the feet of the elders. While doing namaskar both the hands should be folded.

We must understand the greatness of God so as to get inclined to surrender to Him. Spirituality lies in good conduct. God has created everything necessary for the survival. He had made all provisions for our food even before we were born. Before the plant kingdom was created, God had created earth, water, fire, air and space. Before animal kingdom was created, the plant kingdom was created. Even different types of food for different types of animals are arranged. The digestive system of animals is different from that of humans. We humans cannot digest the animal foods. If we break the rules, we will suffer. We lack proper knowledge about the type of food we should take to maintain a healthy body. Even some parents do not have proper knowledge about food because of which they are not able to feed the children properly.

In the scriptures the body is likened to a chariot. Our sense organs and organs of actions are personal godheads. Seeing power is a personal godhead; hearing power is also a personal godhead. Similarly, our tasting power and smelling power are personal godheads. In other words, the divine powers are engaged to protect us; protect our bodies. Without these divine powers we cannot survive. We should respect the divine powers that are residing in us to protect us. Then only we can get more help from them. To the divine powers we must offer sattvic food that is suitable to them. But what do we eat? We take wine and tobacco, smoke cigarettes and take many other intoxicants. In other words, we offer non-eatables to the divine powers residing in us. As a result they would in course of time become demoniac and shall destroy us instead of protecting us. Because of our uncontrolled and indiscriminate food habits, we run into different problems.

Therefore, taking sattvic food, entertaining sattvic thoughts, doing sattvic actions and acquiring divine knowledge constitute true spirituality. We suffer due to many such deviations from the right ways. Hence, we must come back to the right track and properly conduct ourselves in order to get peace, happiness and bliss, and ultimately attain self-realisation.

Divine way of life shall ultimately land us in the vast and limitless ocean of divinity. Everyone is potentially divine.

*****

[34]*["If a man cannot believe even after witnessing the play of the Supreme in guise of the universe, then what else he needs to see to believe? Not being able to believe can be attributed to ignorance.*

---

[34]*Odia Divyadhara Vol 20 Page 59*

Just as a child cannot understand himself and the world, likewise man cannot believe God due to ignorance." (Amritbindu-82)]

Whatever we come across, see all around us are but His mere play. From where so many things have come? Where were they all prior to this? Man cannot understand this due to ignorance. Man is dipped so much in ignorance that even if he is seeing and enjoying everything, he is not able to understand that there is a Creator. Whatever we see were all there in different states. There was no cloud in the sky; the clouds became visible and it rained. Every day the Sun rises and sets. By whom, all these happenings are caused or conditioned? Everything in the Creation is well-synchronized. Who is doing all these? There is some invisible power, which is creating and sustaining the Creation.

Some people think that after seeing God in some form, they can know Him. But without knowledge about the form, how can one recognize Him? God manifests as infinite forms. God manifests as earth, water, fire, and air etc. Man is not able to know that there is a Creator of all these. What else he needs to see to believe the existence of God? This means that we are suffering from cataract of ignorance. If human beings are not able to accept that there is a Creator, then it is most unfortunate. God or Brahman is a naming word. He, by whom all changes do take place, is named as such by the rishis or seers. A human being however great he may seem to be, if he does not believe in God, he should be categorized as a man of lower knowledge. A kid cannot know even who his parents are. Likewise, if we are unable to know God, we are infants only. Man considers himself to be knowledgeable, but he is unable to know God, the Creator. This is a matter of great shame. Lord Jesus had said, "He, who does not see but can believe, is wise." The rishis accepted Brahman as formless. The rishis are wise men. Some educated men also ridicule God. It is a matter of shame. To know a knowledgeable person, we need knowledge. Without knowledge we cannot understand him.

The sentence under discussion (Amritbindu-82) can be understood by the wise only. The rishis without seeing Brahman in form also believed Him. But we after seeing Him manifested as infinite forms and qualities cannot believe Him. Hence, we are ignorant.

People misconstrue a rope for a snake. Since man does not know the Truth, he suffers and remains in fear and doubt. If we do not believe in God, we are as ignorant as a child.

Therefore, everyone should acquire spiritual knowledge and know about the existence and greatness of the eternal and all-pervasive Existence, unitary and infinite.

*****

[35]We have some bhakti towards God but not as much as we are supposed to have. Why are we not having enough bhakti or devotion towards God? The answer is- We are afflicted by ignorance. Due to ignorance, we possess more of tamasic tendencies which bring sufferings to us. A suffering man cannot get liberation. But everyone, including birds or animals, demons or humans, craves for freedom.

Freedom does not mean just going to heaven. It means something else. Freedom means complete peace and bliss, complete independence, and total absence of doubts, fear and sufferings. No one welcomes sufferings. Nobody wants to be in fear. On the other hand, happiness, peace and bliss are sought after by everyone.

---

[35]*Odia Divyadhara Vol 12 Page 5*

Freedom is where there is eternal peace and bliss. Freedom can be attained even while living in samsara. Bliss or freedom is not only there in heaven, it is also there where we live. Heaven is not the name of a specific place or zone. He, who lives in peace and bliss, is said to be living in heaven. Unless you refine your qualities, any place, even heaven, is hell for you. On the other hand, if you possess divine virtues, hell will become heaven for you. It is necessary therefore to acquire right knowledge about these divine qualities wherever you are.

We think that we know so many things. If we are knowledgeable, why do we suffer? We are suffering; it is true. This means, we are in ignorance and so we commit mistakes. So, we suffer. Where is freedom for a suffering man? Freedom is a matter of self-experience. The basis of freedom is knowledge.

Due to ignorance, we are not able to believe in God. Due to ignorance some people believe in God for some time and thereafter again they disbelieve. In other words, they vacillate between belief and disbelief due to ignorance. If their desires are not fulfilled, they start disbelieving. Some people worship God on a regular basis and perform all rituals meticulously. Despite their devotional offerings to God, if they encounter any adversities, they start blaming God for their misfortunes. Even they become atheists. The belief that comes due to limited knowledge or ignorance, does not last long. But the belief that comes after proper knowledge about God lasts forever. Mistakes occur where there is ignorance. But when the truth is known, there is no question of any misconception or consequent suffering. Limited knowledge brings doubt, mistake and fear. Hence, everyone should try to acquire knowledge.

The sages and various scriptures have been reiterating the need for knowledge and exhorting mankind to try to understand the same.

The knowledge to get happiness, peace and bliss is very clearly mentioned in the scriptures. But we are not studying scriptures. Yet we consider ourselves knowledgeable. It is a matter of regret that even though the sages of yesteryears had taken so much pain for doing spiritual practices and handed down the cream of knowledge for our benefits, we do not evince interest in that. Some persons read and remain complacent with getting by heart some verses even without understanding their true meaning. We do not contemplate on the subjects mentioned in the Vedas and Upanishads. He, who can understand and appreciate the true import of the subjects mentioned in the Vedas and Upanishads, can get peace and bliss.

Due to ignorance and resultant ego, we consider ourselves knowledgeable. It is a matter of regret that we do not study scriptures handed down to us by the sages. A child also claims that he knows everything. When his parents point out the mistakes, he retorts, "You do not know." An old man also considers himself to be knowledgeable. This is nothing but a symptom of ignorance. When we were small, we were committing so many mistakes. We were not able to know our mistakes. We were thinking that we were doing things right. When we grew older, we could know the mistakes committed by us during our earlier days. It is quite natural that with limited knowledge, one will consider oneself knowledgeable. Thus, ignorance afflicts us at every stage of life. Therefore, it is important to clear one's misconceptions or mistakes by acquiring right knowledge.

When a person will study the scriptures such as the Vedas and Upanishads etc., he will acquire true knowledge. On the advent of true knowledge, all his past misconceptions about himself and about others, about the external nature and the internal nature will be dispelled, and he will be able to lead a righteous living for attainment of the goal of life. He will realise that he was so far misconstruing the unreal for the real due to ignorance. Truth is far away for the ignorant.

How will a person dipped in ignorance get peace and happiness? It is impossible. True knowledge is very well presented in various scriptures and therefore you should try to delve deep into the same if you are keen to dispel your ignorance. You need not search for peace and happiness outside. You yourself are the store house of all peace and bliss. You need not try to discover any heaven for you outside. The heaven is inside you. Do not ascribe forms to the Gods and Goddesses. It is futile to imagine God as holding some weapons and riding on some animal-vehicle like, bull, buffalo, lion, mouse, owl or swan. God is formless but He can manifest as various forms. We do not know who God is. Lord Buddha said "Truth is God." We have given different names to God. But there exists a great power. It is absolutely necessary to understand that Existence to whom various names like Brahman, Om, God, Param-Brahman and Ishwar etc. are ascribed. Different forms and different descriptions on the single entity make people confused. Different patterns of worships and rituals are in vogue leading to groups and diversified display of religiosity. It is also seen that persons belonging to one sect do not eat the prasad (a sweet or any edible thing which is distributed to people after worshipping God as a blessing of God) from another sect.

There is only one God named differently. If man will realise this truth, he will attain peace, bliss and freedom. There is no scope for any wrangling over which God or whose God is superior. People are not able to know about God's existence and His manifestation. We have merely heard from our parents and grandparents that there is God. But we do not know where He is and how He is. We just follow blindly. We imitate others and accordingly we worship Him for fulfilment of our desires. Our devotion gets tainted by our doubts. In such a situation, how can we expect any blessing from God? Therefore, even though our parents and grandparents had been worshipping God by following some rituals, none had got God's grace.

How can one get God's grace while carrying ignorance, doubt and fear in mind? How can one get God's grace when God (Truth) is not understood properly? To manufacture something, there are some theories in the background. That theory is also truth. If one proceeds step by step in accordance with the theory, one can manufacture a machine or any of its parts. If there is any flaw in applying the theory, he may fail in his mission. Likewise, due to ignorance about truth, we are not able to realise God. God is there as Truth. The reason for remaining far away from God is that we do not possess knowledge about Truth that is ever present everywhere, even inside us.

We have been craving for peace and bliss, but we are not getting the same. Why? It is because we are not keen to know the Truth. To attain the Truth there are many other ancillary truths which are to be known first. Without this, peace and bliss remain a far cry.

First, we do not fully believe in God. It is mentioned in the Puranas that Lord Vishnu holds in his four hands, four weapons such as Panchajanya conch, Sudarshan Chakra, a mace named Koumadika, and a lotus. No one can say that he has seen such a God. Due to ignorance we ask "Can you show me God?" None can bring God for demonstration. At the same time, it is said that God is omnipresent, omniscient and omnipotent. But due to lack of knowledge, we do not understand this nor do we have interest to know.

I am telling you something about God's existence. It is an endless subject. We consider ourselves to be the best. This is an illusion. The ego in us prevents us from knowing the Truth. In other words, due to Maya, we are not able to understand the Truth; Truth is God. To know the Truth, knowledge is essential. By acquiring knowledge one can understand Maya and attain the Truth. At that time, Maya will be dispelled. Maya is the veiling power. Truth is veiled due to ignorance. There is no separate entity by the name of Maya. If ignorance is done away with, the Truth can be realised. Hence knowledge is so essential. This darkness of ignorance creates illusion and all confusions. Light of knowledge dispels the same. Without knowledge one cannot realise God.

Many people do not believe in God. Now the question is how were we created? After our birth, we came across and experienced so many things around us. It is to be remembered that there is some invisible power by which everything has been created. After birth, how do we survive? By whom we are enabled to breathe? Are we breathing by our own efforts? All these are done by some invisible power. Breathing process is going on. Lot of activities go on nonstop inside our bodies. We are seeing, experiencing, hearing, speaking and writing. When we talk or write anything, we pay attention to it but while breathing, no attention is paid by us. This is how the invisible power works in us. During sleep, we do not know anything. We do not know whether we are dead or alive. But we wake up in time. Who wakes us up? The divine power wakes us up. Otherwise, a sleeping man will not wake up. This means, the divine power prompts us to get prepared and attend our work. We possess strength by which we do all work. Do we procure strength from outside to do anything? This proves that, some invisible power is there inside us as our energy or strength by which we can do our work. The knowledge by which we can think of something and apply it through out is also there within us. Even if some knowledge comes from outside, we are supposed to apply the same in time and at appropriate places. Why do we forget? Knowledge is not yours if you forget. Similarly, there is some power within us which can make us blissful and lead us to freedom. He gives us knowledge to speak or work. There is an eternal, all-powerful and all-pervasive Existence who is Truth. All processes and all activities are caused and conditioned by Truth. A seedling grows and becomes a tree. There was no rain; it rained. The Earth revolves round the Sun. Who causes or empowers all these activities? He, who realises that power, gets merged or becomes one with that power. This is the essence of the Vedas and the Upanishads. He, who realises the Supreme Truth, becomes the Supreme Truth who also is the Supreme Bliss. Till such time, man must undergo various kinds of sufferings. In absence of true knowledge, he will be committing mistakes after mistakes. Consequently, he will suffer.

The sages have named that Truth as Atman or Self. He, who gains self-knowledge or realises Atman, will be one with Atman. He alone will get peace and bliss. Whether a tree or a seed, whether a child or parents, whether food materials or other objects for our living, whether the climate or the environment, everything is caused by Him. Unless we know Him and His role functions, how will our problems be solved? We do not understand His plans and designs. That is why we get shocked or surprised. We get surprised by even a small magic show. Once the truth or trick is known to us, we say that there is nothing mysterious in it.

Maya is there in and around all of us. God's one-man show goes on because of Maya. We appear as different actors of His play, but we do not understand this due to our ignorance. Not understanding this brings sufferings to us. Hence, we must acquire knowledge to know truth after truth till we realise the Supreme Truth. At that time only, we shall get rid of all sufferings and attain liberation.

But what we usually do is that out of ignorance, we try to earn wealth to get happiness and rarely hesitate to indulge in undesirable pursuits. Can one get happiness in this way? Wealth is required for our survival but not necessarily for peace and happiness. We see that many wealthy nations also suffer. Even the richest of persons also is confronted with different problems for which he has to spend sleepless nights. It is to be remembered that peace can only be earned by true knowledge. We should be happy that we have been bestowed with some knowledge by which we can earn and make a living. If we take extra training, our skill improves, as a result of which we get better jobs and earn more. That means, by knowledge we can earn money. A thief is able to steal by knowledge only. Behind all our actions, there is knowledge.

By knowledge we can know about Truth or God otherwise known as Brahman, Atman, Om and Ishwar. By acquiring more knowledge, we can realise Him. By possessing some knowledge if we can live, we can also get peace and happiness by acquiring some more knowledge. We will also get bliss and freedom. By means of knowledge, we should find out what suffering is and why we suffer. Then only we can find out ways to get rid of sufferings.

According to Lord Buddha, there is suffering; there is a cause of suffering; suffering was not there; it has come; anything that has come must go. Once the cause is diagnosed, the effect can be done away with.

Human beings undergo happiness as well as suffering but people with tamasic tendencies suffer more. When man suffers, he must try to know its cause so that he can get rid of suffering and be happy. Otherwise, he will continue to suffer.

God has bestowed upon us complete knowledge. We are to arouse and utilize the same to enter the zone of bliss and freedom from the world of sufferings. Therefore, knowledge is one of the greatest gifts of God to the mankind. Man must know the importance of knowledge. By simply lamenting, suffering shall not wane away.

It is to be understood that there is a Supreme Power called God. To realise Him, one needs knowledge. One must take His shelter. One must know the way to get rid of sufferings and live peacefully. "Who is God? How and where is He? How can I realise and attain Him? What is the goal?" One must contemplate on these questions to get peace, bliss and freedom.

The wealth you earn by whatever means such as stealing, robbing or hard work etc. cannot bring you happiness. Happiness is a state of mind. Wealth has got nothing to do with happiness. The truth must be realised to earn peace, bliss and freedom. Upanishads say, "Prajnanam Brahman." It means, "Knowledge is Absolute Brahman; Consciousness is Absolute Brahman." Essence of knowledge is Prajnana. In other words, Brahman who is Pure Consciousness manifests as knowledge. Therefore, taking shelter of knowledge, amounts to taking shelter of Brahman. He, who welcomes knowledge, welcomes Brahman. He will one day realise Brahman, the Supreme Truth.

The sages had realised Brahman. We generally say that the sages are very knowledgeable. We know something and we get happiness to that extent. Realizing the Supreme Truth means realizing God or Brahman. Brahman is there within us as knowledge and power. Without knowledge the energy or power cannot be comprehended. If we continue to remain in ignorance, how can we wish to see God? It is not possible.

There are also persons who believe that by worshipping and propitiating some deities, they get their wishes fulfilled. Bhasmasur also got boon from Lord Shiva. He destroyed himself by misusing that boon. This means if ignorance remains, we cannot enjoy peace and happiness. Seeing some form of some of the deities is also not real but an illusion or Maya only. Every form is a manifestation of the Supreme Truth. The Supreme Truth manifests as Brahma, Vishnu and Maheswar. He manifests as mother Durga, Kali, Laxmi and Saraswati. Witnessing any form does not mean realization of the Supreme Truth. The Supreme Truth eternally exists far above all these manifestations. Realization of the Supreme Truth means at the same time attainment of divine knowledge, self-realization and freedom. Divine knowledge rules out any sort of disservice or injury to anybody. Everything is manifestation of Atman or Self. There does not remain any duality. Ignorance vanishes. Only knowledge and bliss remain.

To acquire true knowledge, one must approach a Sadguru by whose blessings one can unfold the mysteries layers after layers and realise the Supreme Truth.

*****

[36]*["It is not necessary to search for God outside. All our visions and thoughts are His manifestations. In other words, He Himself is all thoughts and expressions. Therefore, He is not something to be searched out but only to be realised." (Amritbindu-56)]*

Generally, people believe that God must be having a human form or some other exceptional form. Due to want of proper knowledge they search for Him here and there. But the God of their imagination remains unseen. Consequent upon their failure to find God after several efforts, they turn out to be disbelievers. Since they are

---

[36]*Odia Divyadhara Vol 13 Page 32*

ignorant about how God exists and whether He is with form or without any form, they doubt His existence. To explain about God, the sages have developed some methodology and therefore, they presented the subject in three steps such as Lila (Divine Play), Greatness, and True Self.

Scriptures say that God cannot be seen. He can be expressed by Himself only and by none other. We see by our eyes. The power by which we see is Brahman. Brahman is to be realised only. But due to our ignorance, we ascribe some imaginary forms to God and wish to see Him. One must acquire more and more knowledge about Brahman, to realise Him and also know His manifestations. Knowledge is the divine eye by which Truth can be realised.

An infant does not know the value of a ten-rupee note. If we give it to him, he may tear it or put it into his mouth. But his response will change after he grows up and understands the purchasing power of the ten-rupee note. He will preserve the same to meet his expenses. Knowledge makes all the differences. By knowledge, everything is understood. Due to want of knowledge about God, man imagines God in a human form with more hands and some divine weapon in each hand. He imagines that God must be handsome, gorgeously dressed and easily distinguishable. There are different divine-vehicles such as swan, peacock, owl, bull, mouse and buffalo etc. for different deities. The truth is that God is formless. He manifests as different forms and qualities. Brahman is Chit-Absolute or Consciousness-Absolute. Can anybody see Consciousness? That Consciousness, by itself, manifests as various forms and qualities. Consciousness has no form. Consciousness is Brahman. But man tries to find God in different places and in different forms. Man makes different preparations to appease God and expects God to appear before him.

Sometimes the devotees claim to have seen Him in a specific form. But this is mere reflection of one's own imagination. When the thought of the devotee becomes intense, it is reflected as such. It is illusory and not real. Brahman is Chit-Absolute. Even He is neither Chit nor Achit. It is childish to say that God resembles a man. Have you ever tried to delve deep into the truth or consciousness present in every form? You may reach the form but not Him who is inside in an invisible state. That formless and invisible existence has taken all forms including the human form. Consciousness expresses itself through different forms. Seeing a specific form does not amount to realizing God.

God is there in everything and everywhere. Due to ignorance we are not able to know Him. He expresses Himself through various forms and qualities. He also manifests as all prerequisites and preparations for the final products and effects. He is formless and therefore He cannot be seen by eyes. He cannot be touched by hand. How can you ascribe any form to Him? By what you will know Him? Only by bhava, you can know Him. Bhava comes according to Jnana.

When Arjun wanted to see the Cosmic Form of Lord Srikrishna, the Lord said that the cosmic form would not be visible to the mundane eyes. He bestowed upon Arjun the divine eyes by which he could see the Cosmic Form. In other words, by the jnana Arjun acquired, the necessary bhava developed in him to understand the cosmic presence of the Lord.

But the idea of the common people on the Cosmic Form is different. They normally imagine God with a very tall figure with long legs and long hands, covering vast space and containing everything. In such case, where did Arjun stand to witness such a colossal and multi-dimensional figure! Further no physical structure, however vast the same may be, can be coextensive with the entire Creation.

Any physical structure implies a finite form and not an infinite existence. For beholding a physical form, the mundane eyes would have been enough. Where was the necessity for divine eyes? It is a matter of realization by jnana and bhava. Realizing the Lord's power, perfection and excellence underlying in this visible Creation, is but visualization of the Cosmic Form. By knowledge, His manifestations as gross forms can also be understood. He spontaneously manifests Himself without the help of any external support. He is the basis of one and all. He cannot be seen by our ordinary eyes.

Hence Divya Darshan says, "God is not to be searched out; He is to be realised." He, who realises Him, can experience His presence everywhere. Where will one go to find Him? By knowledge-eye, when He is realised, it is not necessary at all to search for Him here and there. One can experience Him inside and outside. Whatever happens is He who manifests as such. Seeing, understanding, experiencing and realizing are all parts of His divine play.

If an aero engine is there, it means someone has made it. For each and everything, there is someone at the background who does everything. Be it knowledge or thought or even the visible and invisible Creation, there is someone who has caused and conditioned everything. In absence of the knowledge-eye, we are left with only our mundane eyes by which we try to see God. But it rarely occurs to us that someone is there who has taken all these forms. Who appears as the visible Creation? Who had incarnated as Rama or Krishna? Who has been incarnating in so many forms? He can be realised by the knowledge-eye only. He is named as Brahman. This visible universe is all illusory. The Supreme Truth remains in everything. He is invisible but manifests as the visible universe. But people out of sheer ignorance say that God is to be seen to be believed. Those who are doing idol worship cannot understand and appreciate the all-pervasiveness of Brahman. Scriptures and sages become silent after telling "Neti, Neti," which means, not like this, not this much. He is different from whatever we experience in this physical world. When a seeker realises Him, he will become spell-bound; he cannot speak to describe Him; his imaginations cease there. The Supreme Brahman is eternal and all-pervasive. Therefore, you must try to enhance your knowledge level, elevate yourself to Bhavaloka to realise the Supreme Brahman.

*****

[37]Without proper knowledge about God, we worship Him outwardly. Scriptures reiterate that God is Truth-Absolute. It is not possible to imagine Him even. Scriptures further say, "God is Consciousness-Absolute. Chit (consciousness) is 'sense'. The sages realised Him as Consciousness but what do we do? We imagine different forms and make different deities akin to human form made of wood, stone or clay. God is there as Existence even before we could imagine Him in any form. Sages also say "God is Peace-Absolute, Bliss-Absolute and Freedom-Absolute." He, who knows God to be all-pervasive, understands Him better. He can be in touch with God every moment. He can also realise that God is there as 'Chit' who is the life of his life. He is being controlled and regulated by Him every moment. He is being protected by Him. He is always in close relation with Him. When God is there in the form of Consciousness, are we not meeting Him always? We should contemplate on this always. But since we play and act according to our own imaginations, we are not able to meet Him or feel His presence. In rare occasions, even if some devotees, for a very brief period, could see the deities due to their strong will power, those

---

[37] *Odia Divyadhara Vol 3 Page 16*

are not the real forms of God as they are created out of their own imaginations. God is formless.

We see God or meet God every moment. All our activities are done by Him and through Him or with Him. But since we do not know who God is, we are not able to understand this. At times, people ask questions, "Who is God, where is God, can you show me God etc.?" Some people ultimately disbelieve God. But the fact is that God is all-pervasive. Since He is all-pervasive, He is inside us and around us.

Is there any place where God is not there? Even if He is all-pervasive, we are not able to experience Him due to our ignorance. At times, we say God is there everywhere; but we do not seriously mean it.

There are atheists who seek proof of God's existence. Once the atheist understands whom we call God, such questions would not be there. Some metal is called gold. Another metal is called steel. Since we have some idea about gold or steel we do not ask for proof. Whatever we do not know we call for proof to know the same. When we ask for proof of God's existence, it is our first and foremost duty to know who is called God or who is named as such. If we do not know a particular thing, we cannot get the same even after searching. We may be possessing gold but if we do not know what gold is then how can we search and find gold. Likewise, even if there is God inside us, we are not able to know Him because we do not have any idea about God. We ask for proof. There is no God, we say. We ask further, "Can you show me God?"

He, who knows, ultimately gets. The sages and seers had known God. They had complete knowledge about God. They could experience the presence of God everywhere and always. Since we are ignorant, we only imagine about and search for Him here and there. According to Divya Darshan, God expresses Himself by knowledge. This Creation is but His manifestation.

If man thinks and applies his mind to know God, he can. For any small job also, we must apply our mind and intelligence for successful completion. Even for stealing or pickpocketing one must apply some skill and thoughts. For maintaining a family also, the householder must work hard and think about good education, good behaviour, peace and happiness of the children. Man becomes restless while thinking about the career and future of the children. The sages and seers say that to realise God, so much labour is not required. It is easier to realise God compared to the burden of Samsara. The subject matter of God is quite simple, pure, light and transparent. But the worldly matters make us burdened and preoccupied since the gravity of the spiritual subject is not appreciated by us. We relegate the same to the background and attach importance only to the worldly matters.

The worldly matters are overly complex and hard but spiritual path is simple even though it is misconstrued by people as difficult and complex. We need to find out simple ways to reach our goal. Some spiritual seekers resort to very difficult practices. The followers too feel it very difficult to move on.

When situations and circumstances undergo changes, spiritual practices have also alternative ways which are much simpler. Hence man should try to know simplest ways to attain spiritual progress.

What is the necessity of experiencing Atman?

Man wants happiness, peace, bliss and freedom. He carries on all his activities keeping in view all these. We want happiness, peace and bliss because all these are there within us as Atman who is Peace-Absolute, Bliss-Absolute and Freedom-Absolute. The Atman expresses or identifies itself as 'I'. Atman is ever expressing itself. Hence man is always keen to get peace, bliss and freedom. For this self-knowledge is essential. Man must know himself otherwise he would not be able to know his mistakes. He, who is not able to know his mistakes, is bound to suffer. Knowing the self is '*Swadharma*'. Whatever is done to attain self is '*Swadharma*'. Atman is the be-all and end-all of life. If he is not evincing interest to know Atman it is to be understood that he is committing suicide. Ignorance in him asks, "What is the use of knowing Atman?" But knowing the True Self i.e. Atman is Dharma. He, who is not doing this, is doing *Adharma* only. Everybody should aim at self-realisation.

Our mind only creates the feelings of happiness, sufferings, fear, doubts etc. When man acquires knowledge and goes higher, all these reactions of the mind get eliminated slowly. Mind never gets annihilated. It gets transformed to a reactionless state.

When man acquires higher knowledge, he gets guided by intelligence (buddhi) and not by mind. When he goes further, he is guided by conscience and thereafter by Atman. When he is guided by Atman, he would no longer experience the wants and imperfections which he had been experiencing while being guided by mind and intelligence.

Our base is Atman. Atman has also become everything and assumed all forms and qualities in this Creation. Once one transcends mind and intelligence and is guided by conscience, one will realise Atman.

Those, who are of tamasic nature, are normally governed by mind. Those, who are rajasic in nature, are guided by intelligence. Those, who are sattvic, are guided by conscience. Only people of sattvic nature are better prepared to attain self-realisation.

Everyone is being governed by Atman. Reactions of mind get lost when one is governed by conscience. At that stage, he becomes a fit recipient of self-knowledge.

The first manifestation of Brahman is knowledge. Brahman first expressed Himself as knowledge and thereafter as the Creation. Knowledge covers everything such as mind, intelligence and conscience. Mind (Mana) is controlled by intelligence (Buddhi), intelligence by conscience (Viveka) and conscience by Atman. A person who reaches the stage of conscience is guided directly by the Atman and hence he becomes suitable for self-realisation since at the conscience level, all mental reactions die down. After self-realisation also mind and intelligence remain but they become non-functional as it is conscience that rules.

Question- It is said that unless one develops dispassion, feeling of self-surrender would not come; what does it mean?

Answer- In Yogavashistha Ramayana, it is stated that Lord Ramachandra had developed dispassion. This means that Lord Ramachandra was at the conscience level from the beginning. As a result, he was able to discriminate between truth and untruth, good and bad, justice and injustice. When man remains at conscience level his greed and infatuation etc. born of rajasic and tamasic tendencies die down.

When a person completely reaches conscience level, tamasic and rajasic qualities subside and feeling of dispassion takes over. When a person would acquire more and more of true knowledge, he would develop more and more dispassion. He would accept God's omnipotence and shall be keen to observe His Laws and thus shall enjoy bliss.

The sages and seers affirm that God expresses Himself as Sat-Chit-Ananda. It means God eternally expresses everywhere as Sat, Chit and Ananda. He, who would know Sat-Chit-Ananda, can experience Brahman every moment and everywhere. We meet God every moment as Sat-Chit-Ananda.

We are seeing God every moment and talking to Him. Whatever we do are all due to God. All our activities and all our connections are with God. But since we do not know who God is, we are not able to recognize Him. On the other hand, we ask where God is and sometimes search for Him here and there.

Scriptures assert that God is with forms and without forms. He, being formless, is there inside everything and outside also since He is all-pervasive. It is further stated in the scriptures that Brahman willed to be many. That means He manifests as gross objects also. He manifests as personal godheads and as the Sun, the Moon, man, animals, birds, insects and plants. He manifests as five gross elements and from out of these elements all forms are created. Due to ignorance man is not able to know Him. After acquiring knowledge about all these, he can realise the Truth. At that time, he would not ask, "Can we see God?" God can be experienced by the divine vision or true knowledge. Hence by intensifying the inquisitiveness in us we must know who is called as God. Inquisitiveness is also a divine quality which is God-given and it is there in all beings from the birth itself. But our inquisitiveness remains dormant. If we know Him more and more, we can become closer to Him and experience Him better. This means, always we are in close contact with God although unknowingly.

The sages speak of Him as Peace-Absolute and Bliss-Absolute. They experience God every moment. That is why they are blissful. Since we do not understand God, we suffer. To explain about

God further, the sages say that God is neither Sat nor Asat, neither Chit nor Achit and neither Ananda nor suffering. Nothing can be told about God. Even after experiencing Him also the realiser cannot describe Him. Hence Rishi Yajnavalkya concluded by saying, "Neti, Neti."

There is an existence called God. That existence is expressed by the word Sat. His manifestation is expressed as Chit and the experience is termed as Bliss (Ananda). Hence, He is different from any of the terminologies such as Sat, Chit and Ananda. We must remember that because He exists, Jagat appears as such. All activities are going on because of Him. This Creation shall get merged with that Existence one day.

For complete realisation of God, it must be remembered that He is different from the visible universe. One must realise how He manifests as this visible universe. In other words, how He expresses Himself in the garb of this visible universe. He is eternally self-effulgent. He cannot be realised with material knowledge which is limited. Due to ignorance, man asks different questions about God but does not follow the right process to know Him. Man expects someone to demonstrate God to him. Many people do not believe in God's existence. They advance different logics or resort to argumentation based on intellectual knowledge to refute God's existence. Is there anybody who can disown his own existence? Can anybody affirm that he does not exist, or he is not there? Nobody can. The power by which one can speak that God is there or not, the power by which one is able to raise his hands, that background power is God. By God's power only one is able to tell, "God is there, or God is not there."

When we experience our existence, when the Creation is there, the Creator is also there. A popular story runs like this.

A tiger entered the den of a fox and waited there silently for the fox to return home. After a while, the fox came and while approaching the den observed the footmarks of the tiger. The fox had a doubt and became alert. From a distance it repeatedly shouted, "Is there any one inside the den?" The tiger could not keep mum. The reply came from inside the den, "No one is here". "No one is here" unmistakably proves someone's existence. 'God exists' and 'God does not exist'. Both these statements prove God's existence. We know that in the Creation changes occur incessantly. Who triggers the changes? Who energizes the process of change? He is called God. For every change, location, dislocation, combination, separation, movement, placement, displacement and replacement in this dynamic process of the Creation, some energy is required as the propelling force or as the causal factor. That energy is called God who Himself remains unchanged and unmoved but has the potency to cause and condition everything else. He is known as the Supreme Power or the Supra-Causal Conscious Existence who has been creating and recreating everything in a systematic, phase-wise manner which are all well-integrated and interwoven perfectly to appear as an ever-changing wonderful universe full of thoughts and things, living and non-living, sentient and insentient, colours and fragrance, forms and qualities, plants and animals, oceans and mountains, rivers and rivulets, fruits and flowers, tiniest particles and colossal stars.

Even the tiniest particles are well designed and stuffed adequately to serve the Creation with total dedication and bonding with each other to create newer things so essential for the mega structure to perfectly blossom in a balanced and cohesive manner thereby displaying the perfection and infinitude of the Great Architect called Brahman or God. This kingdom of nature is a great laboratory where everything happens perfectly well. God is the efficient cause as well as the material cause of all thoughts and things, physical and metaphysical.

Nothing can happen without energy which is consciously wielded by Brahman who Himself is Consciousness-Absolute and Energy-Absolute. In other words, He is Energetic Consciousness.

We are not able to realise God even though He always expresses Himself. We do not have inquisitiveness to know God. He, who says he knows God, really does not know Him. He has got some indication about His Existence only. The sages and seers had experienced God. A small boy may say that he knows God; a sage also says that he knows God. These are but gradations of knowledge. The knowledge of the sage is at a higher level than that of the child although both say that they know God.

Lord Buddha had undergone long penance. He said, "Non-injury is the greatest Dharma". A common man may say, "What is new in this?" He might say that he knew it much earlier. In this case also the level of knowledge differs significantly. One may publicly advocate for non-injury but in his personal life he may be ruthlessly killing animals. It is because he has not realised the true import of the statement. He simply hears and utters. His utterance would not have any impact. This is the difference between a common man's knowledge and the knowledge of a sage who having realised Truth conducts himself accordingly.

Whatever a common man knows about God is not adequate. Quite a lot remain to be learnt. He must know that God expresses Himself as 'Sat-Chit and Ananda'. After knowing him completely he would get peace, bliss and freedom. The more man knows about God, the less he would commit mistakes. Due to inadequate knowledge, we commit mistakes repetitively and suffer. Man enjoys bliss only after complete knowledge on God. That bliss is eternal. But the material wealth gives transient happiness. Material wealth is limited and impermanent. Hence the happiness derived from such things is temporary. It cannot stand comparison with the eternal bliss that comes from God-realisation. At that stage man is released from the cycle of birth and death. That is liberation where there is no fear, suffering, doubts or anxieties. This means one must realise the Supreme Truth to enjoy eternal bliss.

When one comes to know truth, one becomes happy. The more one knows truth, the more one enjoys happiness and peace. This world would appear to him as blissful. This is only a matter of self-experience. He alone can understand it, who knows something about God or who is advanced in spiritual knowledge.

The happiness we derive from the material wealth is at mental level. In the *Pitrulok*, the happiness is more because there is no physical body there. As such one is free from the attendant problems arising from food, drink and diseases etc. The happiness level in the *Devalok* is still greater. Like this, if one moves still higher, one will enjoy Brahmananda which is the greatest of all.

A common man remains complacent if he gets some happiness at mental level however momentary the same may be. He cannot imagine what really a blissful state is. Lord Buddha was never inclined towards the material possessions. He was heir to the throne and was entitled to the kingdom. Lord Buddha had realised the evanescence of all those material splendours that would pass away like a floating cloud.

What is important is eternal and unlimited. Man is bestowed with all potentialities to attain eternity. This is the climax of human evolution. This can be achieved only with spiritual knowledge. Since we do not try to acquire spiritual knowledge, we not only suffer in our life's aimless journey, but we remain far away from bliss which is our divine abode.

The more one acquires spiritual knowledge, the more one knows about God. But due to ignorance, we are not evincing interest in self-knowledge which is so essential for everybody. Whatever happiness, peace, bliss and freedom we always seek, are all outcome of spiritual knowledge. Hence it is our first and foremost duty to take to spiritual path and learn more and more about God.

Divya Darshan says, "Whatever religion you may belong to, liberation (freedom from samsara, the cycle of death and rebirth) is impossible without self-knowledge."

We must know Self to attain liberation. Then only we shall get rid of all sufferings. Self-knowledge is our own subject. It is not different from us. True religiosity and self-knowledge are one and the same. Whatever we are doing are all coming under spiritual course. We expect goodness from others. We think about our families and are worried about how they would live in peace and happiness. So far as our work place is concerned, we think of how our superiors would like us. When we crave for 'good' everywhere around us, that means, spiritual knowledge is an essential requirement everywhere. Spiritual knowledge gives the power of discrimination between good and bad, truth and untruth, justice and injustice, divine qualities and demoniac qualities. Without this knowledge, a man cannot tread on the path of righteousness. Self-knowledge is required for healthy individual living, harmonious social living with peace and happiness, and ultimately for bliss and freedom.

In the Kathopanishad, the inquisitiveness of Nachiketa may be discussed here. Nachiketa approached a spiritual master for instructions. The Guru tested the integrity and sincerity of Nachiketa by offering a lot of mundane things for a pleasant life, but Nachiketa did not evince interest in such mundane gifts as they were all evanescent according to him. He insisted on self-knowledge. The Guru was very much pleased with Nachiketa's sincerity and single-mindedness in acquiring self-knowledge. He considered Nachiketa a right recipient of spiritual knowledge and thereafter imparted him the knowledge about Atman. If a mendicant makes sincere efforts for attainment of *Moksa*, he can at the same time acquire 'Dharma', 'Artha', 'Kama' and '*Moksa*'. In other words, if someone chooses to acquire spiritual knowledge, he can at the same time ensure healthy living, harmonious social life full of peace, and attain *Moksa* i.e. Liberation. He gets rid of all sufferings and enjoys eternal bliss.

Hence we must be aware of our divine goal first. Otherwise the entire journey shall be a waste. Everything is possible due to Atman. Without Atman nothing can exist; nothing can happen. Life journey would be smooth and simple once one aims at his divine destination i.e. 'Self'.

Many ask the question, "We have so many bad qualities. Unless we do away with bad qualities, how can we walk on the path of Dharma or spirituality?" Some think that in this birth, it is not possible to bequeath the long acquired bad qualities and therefore it is not possible to resort to Dharma marg. They further say, "First we are to cleanse ourselves and thereafter we would take to spirituality." Such wrong notion is only due to ignorance.

The fact is that whoever will acquire true knowledge or spiritual knowledge, automatically and gradually his bad qualities would go away. When a man would feel that he is going to achieve something greater, he would easily abandon the smaller things or qualities. The more he would be inclined towards goodness, the more he would distance himself from the bad qualities.

It must be remembered that when a person takes shelter of higher truth, the hurdles arising from out of lower truth shall be overcome by higher truth and he shall be protected by the higher truth. A man, who is habitually slaughtering animals for the maintenance of his family, thinks that he cannot live without this occupation. But there are alternative occupations which he can take up and quit the occupation of butchering. Dharma protects us. Knowing the truth and observing the truth is Dharma. We get protected by the same truth which we observe. Because we do not know this truth that butchering is *Adharma*, we go on accumulating sins during the whole life by taking to wrongful occupations or activities.

If we do not try to learn the higher truths, we shall be continuing at the lower levels. Should we not try to get ourselves elevated to higher levels? Our first and foremost Dharma is to develop inquisitiveness in us. To know the Truth means knowing God. He alone is the real practicant (Sadhaka) who is keen to know the Truth and prepares himself accordingly. He is also a real worshipper of God. He, who does not know but worships, does not perform actual worship. Hence man's Dharma is to realise the True Self which is Truth. He acquires virtues while on the path of knowing the Truth or acquiring true knowledge. This means, he is walking on the path of Dharma and getting nearer to God. This is real self-development. He, who goes on acquiring virtues shall one day realise the Self.

It is said that in order to arouse the dormant energy within, a person should approach Guru (spiritual master). By Gurushakti, the accumulated impurities inside get cleared, which cannot be achieved by only reading scriptures. There are three qualities such as sattva, rajas and tamas in everyone. Tamas drags one backward as a result of which one's self-development is adversely affected. Tamas impels a man to habitually procrastinate his duties.

When you are sitting on a chair ready to write something and at that time if your pen falls down, you may not feel like picking up the pen due to laziness. You may wait for someone to come there and pick up the pen for you. At that time, if your father happens to see the pen lying on the floor and draws your attention, you shall immediately spring into action and pick up the pen.

You could have picked up the pen before your father instructed you. The necessary energy was there dormant in you. When the instruction came from your father, the dormant energy got activated immediately in you.

Man is in illusion or Maya. Lord Ramachandra had Maharshi Vashistha as his Guru. Lord Krishna had also Maharshi Sandipani as his Guru. Guru is indispensable for guiding us to perfection. Without Guru it is not possible to attain the goal. Guru means big, heavy and weighty. Gurushakti is the greatest and all-inclusive power. When we surrender to Sadguru it means we are taking shelter of the greatest power who is Supreme. Language fails to describe Gurushakti. By that power we are born, we survive, get peace and happiness, and ultimately we shall attain freedom. Guru is there as everything. Sadguru makes our path clear to liberation. One gets Sadguru due to one's virtues acquired in previous births and due to blessings of parents and personal godheads. There are many ways to identify a Sadguru. Sadguru always rests in *Satya Loka*. He always speaks of True Knowledge. Gurushakti maintains us, protects us, and guides us to liberation. By accepting Sadguru, self-development is assured. A disciple should not think that Guru is at a distant place. After He leaves his mortal body, it should not be misconstrued that Guru is not there. A disciple must know that Guru is always with him. Guru manifests as everything. Guru has already attained liberation. He is not bound by any mundane matters which are all evanescent. He is the Eternal Existence.

*****

[38]Divya Darshan spreads the knowledge on God and His manifestations, His Existence and His True nature. It is quite a common characteristic that everyone seeks peace and happiness. But leaving aside God, it is impossible to get peace and happiness. Many have their doubts over existence of God. Divya Darshan advances the Theory of Change (separately dealt in detail) to prove God's existence. Had there been no change we would not have experienced anything in and around us. We would not have come to existence even. Due to change we could see trees, flowers and fruits. We could get seeds. We can speak one word after another due to change. We can hear due to sound waves that hit our ear drums. Thereafter the same reaches our brain and we are able to understand. Even when we are asleep, many changes inside our body take place. It is raining because of change. The water stream mingles with the ocean due to change. We can put one step after another due to change. God is there behind all changes. It is to be admitted that energy is essential requirement for any change. Without energy nothing is possible. Change is taking place incessantly even in atoms and molecules. This means Atman, the source of all energy resides everywhere and in everything. Because there is Atman, digestion takes place inside and blood circulation goes on. There is role of energy behind all changes. That energy is formless and without any attribute. When it manifests as forms, we find attributes in the

---

[38]*Odia Divyadhara Vol 3 Page 37*

forms. Everything is the play of energy which is all-pervasive. To explain the energy, it is divided into two stages such as Para and Apara. First is Para which manifests as Apara, i.e. as forms and qualities. When man is given this form, human qualities are seen in him. Before assuming forms and qualities, the energy that existed is named as Para. All changes take place due to Para Shakti. A dead man cannot speak or hear. It is because for seeing and hearing, something invisible is either inert or missing in the dead body. Para Shakti remains independently without any intervention from any quarters.

God is Pure Consciousness which is full of energy. Energy is also never without Consciousness. God has no form, but He manifests as all forms. God has no qualities, but He manifests as all qualities. He is invisible. He has manifested as the personal godheads. The personal godheads are also invisible. Only wise persons such as sages and seers know that God is formless and without any attribute. He manifests as everything, i.e. as all forms and qualities. But people in general cannot accept this easily. When an aspirant will acquire spiritual knowledge, he can very well experience God's existence and His manifestations. Not knowing the Self is ignorance. "Ignorance is a great sin," said Socrates. The man, who acquires true knowledge, can know God. Due to ignorance man commits mistakes. A child commits many mistakes due to ignorance. When he grows up, slowly his mistakes get rectified, and he stops repeating the mistakes. Due to ignorance man commits sins. Hence not knowing or not trying to learn is also a sin. All other sins emanate from ignorance. Hence ignorance is a great sin that begets all sins. By knowledge everything is possible. The scriptures exhort mankind to acquire true knowledge and get rid of all sufferings. Hence jnana is to be adored and acquired. Perseverance is required for acquisition of knowledge. By repeated contemplations, truth can be realised and made use of.

This is called meditation. Meditation does not mean closing of eyes. The power by which we understand or explain is called knowledge. To the question, "What have you understood?" the answer will be, "Truth". In other words, knowing the Truth is knowledge.

Scriptures say that God is beyond knowledge. This means that God is neither an object nor subject of knowledge. So how can God be realised by knowledge?

But you believe in the God's existence due to knowledge. You are reposing faith on Him due to knowledge. Man gets more conceptual clarity on God depending upon his level of knowledge. God can be realised by bhava. Self-realisation comes only by His grace

Initially, a seeker develops his idea about God. After knowing more and more about God, he starts getting peace and happiness. In this way when one goes still further, one would know the ultimate Reality by acquiring more and more knowledge. That is liberation. Suffering was there before; it is now there and shall also be there in future. To get rid of sufferings, knowledge is the only panacea. When someone is having sense or knowledge, we say he is alive. When sense or knowledge is absent, we say that he is dead.

Consciousness (Chetana) is divided into four states.

- Waking
- Dream
- Sleep
- Transcendental

Since Consciousness expresses itself in different states, we are not able to understand others' sufferings or pleasure. Waking state does not know dream state. Dream state does not know sleep state. Sleep state does not know waking or dream state. Transcendental state manifests as waking, dream and sleep states. Transcendental state is the real 'I' who manifests as everything. Transcendental consciousness is the Supreme Consciousness or Complete Consciousness, attainment of which is Maha-Nirvana in the language of Lord Buddha. Our supreme duty is to know more and more. For this, knowledge is to be always welcomed.

This is how we are preparing ourselves for happiness, peace, bliss and freedom. Divya Darshan says, "Only you can free yourself." Knowledge is realisation of truth. Sages and seers come and go. They all impart true knowledge. If a man does not accept or assimilate knowledge, he cannot get rid of sufferings. Therefore, knowledge is so important.

A mere assertion that "I have fully surrendered to God." will not help. That level of knowledge essential for surrender must be acquired. People sometimes cite the examples of some great devotees who attained liberation. To reinforce their logic, they say that such devotees did not have any educational background nor had any knowledge. By simple devotion they had attained *Moksa*.

If so, why are we not having devotion? This means that the devotee who attained *Moksa* even without any formal education, had lot of past samskara or spiritual knowledge. By knowledge and contemplation one can know that God is all in all. He is doing everything. He, who knows the truth behind the matter, may be a scientist but he cannot resolve the mystery over matter completely. God remains unattached and independent everywhere. Only a man of sattvic quality would have a spiritual bent of mind and would be eligible to realise truth.

Man thinks that he is doing everything. A sage or seer can tell this in his transcendental state but remaining in a fragmented level of consciousness if one claims like that, it is due to his false ego only.

Different powers of Brahman are called personal godheads. They are doing everything. The rain, heat and cold are all done by the personal godheads that derive power from the Supreme.

What happens when we cook rice? How much water, how much heat and how much rice are to be used? All these are to be determined first. This is called knowledge. The presiding deity of knowledge is Goddess Saraswati. Buddhi is intelligence which is also involved in the process. The God of Buddhi is Lord Ganesh. Boiling is done by fire (Agni). Fire burns due to air (Vayu). Water that is so essential for the purpose is due to Lord Varun. It is clear from the above that all personal godheads such as Saraswati, Ganesh, Vayu, Agni and Varun have done everything. The energy (power, force) that is involved in lifting the cooking vessel belongs to Goddess Durga or Maheswari Shakti. Man is dead without all these. Hence whatever is being done is all done by the personal godheads that are but various powers of Brahman. Even digestion, excretion etc. are all done by the involvement of Devas. On realising this, a man would respect God, and he would be eligible to get God's blessings. Once he possesses complete knowledge about the personal godheads, he would be able to understand and realise Brahman who is the Supreme.

According to Divya Darshan, if someone's parents are happy with him, then the personal godheads are also happy with him. If personal godheads are happy with someone, God is also happy. He, who possesses divine qualities, would respect his parents and would be eligible for blessings from God. Without God's grace, man cannot rise to a higher spiritual level. He must serve his fellow beings including the plants and animals.

A man who has no attitude to serve (Seva) cannot get God's blessings. One should serve both physically and mentally. If one loves all, one earns blessings and goodwill from others. Through service to others, we come closer and acquire truth and knowledge in the process. When we serve a sick person, not only we know about the physical ailments of the patient, we also know about his mental state. Service to mankind is service to God. This is what Swami Vivekananda had emphasised on.

But at times we are averse to serving the visible man while we are keen to worship the God even if he is unknown and invisible. We forget that God appears as different beings in different garbs. He manifests as everything. A person with the attitude of service will have no jealousy, craftiness or complications. He is simple. He would not cheat anyone. He would not be violent to others. He would earn virtues which would help him move faster on the path of sadhana (Spiritual practice)

Everyone should acquire true knowledge. This is what Divya Darshan aims at. Dissemination of true knowledge is a great service. He, who does so day and night, would earn punya (virtues) and shall get blessings from God.

*****

[39]How and where God is there? What about His greatness? Once we contemplate on this, we would like to surrender to God. This visible universe is nothing but His manifestation. In this visible universe, God manifests as names, forms and qualities. Behind everything God is there. According to Socrates, behind everything there is some 'Form' or idea. All names, forms and qualities are the subsequent stages. Hence it would be a misnomer to call each name

---

[39] *Odia Divyadhara Vol 8 Page 25*

and form as God. Likewise, we cannot call Oxygen or Hydrogen as water. We also cannot call ice as water.

There is someone behind this visible universe who is the Supreme Cause of everything. He assumes different forms and manifests as the universe. God alone knows the tricks of this visible universe. Due to His lone existence he has no comparison. In the scriptures, His greatness has been expounded. In the Upanishads, hints have been given about His True Nature. Sadguru only can explain His True Nature. Depending upon situations and circumstances, God reveals His True Self. Many people mistake His subsequent forms for His True Self. This inexpressible and unmanifest True Self must be realised. That is called real *siddhi*. Beyond the kingdom of knowledge there is bhava. One must purify oneself so as to ascend to bhava state to know the Almighty. Everything in the visible universe is subsequent or relative state of the Absolute who is called God. God has made everything. God manifests as everything. The preceding two sentences have some differences in meaning. According to the receptivity of the recipients, different expressions are used. Just as we say oxygen and hydrogen make water. We may also express it a little differently and say that oxygen and hydrogen have become water.

In the scriptures, Shakti, for explanation purpose, has been divided into two states such as *Para* and *Apara*. We come across the *Apara Shakti* always in the kingdom of nature. According to science, matter cannot be destroyed. Matter gets converted to energy. Energy gets converted to matter. Hence different matters in different forms have come into existence with corresponding qualities therein. Example- When energy takes human form, human qualities appear in that form. When energy takes the form of fire, we experience heat and light. All these forms and qualities come under

Apara Shakti. The noumenon manifests as the phenomenon. In other words, the Purusha manifests as Prakriti or *Apara Shakti*. The Purusha expresses Himself through Prakriti. That Absolute Energy expresses itself in and through the kingdom of nature. He is the gross as well as the subtle. It is energy that manifests as nature. That invisible Absolute Energy which is the Supreme Cause of everything is *Para Shakti*.

Energy manifests in innumerable ways. Para Shakti is everywhere. Para Shakti is all-pervasive. *Para Shakti* manifests as the *Apara Shakti*. We are seeing the energy and experiencing the energy all the time by the energy and consciousness present in us. Primarily, Energy is never bereft of consciousness and consciousness is never bereft of energy. There is no difference between energy and nature. The invisible all-pervasive energy is the Absolute Conscious Energy known as *Para Shakti*. There is no dualism at this all-embracing state. You are also a specific state of that all-pervasive energy. If you understand this, you cannot say that God is not there. Man can realise that power within him. In other words, man is himself the Energy; he is none other than He. When we all are there, God is also there. To say that God does not exist, means we are negating our own existence. When we know this mystery, we can know the whole universe. That Absolute Supreme Power is named differently as God, Ishwar, Brahman, etc.

Whom the sages ultimately realise is that Power. The realiser is that Power. He cannot be different from that Power. Brahman is one and secondless, this is what the scriptures reiterate. There is nothing other than energy. Therefore, a true realiser finds no difference but unity everywhere. Play of Energy is on. He, who knows that Power, shall become powerful. You are experiencing that Energy every moment but are not able to cognize. The experience that "I manifest as everything everywhere; my play goes on everywhere," finally dawns upon the realiser.

The space is also a state of energy. None can see the energy; it can only be experienced. By knowledge man can realise both visible and invisible.

When we inflict pain on others, it means we are inflicting pain on ourselves. If someone cheats another, it means he is cheating himself. Not evincing interest to know God is ignorance. "I am not able to understand"; this thought should occur to everyone. Only a true realiser experiences God. Hence knowledge should be adored and taken recourse to. He is not the cause of changes but He Himself undergoes all changes by His Will. The ignorant men imagine and ascribe different forms to God. God may also appear in some specific forms at times. But a wise man experiences His formless form. By acquiring true knowledge, he moves faster towards God-realisation and ultimately gets merged with Him. A spiritual seeker with divine sight power can only realise Him. You are all great, most powerful and the basis of everything. So why should you beg anything of Him. He has provided everything. He, who acquires more and more knowledge, can experience the greatness of God more and more. The idol worshippers would take a longer time. You are so lucky that you are learning about His gross, subtle and causal states in one go. He, who experiences God everywhere and in everything, realises Sat-Chit-Ananda. After knowing thus, he can shed blissful tears. When the Self would love the Self, at that time what amount of Bliss would be experienced cannot be expressed. Experience of Bliss is beyond the Vedas or any other scriptures. Vedas speak of Chit or Consciousness. Once man realises that Chit state, he would realise that there is no death. When Chit takes a form, that form undergoes death. But Chit or Consciousness knows no death. He remains as energy throughout His *Lila*. Man would become powerful once he realises that Energy. God's cosmic form as described in the Shrimad Bhagavad-Gita is only one dimension of Shakti. It is *saguna*. One must realise both *saguna* and *nirguna* to realise Him completely and ultimately to get merged with Him. Without realising the True Self, one cannot get rid of sufferings. Once the feeling comes that God is everywhere in everything, one would start experiencing the divine bliss.

In the Samkhya philosophy, there is mention about Purusha and Prakriti. But Divya Darshan takes a little different stand and advocates Advaita Philosophy. According to it, Purusha (Brahman) manifests itself through nature (Prakriti). Knowing the nature does not lead to liberation. One must know the Purusha who is behind nature and manifests as and through nature. One must transcend nature to reach Brahman. In the Prakriti there are illusory effects. Prakriti is *Apara Shakti* and Purusha is *Para Shakti*. Energy has taken the form of nature. There is energy in nature. Matter never gets destroyed. It is only converted to energy. Energy is again converted to matter. Energy appears in gross forms and as different qualities inside the gross forms. This energy as the forms and qualities is called *Apara Shakti*. The Purusha is *Para Shakti* who manifests as nature or *Apara Shakti*. He is Energy-Absolute. *Para Shakti*, the Absolute Existence manifests as all relativities. We come across gross forms and corresponding qualities therein. That energy is present in the Sun and the Moon. The same energy is there inside a wood that burns emitting heat and light. Because of that energy, man radiates with so much vitality and vigour. Purusha itself is Prakriti. There is no difference. That energy is Rama and Krishna. One will have faith on Him once one learns about His greatness. There is no difference between energy and matter. He is present in everybody as Energy. This visible universe is changeable. Changes are nothing but the play of the Absolute Energy. He, who realises the Energy, becomes the Energy. We are all there. God is also there. He alone manifests as many. When He manifests, we call it *Apara Shakti*. In the unmanifest stage He is *Para*. He is Atman, Brahman, Ishwar or God by whatever name He may be called.

Hence, the wise men do not discriminate based on caste, creed or gender. The Absolute Energy has taken various forms. He, who realises that Power or Energy, becomes powerful. I am all-pervasive and I eternally play like this assuming different forms. I am the Sun, the Moon and all stars and planets. What else would you see to experience God? You are seeing your wife, children, different ornaments etc. You are seeing different matters in the nature surrounding you. But you are not able to appreciate that the same energy has taken all these forms. By divine vision, one witnesses His Cosmic Form. The entire universe (both visible and invisible) you come across is nothing but His Cosmic Form. None can see the Energy. But by the wisdom-eye, one can see Him every moment. By the gross eyes you can see only His gross manifestation. This is the limitation of the eyes one possesses. It is a matter of shame when you say that you are unable to see God. By enhanced knowledge, you can also experience His invisible presence. God appears before everyone as *Apara Shakti*. Only the wise can realise His beginningless and endless greatness. And ultimately he merges with Him. This is called complete knowledge.

*****

[40]For owning and enjoying anything in this Creation, the pre-requisite is our merits or intrinsic worth. We must be the right

---

[40]*Odia Divyadhara Vol 20 Page 6*

recipients to receive anything valuable and important. For example, if we wish to meet some highly placed official, we must first know where we can meet him and his convenient time. We should also have the courage and confidence to speak to him properly. The subject of discussion should also be relevant and significant. We must tell the purpose of visit, obtain his permission and fix appointment. Thereafter only we can meet him and discuss the issues. We may also seek his favour. Similarly a spiritual seeker should purify him by acquiring more knowledge and inculcate divine qualities so that he can move easily and faster towards divinity. From different mythologies, we have learnt that the demons also got boons from Lord Shiva, Vishnu, or Brahma. Sometimes it is seen that Devas award boons to some demons out of compulsion and not out of their free will and pleasure. In such cases, Devas do not help or protect the demons further. But the sages get blessings from the divine beings by surrendering to them. Giving something out of compulsion is not blessing.

To be able to understand and assimilate subtle aspects of spiritual thoughts we must have interest, inquisitiveness and samskara. It should be remembered that we get divine blessings by our good deeds. The demons are deprived of God's blessings whereas the rishis enjoy God's blessings. By way of penance, the demons even enter the fire and inflict different kinds of pain on themselves to get vast powers and immortality from God. But the sages conduct themselves with truth and love and get divine blessings. The demons remain satisfied seeing the manifested divine form of God which is illusory. But the sages acquire right knowledge to realise the Reality.

All forms and qualities demonstrate the greatness of God. Forms and qualities are illusory. All disciples have got Ishta Mantra from Guru. Ishta Mantra represents Sat-Chit-Ananda state. From that state everything is created and again everything goes back to that original state to regain the completeness. The three qualities such as tamas, rajas and sattva constitute nature. Jiva must transcend 'tamas' to reach 'rajas'. 'Rajas' has also to be transcended thereafter to move to sattva. Ishwar state or Sat-Chit-Ananda state is called the causal body. All changes emanate from there. All powers of Brahman are there in Ishta Mantra. This state is the source of all power.

This state is called Mother Durga, the primordial energy or nature. It is also called Ishwar state. From this state, everything such as the mineral kingdom, plant kingdom and animal kingdom are created. Further that mother power, also called as Maheswari Shakti, takes care of the sustenance of the Creation. She also makes all arrangements for the beings to go back to the origin. In other words, all powers that are seen in the kingdom of nature are there in the Mother and everything gets activated by Her.

Mahakali Shakti: Everything occurs in the womb of time. Creation, preservation and dissolution happen in the womb of time. He, who can realise the mystery of time can win over time and get rid of birth and death cycles.

Next is Mahalaxmi Shakti. For the sustenance of the Creation different materials including food and water are essential. It is this power who makes all arrangements.

Next is Mahasaraswati Shakti. Knowledge is essential to know, how to live, what karma is to be undertaken, what food is to be taken and what not to be taken. She is the knowledge power.

Time is life and life is time. All the above powers are active in the kingdom of nature without which our existence would not have been possible.

Our Ishta has thus manifested as the above powers and has been sustaining and serving the entire Creation. We all are on Her lap always. To get Her blessings it is necessary for us to acquire more knowledge.

*****

[41]We have read about God's greatness described in various scriptures. There is mention about many devotees who had great devotion and love towards God. There is mention about some devotees who had completely surrendered themselves to God and merged with God. But the society at present has reached such a state that many do not want to even hear anything about God. In the olden days, people believed in God; had devotion and love towards God. Therefore, they lived in peace and happiness. It was their habit to listen to scriptures and puranas with interest. People are now-a-days averse to reading and listening to scriptures. They are preoccupied with their respective pursuits and seek entertainment from various sources now available. Since people have forgotten God completely, they are suffering. Man does not bother to know how to live in the society in peace and happiness, and also how to deal even with the neighbours for a harmonious living.

There is a tradition in our society to take shelter of a Guru to get guidance from Him to get peace and happiness and walk on the right path to reach the sole destination of attaining God. The sages of yesteryears had known the importance of Guru and that is why the tradition of approaching a Guru for right knowledge is continuing. The sages had known the essence of the Vedas and Vedanta. They had realised Truth and therefore they were imparting true

---

[41]*Odia Divyadhara Vol 10 Page 34*

knowledge. Even divine descends like Lord Krishna and Lord Ramachandra also had taken shelter of Guru. They received true knowledge and had self-realization. There are five types of Guru as mentioned in the scriptures. First Guru is our mother who brought us to this world and taught us so much. The second Guru is our father who made all necessary arrangements for our living and gave us education for a proper living in the society. The third Guru is our school teacher who starting from alphabet taught us various subjects. The fourth Guru is Karnna Guru who whispers God's name into our ears as a part of tradition. The fifth and the most important is Sadguru who teaches us right knowledge about our peaceful living and shows us the path of self-development that leads us to God-realization or liberation.

Sadguru is an emancipated soul. He always wishes for the well-being of the Creation. Sadguru gives true knowledge and highlights the importance of divine virtues which are applicable to everybody in the society irrespective of caste, creed and colour. The knowledge Sadguru imparts to the mankind gets the status of scriptures at a subsequent time.

In earlier days disciples were going to the Ashram of Sadguru and getting knowledge on Satya, Dharma and Nyaya etc. The then kings were patronizing the Ashrams. Slowly the number of sages and number of Ashrams came down. Due to lack of interest for true knowledge, there is increase in the number of atheists.

God Himself descends as Sadguru to liberate the mankind from the bondage. Sadguru upholds Truth and Dharma and inspires the mankind to inculcate divine virtues and walk on right path leading to the greatest common goal i.e. God-realization. Due to right knowledge imparted by the sages and Sadgurus in the past, man is able to maintain his body, live in the society harmoniously with peace and happiness and ultimately attain self-realization. Every person earns some virtues and some sins. One reaps good results for his good actions and bad results for his bad actions. This is the Law of Karma.

One, who gets blessings of the parents, also gets blessings from the Devas. One, who gets blessings from the Devas, also gets blessings from the Supreme. Now the question is- Who has known the Devas as well as God and realised their existence? The answer is Sadguru. Otherwise, we would not have known about God or any other Deva. Therefore, he, who gets the blessings of Sadguru, can get the blessings of the Devas and the Supreme. Who else can explain anything about God other than Guru? The sages have been reiterating that there is God and by Him everything happens. At least this much knowledge everyone should have. Normally people accept Krishna, Rama, Shiva, Vishnu etc. as God. He expresses Himself as everything and He remains in everything. People imagine God according to their understanding. But the truth is that God is formless. Once we know how He is there in everything, we shall have faith and devotion towards Him. Generally, most of the people do not know anything about God but they worship just mechanically. Quite a many worship God for fulfilment of desires. To receive the blessings of God, it is necessary that one should have firm faith, devotion and love towards God. There are many who attain purity by studying the biographies of saints and Sadgurus. People outwardly worship God, but they do not inculcate divine qualities in them as a result of which they do not get God’s blessings. Instead of virtues like charity and service, people possess more of demoniac qualities for which they suffer. After doing charity, one’s heart fills with joy. Due to want of this knowledge, the number of disbelievers is rising now-a-days. Even people in their spiritual pursuits face some resistance from others.

The question is- Should we increase our virtues or lose our acquired virtues by taking to wrong paths? Should we invite sufferings by committing more and more sins? Sadgurus descend on earth from time to time to spread the truth about God's existence and guide mankind to take to virtuous paths for getting God's grace which is the highest achievement of life. He, who takes shelter of Sadguru, Gurushakti shall be transmitted to him. He, who believes in Guru's greatness, would receive Guru's grace. Guru teaches how to observe Dharma properly and shows the way to God-realization. Therefore, it is the first and foremost duty of everyone to acquire right knowledge to move on spiritual path and attain goal of self-realization.

God is Truth-Absolute. Truth protects us. If we do not have faith on the Truth-Absolute, we cannot tide over our sufferings. Everyone should observe Dharma or righteousness to get peace. If we know that God is Peace-Absolute, we shall remain in peace. If we know that God is Bliss-Absolute, we shall be in bliss. If we know that God is Freedom-Absolute, we shall enjoy freedom. The more we know about God, the more we shall be benefited. Whatever we see or come across in this world are all changeable and hence transitory. For example, the sky was clear, there was no cloud; but after some time, cloud appears in the sky. Likewise, changes like day, night and seasons do happen regularly. A child grows into youth. The young become old. Thus there are incessant changes all around. Who is regulating all these changes? Some invisible and unchangeable power is there who manages all these changes. That power remains in everything and everywhere. Only after realizing that power, the sages named Him as God. Hence God is there. Even to assert, "God is non-existent" is propelled by a background power. We owe our existence to that Existence. Had He not been there, we could not have said 'Yes' or 'No'. Let us think for a while before disputing the existence of God. Who made all arrangements for the digestion of our food? How our hearts are functioning non-stop? How our respiratory systems work so precisely? How our senses and different limbs are active? Everything is possible because of Him. But we are not able to know Him. The more we know about Him, we shall be benefited more. If we do not believe in God and do not try to know Him, how can we ask for something from Him with an expectation that He would give us? We crave for peace and happiness, but we are not trying to learn what should be done to get peace and happiness. Without knowing anything about Him, we blame Him, speak ill of Him. But who is giving us everything and is always keen to give us more and more? We are not ready to receive from Him. This is all due to our ignorance about the greatest power.

Many people after knowing something about God claim that they love God. But love comes at an extremely high state. Mirabai loved Lord Krishna. He, who loves God, would get God. God will come to him and bless him. Whatever man wants, he can get once a sense of true devotion awakens in him. Once you have a sense of love towards God, tears will come out the moment you utter His name. You would cry for Him. Hence spirituality starts from belief in God. Subsequently come faith, devotion and love. It ends up with union. If you try to acquire spiritual knowledge, you can know about God and ultimately you can attain God.

*****

[42]Brahman is the root of the Creation. He manifests as the Creation. He manifests Himself and controls Himself. By Him only, we can know Him or realise Him. He is Peace-Absolute, Bliss-Absolute

---

[42]*Odia Divyadhara Vol 20 Page 9*

and Freedom-Absolute. Without Him, no peace or bliss is possible for us. Man wants to live in peace and happiness. His goal is to realise Brahman. First, he should make efforts to know about Brahman. Realization of Brahman amounts to attainment of Brahman.

There are many ways to attain Brahman. The best and the surest way is to follow Sadguru. By Sadguru's teachings and influence, the disciple sheds off his negative qualities and becomes pure. According to Divya Darshan, "Knowledge is Guru". Knowledge makes one pure. By the same knowledge one can realise Brahman. With an impure mind, man cannot realise Brahman. After attaining purity of mind, one can reach out to *Para-Jnana*. By *Para-Jnana*, one can realise the Supreme Brahman. By acquiring true knowledge, gradually the tamasic and rajasic tendencies of the spiritual aspirant wane away and the divine qualities spontaneously come out in him.

Just as a mother takes care of the children, Guru takes care of the disciples to make them clean and pure so that the disciples can move higher and higher to attain the True Self. In the kingdom of nature, we come across innumerable qualities. We name them accordingly. When we find beastly instincts in a man, we compare him with a beast. Man is overwhelmed by jiva qualities. He is called a jiva. This jiva feeling can be eradicated by acquiring true knowledge. Jiva feeling causes all bondages. Once jiva feeling goes away, man becomes free. That is why so much importance is attached to knowledge. All the worldly attachments can be dispelled by Sadguru's teachings, i.e. when He reveals the true knowledge. That is why it is said that liberation is impossible without Guru. Divya Darshan teaches about truth and knowledge. Divya Darshan calls upon the mankind to realise the Self by true knowledge and attain freedom.

Man is mad after money. Man is mad after so many mundane matters which are but short-lived. Therefore, he has no interest to acquire true knowledge. Knowing truth is knowledge. Truth is Self-Absolute. Divya Darshan teaches about *Para-Jnana* and desireless devotion. Without acquiring true knowledge, Brahman cannot be realised.

With limited and fragmented knowledge, people worship God of their imagination. People try to give different shapes to God according to their imagination. They forget that the God they believe in and rely upon is a product of their imagination. People tell different stories about God. They follow many rituals which differ from place to place. They worship different Gods in different seasons. They offer different kinds of eatables as Prasad. To propitiate God, animal sacrifices are also resorted to. All these are done for fulfilment of desires. After worshipping, God is immersed in water. But God is formless and all-pervasive. He manifests as Truth, Consciousness, and Bliss. Divya Darshan lays emphasis on knowing what Truth is and thereafter surrendering to Truth. Divya Darshan teaches the role of God and His greatness. He, who acquires true knowledge, gets peace and bliss. He attains Brahman and attains liberation.

*****

[43]God is there. Even an ignorant person also claims this. But after attaining the highest state of knowledge the sages and seers say, "I am Brahman"; "Thou art that" When a spiritual mendicant realises, "I am Brahman", at that time to whom shall he say that God is there when there is none other than Him? The first step is to understand

---

[43] *Odia Divyadhara Vol 2 Page 20*

that there is God. The second step is to know that everything is full of Brahman or Brahman pervades all and everywhere. But many people even do not understand the first step. Spiritual knowledge is to be acquired in stages. Hence there is nothing to be proud of knowledge. Always more and still higher knowledge remain to be known. Knowledge is infinite. He, who says that he knows God, does not know. He, who says that he does not know, knows to some extent. He, who says that he knows and knows not, knows God. But people knowing little of Him claim that they know God.

According to Divya Darshan, when you are taking recourse to knowledge you are able to know truth one by one. God manifests Himself as various truths. He Himself is the Supreme Truth. Hence Divya Darshan does not assign any form to God. How God is present everywhere? The answer is - He is there as different truths. Hydrogen and Oxygen together make water. This is truth. The proportion in which they mix is also truth. Hydrogen is truth. So is Oxygen. The more we know various truths, the more can we utilise them. Here there is no need to imagine any form to worship Him and beg anything of Him. The more we know the truth, the more can we utilise the same. It is to be understood that we are being benefited by God. It is not essential to see God. God manifests everywhere as form, quality and knowledge but we are not aware of the same. God is everywhere as truth. Many may not accept this truth. When we fall asleep, we do not know when we shall wake up. After we fall asleep our knowledge also vanishes. Who wakes us up? We breathe but we are not aware of the same. Our breathing process is always on. It is automatic. Who is doing all these? Who enables digestion of our food? There is some invisible power that does all these and is present as Truth everywhere and in every being.

When we cook rice, we take the help of many truths like the amount of water, the amount of heat and the quantity of rice. Without knowing all these truths, one cannot cook rice. In other words, rice can be cooked only with the help of truths. Without knowing all these truths if only we pray God, rice cannot be cooked and delivered at our homes. But we do not evince interest to know truths. Without knowledge how shall one know truth as truth? Knowledge is an essential pre-requisite to realise truth. Not knowing the truth is ignorance. Not knowing the truth is darkness. Darkness is nothing but absence of light. Darkness has no separate or independent existence. Light is the cause of it. When we do not know the right answer, we understand things in different ways.

The entire creation is full of truths. Brahman is truth. The more one knows Him, the more one becomes closer to Him. Thus, one day the knower would realise the Supreme Truth.

There are several ways to realise the Supreme Truth. The sages and seers of yesteryears had found out various ways for practice of Yoga. But they may not suit all in the present-day conditions. Further, there are many superstitions which are surreptitiously entrenched in our religious practices over a period. If we proceed in those ways, we cannot reach God.

There are already six systems of philosophy. Question may arise, why Divya Darshan again? Divya Darshan in fact is not a dogma or group or creed or community. It does not belong to anybody. It belongs to all. It is life itself. He, who knows it, gets it.

Self-realisation is such an experience that the experiencer of the Supreme Self cannot explain the non-dual state to anybody else. Therefore, other people often become incredulous of the Absolute Existence.

They ask a common question i.e. "Have you seen God? Can you show God?"

In fact, God is not an object and cannot be shown. God is not a subject to be explained to somebody. Now-a-days people are more inclined towards material science than the spiritual science despite the age-old preaching by the sages urging the mankind to turn Godward. Those who follow material science will not accept Bhakti Marg. Hence different examples are cited by means of knowledge to explain the existence of God. Hence it is imperative for the people to acquire knowledge for experiencing Truth. Everyone wants proof of God's existence. Through material science God cannot be realised. Only way is to acquire spiritual knowledge by which God, the Truth-Absolute would be realised.

The knowledge preached by Divya Darshan is showing the way from darkness to light. Divya Darshan is not presenting the concept of any new Atman or Brahman. It has already been explained by the sages and seers in different scriptures. Divya Darshan says, "Without any yogic practice but only by taking shelter of truth and walking on the path of Dharma one can reach God". God, who remains as Energy-Absolute, can be realised by realising the Energy (Shakti). Hence Divya Darshan lays emphasis on divine knowledge and taking shelter of Truth. By spiritual practices, this can be achieved. When man will realise the essence of the scriptures, he can live in peace and bliss and attain true freedom.

Divya Darshan lays emphasis on Truth by knowing which one can realise God. The subject of Divya Darshan is a matter of self-experience of the spiritual master (Sadguru Sri Sri Arjun). Therefore, it is named as Divya Darshan. Param-Brahman is divine. To realise Him, the divine knowledge is named as Divya Darshan. Divine knowledge and divine virtues are the essence of Divya Darshan. By divine virtues, one can live in peace and attain divinity. By acquiring knowledge, one can move towards divinity faster. When man takes recourse to knowledge, he can forsake his animal instincts faster and would acquire divine qualities and thereafter God. By acquiring knowledge, man would reinforce his faith on God. With knowledge, he would know truth and shall ultimately be merged with the Supreme Truth. This is the Law of Eternity.

Divya Darshan has been advanced in order to dispel ignorance and disseminate knowledge of Truth. There are many scriptures with valuable facts of experience that show to the humanity various paths to attain the goal. Only by memorizing the scriptures, true knowledge shall not come. The knowledge need to be reflected in one's conduct as divine virtues. Without divine virtues the knowledge is incomplete. Many people resort to various religious practices rigorously but blindly, ultimately to get frustrated. It is because ignorance reigns everywhere. Ignorance is the cause of suffering. The essence of the scriptures is not understood in its true spirit. More often those are misinterpreted and misused. Sufferings shall be there until and unless man acquires true knowledge or self-knowledge.

God expresses Himself as knowledge, but we rarely evince interest in knowledge. Man, as well as other creatures, survives because of divine qualities present in the kingdom of nature. Divya Darshan preaches how a man can live in peace and happiness with a harmonious social life and ultimately realise the True Self. This is the fundamental need of all human beings.

A man must know how to live, what to do and what not to do, what goal is to be pursued, from where his journey began, what are the laws/rules to be followed and which path is to be followed to reach the destination, what should be his thoughts, what should be his conduct and how shall he maintain his social life to earn peace and happiness. A man must know what truth is and what righteousness is. Further he must know his duties and responsibilities. Divya Darshan shows the highway to divinity and therefore strongly endorses 'Divine Thoughts', 'Divine Expressions' and 'Divine Actions' as the means to attain the goal. In this process, karma, bhakti and jnana are well synchronised and integrated into one. Therefore, a qualitative and purposeful life is much essential for every human being. A man having been given this rare and fair form must have the prudence befitting the most elevated being of the Creation, to proceed unswervingly towards his goal of self-realisation by continuing with his spiritual practices for acquiring knowledge and divine virtues.

Many people are not aware of the importance of knowledge. Shrimad Bhagavad-Gita has emphasised on karma, bhakti and jnana. Those, who possess knowledge about God, would have devotion towards God and ultimately realise the True Self. Those, who lay more emphasis on karma, attach more importance to the body not knowing that God has given us this body only to carry out spiritual practices. Karma helps in maintaining the body. There is also a subtle body inside the gross body. For the subtle body something else apart from karma is needed. Karma, bhakti and jnana are required for the purpose of self-realisation ultimately.

Divya Darshan says, "If you want to live, be dutiful; if you want peace and happiness, possess divine virtues; if you want freedom, acquire self-knowledge." Divya Darshan preaches monism or Advaita; "All as one and one as all." While doing spiritual practice to realise this, automatically devotion and self-surrender would come. In the path of knowledge, all the three (apparently three but essentially one) such as karma, bhakti and jnana get synchronised, enhanced and perfected so that the seeker can attain the Supreme who is formless, attributeless and blissful. In other words, all the three such as karma, bhakti and jnana as they come under the purview of knowledge, should happen simultaneously and not by trying on the same one after another.

A child after passing the preliminary standard goes to higher class and does not read the courses of earlier classes again. Similarly, karma and bhakti are to be transcended while doing jnana Sadhana. Jnana is all-inclusive. A wise person can streamline his karma, fine-tune his bhakti and do what is best for him to reach the goal. He can choose to avoid the avoidable things and walk straight on the highway that leads to the destination. To proceed faster on the spiritual path, divine virtues are essential. Divine virtues protect us. Divine virtues help us reach our goal uninterruptedly. In absence of divine virtues, a spiritual mendicant will have several stumbling blocks, mistakes, opposition and resistance on his way; the goal therefore shall remain far away. Therefore, he has to simplify, straighten and synchronize himself properly to attain the goal. This is possible only by acquiring divine virtues. If you do not conduct yourselves properly others would not listen to you. So, you are to keep yourself properly tuned and regulated. Karma yoga and Bhakti yoga will take you to the doorstep of Brahman. Jnana yoga will lead you to ultimate immergence with Brahman. The house holders also can carry on with spiritual practice. After attaining Brahman, even if a householder remains in samsara, he is not bound by the law of karma. Everybody's duty is to realise Brahman, the Supreme. Since we are all householders, our spiritual practices start from dualism, but the goal is advait or non-dualism. Bhakti stage comes under dualism whereas love and consequent union is non-dualism. Divya Darshan integrates dualism with non-dualism.

People are suffering because they are saddled with multiple desires. Due to craze for pleasure and enjoyment we usually depend upon others. We can be self-dependent if we can reduce our desires and dependence on others. Peace and freedom will not come if one is dependent on others. We all depend upon five gross elements such as earth, water, fire, air and space. Even the personal godheads depend upon Brahman. The sages and seers who are realisers are independent or free. We must be necessarily self-dependent in order to attain liberation. Divya Darshan says, "You are intrinsically immortal and emancipated, but due to ignorance this great truth is not realised by you."

*****

[44]*["Paramatman is beyond contemplation. All our thoughts and contemplations are His mere play. But we misconstrue this world as real. He is more real than the visible and invisible Creation." (Amritbindu-60)]*

Paramatman is beyond our contemplation. By mind and intellect, man imagines certain things. But He is beyond the mind and intellect. Therefore, all thoughts and imaginations are His mere play. But Paramatman is more real than the visible and invisible Creation.

Thoughts emanating from the intellect are superior to those coming from the mind. Similarly thoughts emanating from the conscience are at a still higher level. Atman is beyond conscience. He, who is stuck up at the level of the mind, cannot appreciate or understand the thoughts coming from the level of conscience. Therefore, how can he realise Atman?

---

[44]*Odia Divyadhara Vol 20 Page 53*

Generally, people discuss about God. Some people speak of Brahman and some others speak of Atman. But man cannot understand these highest states by his limited knowledge. The rishis have experienced the highest state after which they have named Him as such. That supreme state cannot be realised by mind or intellect. Therefore, Divya Darshan says "Paramatman is beyond any contemplation. Contemplation is His mere play."

Man considers the things and happenings around him as real. But these are the divine play of Brahman. Man misconstrues something as good or bad and accordingly he gets pleasure or pain. But in order to realise the Supreme, man has to go beyond His Lila. Through the above enlightening lines of Amrit Bindu you are given instructions to attain the highest level. You are also getting inspiration to move higher and higher to realise the Supreme state. We normally consider this visible Creation as real. But it is not real. This visible Creation has come from something else which is the basis of everything visible or invisible. Innumerable stages come one after another before the gross Creation appears.

We are seeing the ornaments made of gold. Gold is given different shapes or designs. All these ornaments are again recycled into gold. Different earthen pots are there. They are all made of clay and again they become earth or clay.

All these forms or designs of ornaments were not there earlier. There was only gold. Forms and designs came afterwards. Again, they will be one with gold. Like this, the visible and invisible things of the Creation have come from something else. Some invisible things cannot be cognized by the sense organs. But those invisible things can be experienced by intellect, conscience, knowledge and Atman. Whatever we realise by Atman are truths. Out of the five elements, we can see earth, water, and fire. But we cannot see air and ether.

We can feel the air when it blows. There are different waves like radio waves or electromagnetic waves which we cannot see but can experience the same by knowledge. Magnetic force is invisible, but we can see its impact. So is gravitational force.

We cannot see the light or sun rays. When the rays get reflected by some objects, at that time only we can feel the light or rays. Light is travelling from the Sun to the Earth. We cannot see the light in motion. We see it when it hits any object and as a result gets reflected. We discuss about different gods and goddesses who are invisible. We discuss about the spirits which are also invisible. The invisible universe is far bigger than the visible. If man acquires more and more knowledge, he can know more and more about the invisible existence. Brahman is there as the basis of everything both visible and invisible. He is beyond the visible and invisible Creation. He is more real than the visible and invisible world. What we experience by our senses, mind and intellect are all changeable and they are known as temporal truths or partial truths. The basis of these is also still subtler which is Truth i.e. God.

Some examples are cited below.

We imagine things. Who is imagining? Who is there in us who is imagining things? Someone is there in us who is contemplating. He is beyond knowledge and is inexpressible. This means, whatever we imagine, say or do thereafter, everything originates from this inexpressible existence. Everything that emanates from the inexpressible source shall one day get merged in that state which is the root cause of everything.

The wise people know that intellect controls the mind, conscience controls the intellect and Atman controls the conscience. Atman is otherwise known as Brahman or Ishwar. Atman is much above the level of the mind. Mind is changeable. Whatever all mind thinks of, undergo modifications from time to time. Whatever man thinks or does are all controlled and directed by the Atman. Man's body owes its existence to the Atman. Whatever activities man undertakes are all governed by Atman. Atman is beyond intellect, conscience, and knowledge. Whatever we speak about God is all reflected knowledge. God must be realised. From the level of mind, we cannot know God. That is why the sages were doing so much spiritual practices to realise Brahman. The rishis have expressed their experiences through the Vedas and Vedanta. Mind cannot reach there; intellect cannot reach there. By conscience, one gets some indication of God. Atman can be realised by Atman only.

Atman is the basis of everything. To explain Brahman, the sages say, "He willed to be many. This statement is also a thought or imagination. Whatever is created from out of Brahman's Will is all His Lila or play. But due to ignorance, man misconstrues them as real. These are temporal or transitory manifestations. The basis of everything visible and invisible is Truth. All manifested things are unreal and temporary.

Jagadguru Shankaracharya had said "Brahman is real and Jagat is unreal." Truth is Brahman and Brahman is Truth. We misconstrue the changeable things as Truth. The Creation appears as such due to sheer imagination. Truth is always there. Truth is there in us. When man will realise the Truth inside, at that time only he will get rid of all sufferings and realise Brahman or Atman.

When you will meet Him whom you are seeking for long even for births after births, how happy you will be! Everyone can get Him provided one possesses strong inquisitiveness to know. Until you know about who God is, you remain far away even though God is always near you. After realizing Him, you will say that you were all along searching Him outside although He is inside.

You are in intimacy with the evanescent objects. When you know Him, you become one with Him. Without knowing Him how will you be one with Him?

*****

[45]How can we maintain relationship with someone about whom we do not know? How shall we get favours from him? How can we utilise his services? Common men do not know about Brahman. In other words, they do not have clear idea about Brahman. That is why they do not have faith and devotion towards Brahman. The sages and realised souls had realised Brahman. But the common people instead of trying to know Him, make some outward arrangements for worshipping and chant prayers to appease Him. It is nothing but groping in darkness. We form a picture of God out of our imagination. It should be remembered that it is essential to realise Brahman to get rid of sufferings.

God of our imagination is at a particular level. A devotee keeps his faith on the imagined God; he gets some experiences or may witness God according to his bhava. But Brahman is different from all these. He is beyond imagination. He is the Supreme Existence, all-powerful and omnipresent. The all-pervasive power by which everything is caused and conditioned including our thoughts or reflections, is known as Brahman who is inexpressible. He is the background existence. Common people do not know this and therefore they ask, "Where is He? What are His Laws?" They simply go on begging one favour after another just to satisfy their endless

---

[45]*Odia Divyadhara Vol 6 Page 13*

desires. How can one expect anything from someone who is unknown? Man worships various personal godheads who have only limited powers delegated to them. For example, Goddess Laxmi can give wealth, Goddess Saraswati can give knowledge. Likewise, Brahma creates and Vishnu sustains the whole Creation. But without knowing this, man asks for everything from some personal godhead. It is not possible to get everything from any particular personal godhead.

Man must acquire true knowledge and after knowing about Brahman's greatness he must surrender to Him to get His blessings. By conscience only, man can get some indication about God. Hence man must rise from the sense plane (Indriya level) to the mind plane, from mind plane to the plane of intellect and from the plane of intellect to the plane of conscience. Since man habitually operates at sense level, he is unable to know about Brahman who transcends everything.

Who can give the right knowledge about Brahman? He, who has realised Him, can show the right path. Common people give some name to God of their imagination, ascribe some form and qualities and accordingly worship. But scriptures say that Brahman is formless and attributeless. He has neither any beginning nor end. He is indescribable. Rishi Yajnavalkya concluded by saying, "Neti Neti", which means, "Not like this, not this much." Brahman is smaller than the smallest and bigger than the biggest. Hence, He is inexpressible. It must be remembered that the unitary existence is the Creator and Protector of the universe. He is there in all beings; He is the life of our lives. He is our vital energy. He has made all arrangements for us to survive, live in peace and happiness, and also He has given us everything by which we can attain eternal bliss and freedom. Earth, water, fire, air and space are all created before we were born. Where shall we take birth; what and how much shall we enjoy are all predetermined by Him. Law of action is in operation. Whatever we enjoy, nothing is ours. Everything belongs to Brahman. Such being the case, we should return everything we possess since everything belongs to Him. But if we return everything to Him, there shall not be any question of our existence. Our body is made of five gross elements such as earth, water, fire, air and ether. Even if only one element is withdrawn from us, we shall not exist. He, who understands this, will be eager to know Brahman and shall cry for Him. When he would go on knowing more and more about Brahman, he would ultimately realise, "I am Brahman."

Realising Him amounts to attaining Him. He, who knows Him would become more and more powerful and would be able to get rid of all sufferings. God is Sat, Chit and Ananda (Existence, Knowledge and Bliss). This means that Existence manifests as Consciousness; Bliss is experienced by Consciousness. By Consciousness, the Existence is also realised. Brahman is the basis of all divinities and glories. He is Peace-Absolute. By knowing Him as Peace-Absolute, man gets peace. By knowing Him as Bliss-absolute, man gets Bliss. He, who knows Him as Freedom-Absolute, gets freedom. He, who attains Brahman, becomes Brahman. He gets Bliss and Freedom. He becomes everything. Ultimately, nothing remains to be known; nothing remains to be attained. Hence preparation for realisation of Brahman or spiritual practice for self-realisation is real worship. He, who worships like this, gets blessings and gets rid of all sufferings. He breaks all chains of births and deaths. This is man's goal.

*****

[46] *[Our knowledge is improper and meaningless if we do not have sense of love and devotion towards God. It is only by Jnana that we know God's greatness and as a result, sense of devotion wells up in our heart. In the next stage, devotion (Bhakti) is transformed into love (Prema). Once there is love towards God, there is no necessity of Jnana. (Amritbindu-113)]*

Brahman is one, not two. The one only appears as many. Those, who take Brahman as many, realise neither Brahman nor His Lila. Generally, Brahman and God are used interchangeably. He is also called Ishwar and Atman. To explain the subject at varying levels, different terms are used by the sages. The Unitary Existence has innumerable names. He appears as many. This means, He has unlimited powers. This is indicated by the term greatness or Lila. We all are products of His manifestations. We therefore consider ourselves as individual beings and not as manifestations of the Unitary Existence. Multiplicity of names, multiplicity of forms and qualities create confusion in us. If we do not realise the Unity, we will remain in illusion born of ignorance. Therefore, people imagine their own gods in their own ways. They ascribe different forms and different qualities to God although He is beyond all these.

Brahman is one. He has infinite powers. His specific powers are named as different gods and goddesses. People keep on shifting their devotion from one Deva to the other until their desires are fulfilled. For them the Deva who fulfils the desires is the greatest and most powerful. By acquiring knowledge about Brahman, you will be convinced that Brahman manifests as everything visible and invisible. Many people have heard the scriptural saying that Brahman is one. But still they worship different deities. This is because what

---

[46] *Odia Divyadhara Vol 15 Page 53*

they have heard about Brahman is not enough. Brahman is the material cause as well as the efficient cause of everything. He is the basis of everything. Everything has emanated from Him. He is the Witness-Consciousness. He is seeing everything that we do or even think of. He, who is present everywhere and always as primal cause can witness everything of the Creation. He dwells in everything of the Creation. He is Antaryami. He knows the heart and mind of everyone. He is the basis of all. He is infinite. Since He is eternal, He has neither birth nor death. He is formless and unchangeable. While explaining about Brahman, the sages have likened Him to the space which is infinite, formless, beginningless, endless and all-pervasive. From the space, everything else has been projected or manifested.

Since we are not interested to know about Brahman, we remain ignorant about Him. He is one without a second. By His Will, everything else has manifested. That Unitary Power only should be worshipped. Knowing Him is the goal of everybody. Liberation comes on attaining the goal. He can be realised or attained even in one birth. But if you do not want to know Him, you will never get. You must understand first that everything in this Creation is manifestation of Brahman. Brahman is the only Reality. In arithmetic, we start from one. One is present in all numbers. All other numbers are additions or products of one. If one is not there, other numbers will not be there. One is the only constituent of all numbers.

Ignorance is a great sin. Ignorance is the cause of sufferings. Knowledge of Brahman is essential to come out of doubts, despair and all sorts of sufferings. Brahman being all-pervasive need not be searched for in any specific place or in any forest or mountain. He will listen and respond wherever you will remember Him. He, who searches for God here and there, has not understood the all-pervasiveness of Brahman. We all shall be merged with Him one day.

One manifests as many. Many will be merged in one. This is the Law of the Universe. This is the theory of monism. Every form is a form of Brahman. Every quality is a quality of Brahman. Every name is a name of Brahman. Every power is Brahman's power. Every flicker of consciousness is Brahman's consciousness. All knowledge is Brahman's knowledge. Every truth is a manifestation of Brahman, the Truth-Absolute. Brahman must be realised to get rid of all sins and sufferings, to be released from all the worldly bondages, and to get bliss and freedom. Brahman is the Supreme Truth. He is the goal.

*****

[47]*["There is Maya in Lila. Behind the Lila is its maker. Unless He is understood, Maya cannot be comprehended." (Amritbindu-64)]*

Brahman is Sat, Chit and Ananda (Existence, Knowledge and Bliss). He is beginningless and endless, all-pervasive and all-powerful. He is eternal and self-effulgent. Divya Darshan says, "Someone exists, who illumines Himself, regulates Himself and reveals Himself." He is Brahman. He manifests as this Creation. His first manifestation is knowledge.

Hence in the Aitareya Upanishad, He is known as 'Prajnanam Brahman'. Whatever occurs or happens in this Creation are all His Lila. There is Lila in the process of manifestation. Who is behind the scenes? Brahman is there behind all these occurrences and happenings. That means, everything is caused and conditioned by Him. This is called Lila. But we are not able to understand the truth behind Lila (Divine Play). Unless Lila is understood, Maya cannot be comprehended. What is there in Lila? Maya is there in Lila.

---

[47]*Odia Divyadhara Vol 13 Page 42*

What is Maya?

Not knowing the Lila is Maya or Ajnana (ignorance). Who is the maker of Lila? How does Lila take place? He, who does not know the answers to the foregoing questions, is in Maya. There is no separate thing like Maya. Since we are not able to understand the Lila, we get surprised and at times shocked by the transitory happenings. This is due to our ignorance. Due to ignorance, we get confused. We fumble and falter. Not knowing the truth or Reality is Maya.

In everything there is some truth. Many people do not know how water is formed. The scientists know the truth behind water. They say that water comprises Hydrogen and Oxygen. There is a definite formula for formation of water. Divya Darshan says that water is truth. Similarly, Oxygen is truth. Hydrogen is truth. The definite formula for combination of Hydrogen with Oxygen is also truth.

Let us take one more example. It is raining now. There is cloud in the sky. But there was no cloud in the morning. It appeared thereafter. Wherefrom did it come? How was it formed? How did it rain? If we do not know answers to these questions, we get surprised. He, who knows the answers, will not be wonderstruck to see the cloud and rainfall. Hence Maya is nothing but not understanding the truth. If Lila is there, Maya is also there. If Maya is there, Lila is there. There is Maya in Lila. If there is no Lila, Maya is also not there. In that case, there would not have been any plant, animal or man. In that case there is no question of Maya. If the Creation is there, there is a Creator also. If Lila is there, there is a maker of Lila. If Lila is there, God or Brahman is also there. Had there been no God, the Creation would not have been there. In that case, there is no question of Lila or Maya. Unless Truth is known, we will continue to be mystified by Maya. Unless the Creator is realised, His

Creation cannot be understood properly. God is the cause of both Lila and Maya.

When God is realised, the mystery of both Lila and Maya vanishes and therefore they cannot confuse us anymore.

We suffer because of Maya. When someone dies, we cry. This is due to Maya. When someone blames us, we get angry; this also is due to Maya. When we get attracted towards something and get tempted to acquire the same, we are in Maya. We are all ensnared in Maya. Therefore, we suffer. The children cry for chocolates, but an adult does not cry for chocolates. The children do not know that chocolate is harmful for teeth. But an adult knows that the chocolate may harm him. Hence, he does not cry for the same. Therefore, if our level of knowledge increases, our sufferings shall get reduced. He, who knows the intricacies of Maya, can tide over Maya. In other words, Maya will not affect him. Someone's sufferings indicate that he is afflicted by Maya. Unless Maya is known and done away with, sufferings will continue.

Due to our ignorance, we commit mistakes in knowing the truth. We are totally in Maya or illusion. We are not able to understand the truth. That is why Divya Darshan imparts knowledge about Brahman, about Lila and Maya. Divya Darshan also explains the greatness of Brahman. Finally, we will acquire knowledge about our True Self. Not being able to realise Truth behind this Creation is Maya. In other words, Maya will be dispelled forthwith once Truth is realised. Maya is with the ignorant and not with the wise. In the foregoing chocolate example, Maya is there with the child but not with the adult. Therefore, in order to get rid of Maya, we must try to realise Brahman.

There is knowledge in Lila. Knowledge is the power by which we know how the Creation has come into existence and who is the Creator. By acquiring true knowledge, we can correct ourselves and get rid of Maya. To know how to cook rice or how to prepare a cake is the contribution of knowledge. Knowledge is involved in everything and everywhere. Avadhut had 24 Gurus(besides his own Atman) such as- The Earth (tolerance, patience and forgiveness), water (quenching thirst of every one, pure and transparent, serving all), fire (brightness with no extra storage place), air (pure and odourless), sky (infinitude and remaining unaffected), The Moon (waxes and wanes without getting affected), The Sun (evaporates water but returns the same back without attachment), pigeon, python, the ocean, moth, honeybee, honey gatherer, elephant, deer, fish, the dancing girl Pingala, the kurari bird, child, the young girl, arrow maker, serpent, spider and wasp. This means, he had acquired knowledge from the nature.

This indicates that everything around us is Guru. You can get knowledge from everything around you and from within you. You can learn from a plant and even from an ant. Like this if you go on learning from nature, your knowledge shall improve to higher level and then you will be fit to acquire still higher knowledge. Ultimately, you can realise the Supreme Truth.

The Creator is beyond knowledge. He manifests Himself as many through knowledge. He creates, He maintains, and He transforms by means of knowledge. He manifests as time and space, fulfils all necessary pre-requisites for the sustainability and sequential development of the created beings in accordance with the Law of Eternity in a perfect manner.

To realise Him is not that easy. Due to ignorance, the Truth is far away. Knowledge pertains to His Lila. How and when did the Lila begin? Answer to this can be had at a higher stage of spiritual knowledge. First there was no quality or any form. The tri-qualities came from 'Om'. Myriads of qualities and matching forms came into play thereafter. This means, from the Supreme Truth, all other truths such as qualities and forms have emanated. The 'One' appearing as many in different roles on a stage is His Lila. At His True Self, He is eternally unitary and there is no question of any Lila. Not understanding His Lila involving innumerable characters is Maya. You and I are all parts of His Lila. On realization of Brahman, Maya vanishes along with all sufferings. He realises that he is Bliss-Absolute and Truth- Absolute.

Fear of death is the biggest fear. Everybody will depart one day. But many people do not know that after death also the subtle body exists. The subtle body survives the mortal physical body. Therefore, you are always there. Death cannot eliminate you. He, who knows like this, gets rid of Maya. In course of Lila, whatever occurs or happens, there is knowledge in everything. Knowledge is there up to this side of 'Om'. The other side, there is Supreme Brahman who can be realised in bhava state. Hence by knowledge He cannot be realised. In other words, knowledge is necessary to proceed but it cannot bring in realization of Brahman. Creation has emanated from 'Om'. When a spiritual mendicant reaches bhava state, at that time knowledge is unimportant or immaterial.

Bhava is the essence of jnana. When the wise men say 'Brahman', it is bhava. When they explain or describe the concept for the ignorant to understand, it is all knowledge. In bhava state, they get established in Brahman. There is no scope for further imagination or contemplation. Another example may be cited here. When we say 'rose', it is bhava. When we describe its colour, fragrance and petals etc. it is all knowledge. The essence of all narratives is 'rose'.

Similarly, Lord Shiva is a bhava. When we describe about his physical features, get-up, vehicle and consort, it is all knowledge. The spiritual mendicant moves to bhava state after acquiring jnana. At that time, he can realise that there is only one Supreme Brahman who has caused and conditioned everything. He will lose interest in Lila and prefer to get established in the Supreme Brahman. If somebody remains within the knowledge kingdom, he cannot realise the Supreme Brahman. With lot of spiritual knowledge, he will have the power to explore still greater truths. Man must move to bhava state for realizing the Supreme. He will realise that Brahman is everywhere. His Lila (divine Play) goes on and He goes on manifesting Himself. It is all His greatness. Therefore, we come across the diversities. It is called Maya or illusion. It is due to our ignorance about the Unity. The people out of ignorance undergo chains of sufferings and they wail and mourn. But the sages or the enlightened souls are always in blissful state. They realise that people are unnecessarily crying like children for losing something or for not getting something. They know that the people who are craving and crying are in Maya. They misconstrue a rope as a snake. The sages keep on advising us that it is all Maya and there is no reason to grieve for anything. They impart true knowledge to us by which all sufferings vanish. There is knowledge in Lila. By knowledge Lila can be understood. As a result, 75% of the total sufferings will go away. Once we know the maker of Lila, sufferings will vanish totally. There will be total absence of fear, doubt and despair.

The children may be afraid of seeing a fearsome picture some artist has drawn. But the artist who has created the picture will not be afraid of seeing his own art however awe-inspiring the same may be. Similarly, when a realiser realises the Supreme Truth, he can well understand the true nature of the Creation. He realises, "It is a play by the Unitary Existence. I am that Being. All other things, happenings and occurrences are my becoming. I manifest as such." As this truth is unknown to the people, they suffer, meet with death and undergo the cycle of birth and death.

All bliss is there with the Supreme Truth. For this, one must acquire spiritual knowledge to know oneself and the Supreme Brahman. Without self-knowledge, it is impossible to get freedom from all bondages and consequent sufferings. Now it appears that, you feel complacent having understood what I said. But this is not enough. This is only the preliminary stage. Till you have not gone to the ultimate stage, you must be with Guru and keep on practicing this spiritual science. You must meditate and contemplate on the Supreme Truth till you attain perfection. "Knowledge is present everywhere and in everything. Knowledge is there in the nature. Brahman has taken all these forms for my well-being and also to give me knowledge. He has become various kinds of plants and animals, various stars and planets, and what not. To give me knowledge He has come as my Guru. He is the undivided whole; I am not different from Him. I am always there." Thus the spiritual mendicant will ultimately have unwavering conviction that he is That.

*****

[48]**Maya:** Maya is an oft-repeated concept, although still elusive and obscure. Today's man is not able to comprehend this mysterious term 'Maya'. Learned men talk of Maya but they are not aware that they themselves are caught in the snares of Maya.

From the point of view of the Supreme Truth, there is nothing called Maya. The term Maya is used to indicate a state of the Unitary Truth. The goal of man is self-realisation. From self-realisation point

---

[48]*Odia Divyadhara Vol 6 Page 39*

of view, there is nothing called Maya. What is Maya? What is the role of Maya? Everyone should know this. Whether Maya is there or not? If it is there how it is there and when it is there? If it is not there, then how and when the same is not there? Maya should be understood well. Now we shall discuss about Maya. Wherever there is ignorance or the truth is not known, one is mistaken for the other or one subject or event is not perceived correctly, it is to be inferred that there is Maya. Where renunciation is absent, we are overwhelmed by greed. This is called Maya or ignorance. Maya is due to ignorance. In other words, ignorance is Maya. Everyone is affected by Maya or ignorance. Only a free soul or a true realiser can say that he is above Maya. Those, who are on the righteous path trying to acquire true knowledge or trying to know God, are least afflicted by Maya. The more the ignorance, the stronger is the spell of Maya.

The power to realise truth is knowledge. Where there is true knowledge, there is no Maya; there is no suffering. Maya is there in the kingdom of nature. Everything in the kingdom of nature is changeable. Since man does not know the Law of nature due to ignorance, he suffers when changes occur in and around him. If someone dies, the close relatives are in grief. Butthose, who know the law of nature, would not grieve on the death of someone. He, who is childless, suffers from mental agony imagining that a son would have helped him in his old age. There is no certainty that a son would support his father in old age. God takes care of everyone. He is aware of what is good for us. We suffer because we are not aware of the natural laws, God's Will and the Law of Eternity.

Now let us discuss about whether Maya is there in the kingdom of nature or elsewhere? Three qualities such as sattva, rajas and tamas are created from nature. It would not be fully correct to say that Maya is there in the kingdom of nature. It may be partly true.

But the truth is that Maya remains with everybody and nowhere else. If we have not understood nature, it means Maya is within us. When we shall know that Maya is within us, we can get rid of Maya. We are suffering because we are not aware of Maya. He, who would be able to understand the nature of Maya, would be freed from Maya. Ignorance is therefore nothing but not knowing Maya within us or not knowing nature. Wherever there is ignorance there is Maya. The sages therefore say that since man is afflicted by ignorance, he is dipped in Maya.

When a child puts his fingers into the fire, he cries. Seeing him cry, his parents also cry. Both are affected by ignorance or Maya. Since Maya is in everybody, if someone does something wrong, others are also affected. If someone does something good, others get benefited. It is clear from the above that not knowing the truth is ignorance and that is Maya.

We all suffer from Maya. But we do not know how to get rid of the same. Maya is not any gross thing that we can remove or throw it away. If true knowledge is acquired, Maya will go away. How to get this true knowledge? The giver of true knowledge is Sadguru. If a person surrenders to Sadguru or takes His shelter, Guru will identify the Maya in him. Guru also would not remove or stave off Maya from the disciples. Guru knows the tricks to dispel Maya. Guru will teach the tricks to the disciple. When the disciple would acquire true knowledge or spiritual knowledge, Maya shall vanish. At that time, the sufferings arising out of Maya shall come to an end.

Most of the people are not aware that they are all bound by Maya. It should be remembered that no one can dispel another's sufferings. One must try for oneself; one must make necessary arrangements to acquire required knowledge to get rid of sufferings. One blind man cannot show path to another blind man. Only a person with proper vision can show path to the blind.

If the parents are not aware of the spiritual knowledge or true knowledge, how will they be able to show right path to the children to live in peace and happiness? The future lives of the children also become gloomy due to improper guidance. Hence the children without knowing the righteous path or true goal of life are bound to suffer. It is also seen that some parents compel their children to take non-vegetarian food. Is it so important? Are there no alternative diets to keep the body healthy and strong? Due to improper food habits, we suffer from various diseases. Due to our ignorance, we cannot impart good training to the children on righteousness and morality. At times, we impart opposite knowledge. How can our children remain happy? The parents themselves do not have sense of duty and righteousness because of which the children also grow up in an improper environment. Hence sufferings are on the rise. By shouting that Maya should vanish, Maya won't. Only by acquiring true knowledge, Maya shall be dispelled. Everyone in this samsara has a different road map. Everyone has come to this samsara to enjoy the fruits of his actions. We come across many co-passengers while travelling in a train. Every passenger shall get down at his destination station. This samsara is like that. We weep for others due to Maya. Maya is not there in a wall or fence. Maya is not there in the insentient objects. It is in our mind. The only way to get rid of Maya is to acquire true knowledge by which we can get rid of sufferings. Divya Darshan says, "Ignorance is the cause of sufferings." Some disciples say that Guru has not taken away their sufferings. This is not correct. Guru would impart true knowledge. He would not interfere with the Law of nature. We have to acquire true knowledge. Then only we shall get rid of sufferings. If a disciple does not follow Guru's teachings, how would he get rid of sufferings? We crave for so many things and suffer. To get rid of the desires, we must acquire tattva jnana (True Knowledge). Devotees with bundles of desires worship God for the fulfilment of desires. They are in Maya. But those, who move on jnana path and practise desirelessness, would not be bound by Maya. By the fire of knowledge all the accumulated dirt of their previous births shall get burnt. On the advent of true knowledge all sufferings would vanish, and God can be realised. Divya Darshan says that we have bound ourselves by Maya. We ourselves can come out of it by resorting to sadhana. One must take the shelter of Sadguru, acquire true knowledge to get rid of Maya and realise God. The most infallible path is Divine Thoughts, Divine Expressions and Divine Actions. This is complete Yoga as emphasised by Divya Darshan. It is an integration of Karma, Bhakti and Jnana. By entertaining divine thoughts, divine expressions and performing right actions with sense of duty and responsibility, one can get rid of Maya very soon. While doing this, the mendicant would reach a state when he would realise the True Self and experience, "I am Brahman." This is called liberation or *Moksa*. Those, who are in jnana path, can earn good impulses (samskara) in a single birth which would have otherwise taken many births. 'Jnana Marg sadhana' is like moving in a rocket. Everyone should know the intricacies of Maya and sincerely try to get rid of sufferings. This is the sole objective of human birth.

*****

[49]In this world, Maya is ever active. Lord Srikrishna explains to Arjun about the role played by Maya. Maya is especially important from spiritual point of view. Knowing Maya almost amounts to knowing Brahman. Without knowing Maya, Brahman cannot be realised. I (Sadguru Sri Sri Arjun) am speaking to you about Maya because you are all caught in the snares of Maya. You are gradually

---

[49]*Odia Divyadhara Vol 20 Page 39*

learning more and more of spiritual knowledge. In this process, you are getting to know Maya also. I am imparting you true knowledge by which you can get rid of Maya. By this you can penetrate the coverings of Maya and attain Brahman. I am imparting this knowledge to open for you the doors of good fortune. If you do not listen and receive carefully, you are missing a golden chance.

If you look at the kingdom of nature, you can see the Lila of the Almighty. Wonderful things happen in the kingdom of nature. The tortoise lays eggs and covers the eggs by sand. From a distance the tortoise keeps its eyes on its eggs. It is by sheer will power of the mother tortoise that eggs are hatched. A hen sits on its eggs for hatching. Here there is difference between the two species. The crocodile lays eggs in water. Many water animals also lay eggs in water. A bat stands in between a bird and animal. This world is thus full of diversities. These diversities are all due to Maya.

Mahatattva is Buddhitattva. It is known as intellectual sheath. Unless intellectual sheath is known, the blissful sheath cannot be known. The Earth revolves round the Sun. Are we able to experience this? But the scientists by their persistent pursuits had realised this.

We all know something about the physical sheath. But we have lesser clarity about vital sheath and mental sheath. How much wise they are, who can see the invisible things! This Creation is replete with wonderful things and processes.

In this Creation, all divine powers are at work. All activities and processes in this Creation are handled by the divine powers. Those divine powers are named after various gods and goddesses. The more we know about the benevolent arrangements of the Creator, the more shall we be benefited and the more shall we love Him. Desireless love will come after knowing the greatness of Brahman.

The same Atman resides in me as well as in you all. One loves the other. This means one loves oneself. If one hates someone, it means one hates oneself. Desireless love will create universal love. In fact, self loves the self. In Shrimad Bhagavad-Gita, Lord Srikrishna told Arjun, "There is absolutely no difference between you and me. It is a top secret. Since you are dear to me, I am disclosing this secret knowledge to you. If you love me, you will come to me." When you will follow my instructions, it means you love me. When a disciple is eager to know Guru, this means that he loves Guru. Guru also loves the disciple. If you know the location of a gold mine, you will disclose the address to your nearest and dearest person. Likewise, Guru imparts to the disciple true knowledge which leads to self-realization.

Only Guru can tell about the greatness of Guru. Guru can also give all answers about the True Self. You love Guru. That is why you are asking these questions. Due to good impulses acquired in the past, one becomes keen to acquire knowledge. There is no difference between Knowledge and Guru. Guru and jnana are one and the same. This has been told to you from the beginning. He, who loves knowledge, loves Guru. He, who loves Guru, loves knowledge. Guru can know how much you love knowledge. Knowledge is there in everybody. Nobody can cheat his own knowledge. Similarly, nobody can cheat Guru.

*****

[50]God's greatness has been dealt elaborately in the Shrimad Bhagavad-Gita. Since we have little knowledge about God's greatness, we are not able to know the important role He plays. Many people are under the impression that if we pray to God for

---

[50]*Odia Divyadhara Vol 8 Page 4*

something, He will give us and rescue us from all misfortunes. This is devotion with desire. If man does not understand God's greatness and His role functions, till then desireless devotion would not come. Peace in the world shall come only after people possess desireless devotion. Divya Darshan lays stress on His greatness and role functions.

He is subtler than the subtle-most. He manifests as poison as well as nectar. There is nothing which He cannot become. This is His greatness. One form gives us pleasant feelings while another form or object overwhelms us with fear. This is how He manifests by His greatness.

I (Sadguru Sri Sri Arjun) have told you in earlier occasions that without five gross elements we would not have got this body. He has manifested as earth, water, fire, air and sky (ether). He is the cause of rain and therefore the cause of flora and fauna. The morning is different from the evening. He has made so many arrangements for us to provide us comfort, happiness and peace. God is Truth-Absolute. He manifests as various forms. He is the Supreme Truth. In other words, He is the Truth of all truths. He alone manifests as various truths. Every truth has some link with another truth. Whatever we enjoy or utilise are all different forms. All these forms are gifted to us for our enjoyment. For our survival, different foods are there with different tastes. If we suffer from any disease, the medicines and doctors are all available for our survival. Diseases, medicines and doctors are different truths. For a harmonious social living we are to maintain healthy social relationship. After our birth, if our mother would not have served us well, we would not have survived. What all are necessary for us to survive are all provided by God. He has also bestowed upon us the necessary knowledge for making use of His provisions. Even before man needs, God has made all arrangements perfectly well. Has He kept anything unfulfilled?

But the ignorant man is not able to understand God's scheme of things. Even after making all arrangements, God has been making more and more provisions always. God has been showering His grace on all of us. This is how He acts so perfectly, taking timely care of one and all. Even though we are getting the benefits from out of His grace, we are not able to understand Him or believe in Him. That is why the sages and seers speak of God's greatness and His role functions so that the ignorant man can have faith on Him.

Divya Darshan says that since we are contaminated by so many bad qualities, we are not able to understand His grace. The parents and teachers all along try for the improvement of the children but due to ignorance, the children do not understand the same. At times children disobey their parents and move in their own ways ultimately to suffer. For our happiness, peace and bliss, God has been doing so much. If we deeply contemplate on this, we would be lost in His greatness. Since we are not able to understand all these due to our limited knowledge, we are not getting the benefits as much as we should. For us to grow from childhood till we become adults, the continued services of our parents, the availability of medicines and doctors when we are ill, keep us alive. Are these not arrangements made by God for our well-being? To proceed further, God has made all sorts of arrangements for us to live in peace and happiness and ultimately attain freedom by realising God.

*****

[51]We are suffering because we are not aware of the secrets of God's blessings. Of all blessings of God, the most precious is knowledge. By knowledge everyone gets benefited and gets rid of sufferings. By acquisition of knowledge the thought process gets modified. There is no greater wealth than knowledge. Real siddhi is nothing but attainment of knowledge. Lord Buddha was never meditating on Brahma or Vishnu. He was only contemplating on that true knowledge by which the people would get rid of sufferings and live peacefully. Finally, he attained divine knowledge. Attainment of true knowledge is attainment of God. By God's blessings only, true knowledge is gained. True knowledge brings Supreme Bliss. The more one gets His blessings, the more the worldly bondages get cut-off. It must be remembered that by knowledge only we are born, we survive, and ultimately we shall attain liberation.

True knowledge or self-realization can be attained even in a day. Therefore, the aspirant should make himself fit to receive His blessings to realise Him soon. The sages have prescribed everything in the scriptures by following which an aspirant can get God's blessings. The teachings of the sages are blessings for the mankind in the sense that man's thought process and tendencies are changed so as to become fit for receiving God's blessings. The words of the sages are power packed. Likewise, Guru's words are power packed. The more a disciple assimilates Guru's words, the more and faster he would be benefited. It should be remembered that Shakti is knowledge and knowledge is Shakti.

Immortality: Of all fears, fear of death is the worst. Fear of death brings sufferings. Those who are wise and conscientious make spiritual practices to conquer death. Death can be conquered by

---

[51]*Odia Divyadhara Vol 10 Page 7*

acquiring knowledge only. Thereafter one can say that he is always there. He is ever existent. He can say, "I am immortal and free." It is stated in the Shrimad Bhagavad-Gita that Atman cannot be cut by the sword, cannot be drenched by water, cannot be burnt by fire, and cannot be dried up by air. When everything is Atman, how can water drench itself, how can fire burn itself? Where there is fear and misery, there is no liberation. We know Atman knows no death. When any form is destroyed or gets transformed, we call it death. In reality, nothing gets destroyed. Only transformation takes place.

You fear death and at the same time you are busy in accumulating mundane wealth. To save yourself from death, try to realise Atman. By acquiring true knowledge, Self can be realised. Fear of death shall vanish on the advent of true knowledge. You must know about death first. Lord Jesus has told, "Conquer death to be immortal."

There is no question of rebirth once death is conquered. If man does not acquire self-knowledge, he will be caught in the chains of birth and death. He, who is keen to acquire knowledge every moment, is intelligent or wise. "Ignorance is a great sin", this is what Socrates laid stress on.

Jnana and Vidya: Knowledge is expressed through karma but not to the extent of full and perfect knowledge. Because through karma alone, some amount of knowledge remains unexpressed. Whatever is expressed through karma is vidya. Whatever is realised is jnana. When realization is expressed, that becomes vidya. When we show something or explain something to others that is vidya but not jnana. Whatever we learn in schools and colleges, those are all vidya. When that vidya is assimilated and experienced, it becomes jnana. The sages have clearly stated that God cannot be realised through scriptural knowledge. From the scriptures we acquire vidya, not jnana. From the scriptures we get some idea about God. By jnana only, God can be realised. Hence God can neither be demonstrated nor can be seen by the naked eyes. Experiencing Supreme peace and bliss is called self-realization. Therefore, everyone should make continuous efforts to attain self-realization. This is the first and foremost duty of everybody to make spiritual efforts to attain this goal of life.

Manifestation of God: God is present everywhere as Satya, Dharma and Law. These cannot be seen by eyes. These are to be realised only. When someone cheats another, we say that the man has been cheated. It is *Adharma*, we say. In this case Dharma has not been observed. Where there is Dharma and fairness, there is peace. When there is no Dharma and fairness or justness, there is no peace. Due to the underlying principle of justness, everything in this Creation gets manifested and continues to exist. For creation of water, exact proportion of Hydrogen and Oxygen is essential. Water cannot be formed if there is any deviation (want of either of the components in right proportion). That means there is truth and law behind formation of water. Hydrogen is truth; so is, Oxygen. Both Hydrogen and Oxygen mix to create another truth called water. What should be the right proportion and right condition? There, Law is essential. That is called Law of Eternity. That Law is also Truth. God manifests everywhere as Truth, Law and Dharma

God blesses him whoever observes the Truth, Dharma and Law. On the other hand, the delinquents are bound to suffer. God expresses Himself as knowledge. Human beings must acquire knowledge to avoid the shortcomings and pitfalls and be on the righteous path. Not evincing interest in knowledge amounts to disobeying God's Will. God has been all along rendering greatest service to us by enriching us with knowledge for alleviating our sufferings. We all are here due to compassionate attitude and services of our parents. God expresses Himself as benevolence and compassion. Due to paucity of knowledge we are not able to know that God is always with us and in us. We ascribe different imaginary forms to Him. Once we become aware of God's all-time association with us and His ever conscious presence in us, we shall get peace and happiness. God expresses Himself as divine virtues like love, truth, service, restraint etc. Hence, we should bow down before the divine virtues and consciously try to practice them till they blossom as our natural expressions. Sadguru imparts knowledge about Truth, Dharma and Justness to the disciples to prepare them to move towards the goal of liberation. Sadguru enables the disciples to come out of the illusions and put an end to all sufferings. If we do not acquire the right knowledge, we cannot realise God. Not having the right knowledge is Maya.

Significance of Guru: Most of the people are indifferent towards God. They are so much busy in their occupations and are burdened with worldly life that they do not find time to think of God considering it as an extraneous subject. As a result of this, they do not feel the need to approach a Sadguru to acquire that life-saving knowledge i.e. right knowledge. Hence quite a major chunk of the population lives in fear and frustrations which are opposite to peace and happiness. In the olden days, the disciples were worshipping their Guru as the divine descend. Once one acquires the right knowledge from the Sadguru, one can truly feel to be the scion of immortality and divinity. Ultimately, one can realise True Self on acquiring self-knowledge. At that time, one realises, "I am divine, pure and immortal Atman." A realiser is above any kind of narrowness. He never boasts of any caste or clan, creed or community. Everybody irrespective of all apparent differences is the scion of divinity. Everything is essentially the Self only. By being indoctrinated by a Sadguru, one would enjoy peace and happiness free from any fear or tension. Ultimately, he would attain True Self. Without serving to Sadguru, service to any other deities would not bear fruits. A Guru should always be respected by one and all whether they are disciples or not. You may not accept a Sadguru as your Guru, but you must pay your respect to him. A time may come when your children or grandchildren would accept him as Guru. For the appeasement of Sadguru, what can you offer? There is nothing in this Creation which can be offered to Him for his appeasement. There is no companion like Guru. Being associated with Him, a disciple attains God. No kith and kin can be equal to Guru. There is nothing in this Creation by which the debt owed to Sadguru, who has imparted the mono-syllabled Mantra, can be repaid. He, who has received this mono-syllabled Mantra, is great. From this mono-syllabled Mantra, all other Mantras have emanated. When the disciple becomes a Guru and passes on this Mantra to others for alleviation of sufferings and enjoyment of peace and bliss, then only it is to be understood that the disciple has fulfilled the wishes of Guru. One should not abandon Guru in the search for God. Such quest shall never be complete. When a disciple shall realise that he is getting rid of the three kinds of miseries (Adhi-bhoutik, adhi-daivik and adhyatmik) then only he would realise that there is none bigger than Sadguru. He, who knows Guru like this and accordingly gets devoted to him, gets Guru's blessings. Unless there is Guru's blessing, no other deities or divine powers shall bless. Those, who ignore and overlook Guru, cause untold damages to themselves. Due to virtues acquired in several past births, man gets the chance to prostrate before a Sadguru and serve Him in this birth. Only by Guru's grace, one realises True Self. But it is regrettable that people do not understand the greatness of Guru. By doing so, they get deprived of the right knowledge which is the only key to peace, bliss and freedom. It is by right knowledge that we can get rid of all doubts, sufferings, fear and frustrations. By taking initiation from Sadguru all delusions vanish; all sins vanish. Divine knowledge dawns upon the disciple. He becomes immortal and eternal.

*****

[52]**Yoga:** Yoga is necessary to attain God. We are under the impression that only a yogi can do yoga and none other. Some people also think, "What is the necessity of yoga? Everything is going well."

Every person should do yoga. Keeping contact with God is yoga. We stay connected with food, property, money and gold. This is yoga with mundane matters. But since we do not evince interest to know about God, we do not remember God. We are not able to establish yoga with Him. It is to be remembered that the more one stays connected with God, the more one is benefited and becomes eligible for His blessings. You keep the photos of different Gods and Goddesses in your house and worship them. This is also yoga. But due to inadequate knowledge, you are not able to know that you are in yoga (union) with God. Therefore, you are not able to get rid of sufferings. If you stay connected with good things you would be good, and goodness shall blossom in you. Similarly, contact with bad things shall contaminate you.

God is the root of all wealth and goodness of the Creation. Once we keep contact with Him, how much benefit we may get, we cannot imagine. We feel happy to be in friendship with a prominent person. If we establish regular contact with the Supreme, how much happy we shall be! It is therefore quite necessary for everybody to establish yoga with Him. Different kinds of yoga are there such as – Karma Yoga, Bhakti Yoga, Jnana Yoga, etc. Whatever preparations are to be

---

[52]*Odia Divyadhara Vol 10 Page 39*

made to attain God's grace is called yoga. Where is God? How is God? How does God manifest Himself? How does He remain in everything and everywhere? What all are His greatness? All these enquiries come under Jnana Yoga. In other words, spiritual practice is yoga.

The practice of yoga or sadhana by the demons is different. They undertake torturous practices by standing in water or entering into fire to get boons from the deities. But these are not real spiritual practices. They get some boons, but they do not attain God. Nor they attain liberation. The example of Bhasmasura can be recollected here. He got the boon by which he destroyed himself due to sheer stupidity.

Those, who are on knowledge path, can fully realise God and they are the true enjoyers of liberation. It is to be remembered that when God appears in any form, that form is not God. Form is created by illusion. Yogi Aurobindo and Swami Shivananda had seen God in the forms of Krishna but they were not satisfied with the forms since they knew those were illusory. They continued their spiritual practices still further and got enlightenment thereafter. Likewise, many sages had different experiences. Swami Nigamananda Paramahansa had seen Goddess Tara Devi. Thereafter he took shelter of four gurus one after another and got enlightenment.

The question is- "Who is appearing in all these forms?" Hence the sages were carrying on spiritual practices for years to realise the formless, eternal, all-pervasive, omnipotent and omniscient existence, who is infinite indivisible whole. Once a mendicant knows how God remains inside and outside, and regulates everything, at that time he will surrender to God. Unless you know who God is, you will not have belief or faith on Him. By His Grace, you will get divine knowledge and will get rid of all sufferings. We are not able to wriggle ourselves out as we are tied with many knots carried over from our previous births. By divine knowledge, all these knots would be cleared away one after another and ultimately the aspirant will set himself free. He, who realises God, realises everything. He becomes all-powerful.

God owns everything we come across around us. He is the wielder of the results of our actions. No other deity has the discretion to award any fruits of our actions. Hence, the unitary omnipotent God only is to be worshipped.

God is Peace-Absolute. He is Bliss-Absolute. He is Freedom-Absolute. He, who contemplates like this, gets peace, bliss and freedom. In other words, as one contemplates and realises, one becomes that. Worshipping with some desires would not benefit much. One may get only the desired object for some time. But he, who keeps regular contact with Him, gets everything. By divine thoughts alone we can reach nearer to Him. Beyond bhava, there is one more state called Mahabhava. It is a state of total immergence. Some give emphasis on Bhakti. But it would take long time to attain God by Bhakti. Love (Prema) is superior to Bhakti. He, who can love God, is great. Bhakti means faith and respect. But love shall culminate in union with God. Although quite a good percentage of people are on Bhakti Marg, many of them do not even know that God is one. Our contact with God starts from our belief. Thereafter, come faith and devotion. But by knowing the greatness and His role, one starts loving Him. When love comes, all differences vanish. All become one.

Everyone should think of attaining God. Those, who take shelter of any wise soul or Sadguru, would acquire divine knowledge and will quickly attain God. He, who has not taken shelter of a Guru, cannot attain self-realization. It took about 16 to17 years for me (Sadguru Sri Sri Arjun) to realise the True Self. But my disciples will take less time to attain self-realization. He, who is inquisitive to attain God, will surely attain the Supreme Truth. Many spiritual mendicants are doing yoga but not to the extent required. That is because, the anxiety or urgency is lacking in them.

The more one knows the value of something, the more one gets attracted towards it. We do not know the value of God. That is why our mind does not get attracted towards Him. Although there are a large number of spiritual aspirants, only a few attain Him. Some go up while most others fall. It is not that easy to attain God. To attain Him, a lot of qualifications and qualities are required (knowledge, divine qualities, courage and capability). A weak man cannot get Him. Hence to attain the omnipotent Brahman, one must muster up power.

To be powerful, one must be righteous and pure. For that, divine knowledge is essential. This is the surest and simplest path to God-realization.

*****

[53]There are differences in opinion about Jiva and Ishwar. Both the concepts are important but very much misunderstood from the point of view of spirituality. Unless someone reaches a minimum level of knowledge, he cannot understand the concepts clearly. They are different from each other but essentially, they are one. This dichotomy requires explanation. When the Unitary Existence called Brahman manifests as many, there appear different stages of manifestation. Tree, animal, man, the Sun, the Moon etc. are the various manifested forms. He, who manifests as such, eternally

---

[53]*Odia Divyadhara Vol 15 Page 14*

remains unchanged as Unitary Existence. The sages named Him as Brahman. Brahman is there in everything and everywhere.

An example may be cited here. It is water that takes the form of ice. In these two cases, names are different, qualities are different, and appearances are different. Ice is solid whereas water is liquid. But essentially both water and ice are nothing but one substance.

We all know a seed has become a tree. Tree has the potency to create seeds. Seed has come from the tree. Both the forms are one in essence.

Similarly, Brahman has become Jiva; jiva will one day be merged in Brahman. In accordance with the Law of Eternity, through the process of change, Brahman has become jiva or has manifested as jiva. Although Brahman and jiva are apparently different, essentially, they are one and the same. It is the uniqueness of Brahman that, although He remains unchanged in His true nature, He can at the same time manifest as different forms and qualities.

Water becomes ice; ice becomes water. Not that all water becomes ice at once. Nor all ice becomes water at once. Ice and water co-exist. The process of water becoming ice and again ice getting transformed to water happens always. Likewise, the seed to become a seedling and thereafter a tree, so many conditions are necessary. Similarly, when Brahman manifests as various forms and qualities, so many conditions, situations, circumstances, surroundings, settings and environments are necessary. Brahman Himself manifests as such. Brahman Himself is everything. Brahman being all-pervasive, whatever happens is but Brahman who is self-effulgent and spontaneous. This is His greatness. The gross universe is made of five elements such as Earth, Water, Fire, Air and Ether. But things appear differently or in different forms with different qualities in them due to the differences in their mixing patterns. Different names are ascribed to them.

By spiritual sadhana and knowledge, you can one day realise that your present jiva form is temporary manifestation of the eternal Brahman, and you are That. Jiva feeling will vanish and you will be free from all sufferings. To attain this state of true knowledge, past samskara, spiritual practice and Guru's grace are essential. Remain alert and move on. Be sure that you shall reach the goal.

*****

[54]**Shakti** is all-pervasive. With our limited knowledge, we understand something about this infinite energy that pervades the whole Creation and appears as the whole Creation. That energy takes different forms such as power, force, pressure and strength which vary in different situations and circumstances. Brahman also manifests as knowledge or consciousness. Brahman is ever present as consciousness and energy everywhere. Brahman is without qualities but manifests as various qualities. Brahman is formless but manifests as various forms. He again goes back from manifested states to the unmanifest. He is simultaneously there both in manifested and unmanifest states. He is simultaneously formless and is with forms, with qualities and without qualities. It is His greatness and uniqueness. He, who understands His manifestation, gets peace and bliss. "He manifests as the Creation; He also does not manifest as the Creation"; to speak like this is also his manifestation. (When we say, He manifests as the Creation, it is His manifestation. When we say, He does not manifest as Creation, it is also His manifestation.) Whatever we experience or see are all his

[54]*Odia Divyadhara Vol 17 Page 21*

manifestations. The whole Creation is pervaded by Brahman. He is always complete. There is no decay, no increase or decrease. But the ignorant man cannot understand this. He does not understand that he is himself the manifestation of Brahman. Brahman is only to be experienced. He cannot be expressed or explained through words.

We see something and say it is beautiful. But how much beautiful it is cannot be expressed. Similarly, we cannot express how much ugly something is. There is nothing like beautiful or ugly, good or bad. Any comparison is also misleading. Every form is a manifestation of the Supreme Brahman. Brahman presides everywhere and in everything without any discrimination. In other words, the Creation is completely filled with Brahman. A sincere mendicant by Guru's grace can realise His oneness and get lost in the oneness. Such rare realization comes after lot of spiritual efforts, virtues and past impulses. There are diversities in His manifestation. We come across diversities and get confused. We are not able to comprehend the unitariness in all diversities. Everything is Brahman's manifested state. This means, the nature we see around us is verily Brahman in guise. It may be mentioned here that all matters are but forms of energy or Shakti only. Manifestations appear many and varied with varied qualities therein. It must be remembered that nothing is destroyed. Brahman is therefore always complete as the undivided whole. The process of transformation, governed by the Law of Eternity, goes on non-stop perennially. To realise the presence of Brahman everywhere, is called equal vision. Only the realised souls have equal vision. Be it water or fire, everything is manifestation of Brahman. Different qualities are seen in different manifested things. That is how multifarious needs of the Creation are taken care of. Be it earth or water, fire or air, everything is of service to us. He, who can perceive the homogeneity in all the apparently varied matters, realises Brahman. Those, who reach the final stage of spiritual efforts, realise this. Whatever all they wish get fulfilled. They are independent or free souls. They can do everything as they will. It is difficult to recognize a sage or realiser. We are only specific forms of the total form. But the realisers realise all forms or the total form. They realise that they are there in every form. Since the sages know all forms, they accept everything. They can say, "Everything in the Creation is my manifestation. I am there as Atman in everything and in all beings." This realization is siddhi. A sage does not express openly that he is Brahman. Only in some special circumstances, he may disclose his identity as Brahman or Atman.

Lord Srikrishna had shown His Cosmic Form to Arjun. He had clearly said, "I am the Sun, I am the Moon, I am the mountain, I am the river, I am the ocean etc." He, who is in Brahmi state, can tell this. There is none superior to Atman or Brahman. Brahman or Atman is supreme. Someone is listening about Atman. This is a form of Atman. Someone is not willing to listen about Atman. This is also a form of Atman. From out of some forms, we can make some other new thing which is another form. As told earlier, we are in specific forms. But the sages know all forms or the total form. That is why we are not able to understand the sayings of the sages. Even if others blame them or criticize them at times, they do not pay heed to those talks. The sages always remain in bliss. They have realised all forms. The realization, "I am everything", is always with them. "I am the all-pervasive Atman. I am the all- pervasive Brahman." When they remain established in this form, where is suffering? When they remain in nirguna state, they are nothing. When they are in saguna state, they are all forms. We talk about the suffering of the sages; that is also a form. Whatever you see and experience are all His manifestations. Wherever His manifestation is necessary, He manifests according to situations and creates appropriate situations in different places. "I am expressing myself as suffering and bliss, different forms and qualities. But my True Self is pure, uncontaminated, divine and motionless." He, who realises both the aspects such as His Lila and the True Self, has realised Brahman in toto. But we come across His Lila and do not realise the True Self. We say that the sages sometimes cry or laugh. These are only outward expressions. It is almost impossible to know a sage. Only a realiser can know another realiser.

*****

[55]**Chanting God's name:** "I meditate upon the Supreme Truth every second, every moment, said Guru Nanak. Day and night, I meditate upon the Param-Brahman. Oh Lord, you are infinite and formless. None can express you. None can write about you. None can estimate you." Tears used to roll down Nanak's eyes when he was contemplating like this. Therefore, occasional remembrance of God or casual chanting of God's name would not help.

I (Sadguru Sri Sri Arjun) recollect my sadhana days. How much pain I was taking but I was not feeling the pain. I was always immersed in the thought of achieving the goal of my life. I was not paying much attention to life, property, and maintenance of family, status or prestige in society. Day and night, I was eager to attain the Supreme Truth. I had no feel of the difficulties or troubles that I faced.

Those who are steeped in greed and infatuation, they are stupid even if educated. Such persons can never attain God. Those, who do not realise the importance of God, are ignorant. Those, who are keen to realise the importance of that great Existence, are really qualified and wise. Whatever book you read to acquire knowledge, there

---

[55] *Odia Divyadhara Vol 9 Page 25*

should be description of God's greatness in it so that you can add to your knowledge about God. God realisation is the sole purpose of this great human birth. Hence, the sages say that God's name should be chanted always. By attaining Him nothing else remains to be attained. By following Guru's instructions, one can attain God.

If only by reading books about God it would have sufficed, what is then the role of a Guru? Or where is the need for a Guru? Only by reading any book containing God's names, problem would not be over. Many people believe that by reading or chanting God's names one lakh times, they would attain God. You may chant God's name as many times as you can but if you do not go beyond the meaning or bhava behind the name, nothing significant is going to happen. Therefore, it is said that without Guru's instructions, you cannot delve deep into the bhava behind name. The reason is simple and clear. Only an inquisitive disciple with good impulses (Samskara) can realise True Self even in a second. The greatness of name can be explained by Guru only.

There are many impurities in us. When we chant God's names, we recollect Him. Unless we do that, we may not remember God. There are many devotees who remember God only till all their desires are fulfilled. After that they conveniently forget God. There are some devotees who lose faith on God if their desires are not fulfilled in time. Hence desireless bhakti is the real bhakti. They always remember God without waiting for some conditions to happen. God is the best and highest wealth. By surrendering to a Sadguru, the disciple becomes fit to receive the divine wealth. There are people who cry and shed tears (out of extreme happiness) while chanting God's name. Others do not have any such feeling. It is clear from the above that the effect of chanting God's name is different on different persons. Only parroting God's name would not help much. No mechanical process of chanting God's name would be fruitful. Guru's instructions in this regard are essential to have greater effect of God's name. Without sincerity and devotion, it is fruitless to chant God's name. By crying out for money, money does not come; necessary efforts are to be made for that. If bhava behind the name gets aroused, one will start feeling ecstatic. All vikaras from the mind should get cleansed to enjoy the bliss. If bad qualities in us are not staved off, then whatever knowledge we have acquired, becomes fruitless or meaningless. If our conduct gets refined due to good tendencies, it is to be understood that we are benefited from chanting God's name. If someone realises the greatness of God's name, his mind gets cleaned and sins are washed away. This is not possible without Guru's instructions. The disciple comes to understand the significance of God's name and blissful tears trickle down from his eyes.

God is Truth-Absolute. All sages have tried to explain Truth in the scriptures. He, who follows Truth also welcomes Truth and realises Truth. He, who knows, will get. Truth is the life and vital energy of everybody. Due to Him alone, all others come to exist. But it is regrettable that man does not want to know about his own life and vital energy. He, who does not like to know about God, is not conscious. He is like an insentient matter only. He alone can realise God in whom spiritual awakening is there. Since we all possess consciousness, we can grasp something about God. Consciousness is there everywhere. The plant called 'Touch-me-not' reacts immediately to touch because of consciousness. Since we are not interested to know, we are unable to understand God.

Man seeks peace and happiness which indirectly means he seeks God, who is Peace-Absolute and Bliss-Absolute. But man is not able to realise God because he is not conscious about it. God is there in everybody as light who is ever-shining. The sages have tried to explain this in several ways. But language would always fail to explain Him. He can only be experienced. Self can be experienced by Self only. That divine light is much more than the combined light of millions of Sun. We can experience the Sunlight, but we are not able to experience the divine light. That light is Supreme Light. There is nothing equal to it. That light is beyond words. It is inexplicable. That light is hotter than the hottest, cooler than the coolest. You cannot speak in absence of that light. You cannot understand anything without that light. No one can exist without that light. By that light, you can identify something even by closing your eyes, and also experience things. Small or big, pleasure or pain, good or bad; all are experienced due to that light. Whatever light we come across, is activated by that Supreme Light. Hence the Supreme Light is beyond words.

He, who possesses many things, is the wealthiest person. God is another name of Truth. Whatever man feels or experiences are all truths. This Creation is full of truths. It is not that easy to realise this. By whom we can understand or experience is also Truth. Brahman is the owner of everything in this Creation. The Creation is filled with Truth. All materials needed by man are all truths. Brahman is the Truth of all truths.

Those, who know God like this, are in Satya Loka. We have not been able to know God in this manner. The sages and realisers remain in Satya Loka and they impart knowledge on Truth in this manner. Satya Loka is beyond Swarga Loka. Sufferings are there in this Bhulok. The more we transcend higher and higher, our sufferings shall be lesser. In the Satya Loka, there is no suffering. It is all bliss and bliss. There is total absence of sufferings. Always there shall be divine experiences and bliss like we enjoy the mild breeze throughout the spring season. But we, being ignorant about all these, seek pleasure and nibble at the mundane matters even if we are surrounded by hostility, crookedness, deceitfulness and harassments etc. in this world. We are not aware that we can also get rid of all these. That is why we are not making efforts. Thus, having been born in samsara, we are always afflicted by samsaric feelings and therefore lead a life full of drudgery. Those, who want to get rid of all these sufferings, are wise men. There are many people who possess demoniac qualities. It is said that the Devas drink nectar and they live blissfully but the ordinary man takes to opposite path and suffers. If we observe the food habits of some persons, we can easily observe the demoniac qualities. Hence sufferings are there in this samsara.

If everybody tries to acquire true knowledge and divine virtues, Satya Yug may also reign here. The sages descend to preach this knowledge of Truth. Due to ignorance we do not listen to them. They teach us how to get rid of sufferings. They do not expect anything from anybody. They do not have any want. They always reside in Truth although they lead ordinary ways of life in the world. They remain detached from the worldly affairs. They always wish for the good of the world.

*****

Gurutattva

[The most important aspect in spiritual knowledge is to get the blessings of Sadguru who has already experienced the Truth; who is God incarnate and has descended to teach others the mechanism of knowing and experiencing the Truth for He alone can lead us to the highest goal. In the following discourses, Sadguru Sri Sri Arjun explains Gurutattva and how a disciple should conduct himself to attain self-realisation, which is the only goal of life]

[56]Gurutattva is not an ordinary subject. Guru means heavy, weighty and great. Knowing Guru is same as knowing Brahman. The play of Brahman is expressed through Guru. According to the scriptures, Brahman willed to become many. Brahman was first nirguna (unqualified) and thereafter became saguna (qualified). This is what scriptures explain. The Law of nature is that qualities will be there according to forms. In man, man's qualities; in tree, the qualities of a tree; in water, the qualities of water are manifested. Before Brahman manifested as forms and various corresponding qualities, He Himself remained as Knowledge or Guru so that the manifested forms can again go back to the original Form by Guru's guidance. Scriptures have explained like this. Do not therefore limit Guru to form. Knowledge is great and weighty. Archimedes advanced his lever theory and claimed that he would be able to lift the Earth by a lever. This indicates the power of knowledge. God too can be

---

[56]*Odia Divyadhara Vol 9 Page 39*

realised by knowledge or Guru. In the scriptures there is mention about five Gurus such as Mother, Father, Schoolteacher, Karnna Guru and Sadguru. Only Sadguru can guide a disciple for realisation of the True Self. By knowledge only, we can understand the value of gold. If we go still further we reach a stage where there is no quality of gold in its nucleus stage. The concept of God is so deep that with ordinary knowledge one cannot comprehend anything. The knowledge, by which the greatness and role of God can be explained for ultimate realisation of True Self, is called Sadguru. In other words, He, who imparts knowledge about 'Sat', is called Sadguru. People, who consider Rama or Krishna as God, do not have complete knowledge about God. They limit God to some forms, which is not correct. It is essential to know who incarnated as Rama and Krishna. That eternal and unitary existence only manifests as different forms. Therefore, it is essential to know Him. Ramakrishna Paramahansa was also talking to Mother Kali but subsequently he surrendered to Guru and realised God.

Similarly, Swami Sri Shivananda and Yogi Sri Aurobindo even after they saw Lord Krishna in physical forms, continued their yogic practices and attained the Supreme Truth. God Himself descends as Sadguru and imparts true knowledge. Santha Kabir said, "If I happen to meet Guru and God at a time, I shall first prostrate before Guru, because Guru has enabled me to attain God." When one prostrates before a Sadguru, it means, one surrenders to knowledge. Body may disappear but knowledge shall never go waste. Knowledge is there in forms of mother, father and teachers. From whomever we get knowledge, he is Guru. Guru is there in everything such as earth, stones, lower creatures and human beings. Sometimes we ask questions to ourselves, and contemplate on that. We also get the answers from within. It means that Guru is inside us also. Guru is there both outside and inside.

He is Guru who dispels the darkness of ignorance. So, the scriptures reiterate that Guru is Brahma, Guru is Vishnu and Guru is Maheswar. Guru is Param-Brahman in person (embodiment of Param-Brahman). People very often chant this, but they do not understand the real secret of this. He, who knows Guru like this and remains in contact, one day he would become a Guru. Just as darkness becomes light in contact with light, similarly, the ignorant disciple also becomes wise in contact with Guru. If we disbelieve Guru, we cannot possess knowledge and Gurushakti. If we want self-realisation, we must be in touch with Guru. In the Mahabharat, when Ekalavya was denied admission by Dronacharya, Ekalavya, by his strong will power, acquired all knowledge by means of Gurushakti. There are many examples to prove that the sages, who revered Guru as such, had attained the Supreme.

In the Upanishads, knowledge is regarded as Brahman. 'Prajnanam Brahman' means Pure Consciousness i.e. knowledge is Brahman. But many people disregard knowledge without knowing the importance and indispensability of knowledge. By knowledge alone we excel in all matters and achieve things. By gaining knowledge from Sadguru, we cannot imagine to what extent we are benefited and how much powerful we become! Since we do not understand and appreciate Gurutattva, we become weak or powerless. He, who possesses this inner power, alone gets peace and happiness.

Join Satsang with shraddha. If you do not attend satsang, how can you enhance your knowledge? Not attending satsang means you love neither Guru nor knowledge. Satsang is greatly beneficial to everybody. Try to assimilate knowledge that would lead you to self-experience. Acquiring self-knowledge and disseminating the right knowledge is a virtuous deed. You must feel happy to meet those persons who impart knowledge to you.

I (Sadguru Sri Sri Arjun) have my first teacher who is alive now. Tears trickle from my eyes when I meet my first teacher who taught me alphabet. Scriptures say that he, who tortures or causes any kind of harm to the Guru, becomes Brahma rakshas in the next birth and wanders in dense jungles. He, who inflicts pain on Guru or insults Guru, gets lower births. Guru is Truth-Absolute. There is righteousness and Dharma in Satya. He, who is not righteous, goes to hell. Brahman manifests as truth, righteousness and Omkar. We are benefited by a thing or subject to the extent we know it. As much a disciple knows Guru, to that extent he is benefited. The depth of one's knowledge means how much one has penetrated a subject. Accordingly one enjoys. In other words, the more one knows, the more one enjoys.

It is to be understood that by attending satsang, our knowledge gets enhanced and we are benefited to that extent. We get peace and happiness accordingly. We become purer day by day. We earn virtues and move along the path of self-development. Once we know this, we can easily earn virtues otherwise we shall be accumulating vices only. Many people think that by doing charity and going on pilgrimages, virtues are acquired. They do not know that without spending money and without any physical pain also, one can easily earn virtues by attending satsang. We attain goodness by attending satsang.

In the scriptures it is mentioned that if one believes in God, one remains happy. If we serve Him, we get His blessings. Believing in God is a virtue. Serving others is a virtue. Similarly, to trouble others or to do harm to others is a vice. Hence everyone should wish good to others. By developing such qualities, we can easily earn virtues without spending money and without undergoing any physical stress. 'Sarve Bhabantu Sukhinoh', this is what we chant at the end of satsang. The sages of yesteryears also chanted this mantra. This mantra should be chanted wholeheartedly. God is blissful. All His arrangements are for the good of the Creation. We should also wish good to others. Goodness shall come to us from all sides. Dissemination of spiritual knowledge or right knowledge would do good to the people. We can ourselves be good also. Spiritual knowledge which is divine knowledge is inexhaustible. You can disseminate more and more, farther and farther. It shall never diminish. Through satsang not only we remove our doubts, we also become fit to experience the Truth.

Guru always wishes to give away His knowledge to the disciple. He becomes happy when a disciple receives the knowledge more and faster. We take initiation. The purpose is that by doing so our capacity gets enhanced and we become stronger. We can acquire maximum knowledge within a short time. That means we can understand the Truth better. A young student, who learns various subjects by tuition and coaching, acquires more knowledge than an aged person who never evinced interest in learning alphabet even. Through initiation, Guru's thoughts (bhava) get implanted in the disciple's heart. By taking initiation a relation is established between Guru and disciple. Guru is the store house of all knowledge and power. He, who keeps relation with Him, receives more power from Him. The disciple can become pure by meeting Guru, just as an iron rod when put in fire becomes bright. Guru-tradition is there from olden years and finds mention in various scriptures. But many people, out of sheer ignorance, feel complacent by worshipping God without knowing what it is. They do not feel the importance of Guru. He, who wants happiness, peace and freedom, should approach a Sadguru who would guide him to the destination. Guru Nanak said,

"He, who gets Guru, gets God." By taking initiation, we get Ishta Mantra. By chanting Ishta Mantra, we get blessings from Ishta. All divine powers become supportive to us and save us from adversities. Gurushakti and all divine powers help us not only in the life here but hereafter also. Paramahansa Nigamananda said that those, who are not initiated, take longer time after death to get rebirth. They remain in Preta Lok for long time and undergo various sufferings. Since Guru takes the responsibility of ensuring freedom of the disciples, He always works for the disciple's self-development and creates proper surroundings not only here but in the next birth also so as to enable the disciple to proceed in the right direction. Those, who have not taken initiation from Guru, after death their subtle bodies appear smoky whereas those who are initiated and virtuous, their subtle bodies appear bright. The subtle bodies of the virtuous can rise high. Because they have knowledge and power, they can go anywhere they like. On the other hand, the vicious souls cannot go higher than 50 feet from the earth's surface. He, who gets initiated, gradually learns that he is immortal. As such he has no fear of death.

Lord Rama and Lord Krishna had Vashishtha and Sandipani respectively as their spiritual masters (Guru). By Guru alone, Gurutattva can be realised. There may be many in the society now-a-days, who falsely claim that they are Sadgurus. Sadguru does not depend upon anybody. He does not ask for anything from the devotees or disciples. Only Sadguru can give us freedom. After having a Sadguru, one should not go for any 'Karnna Guru'. He, who has already got a Karnna guru, should go for a Sadguru. A Karnna guru cannot impart right knowledge or true knowledge. He can only give God's name for chanting.

Divya Darshan exhorts everyone to acquire spiritual knowledge. Divya Darshan gives stress on knowledge. Bhakti Yoga and Karma

Yoga are phases of Jnana Yoga. Now in the society, everyone understands the importance of knowledge. A time will come when more and more people will be attracted towards jnana marg. By the Will of God, Satya Yug would again prevail in the world. When more and more people shall take to knowledge path, Satya Yug will rule everywhere. In the jnana path, a Guru cannot deceive a disciple, since in this path the knowledge of the disciple also gets enhanced.

It is to be known for certain that one should approach a Sadguru to get happiness, peace and freedom. By this, one gets cleansed up and attains divinity. By this, all basic needs of a man can be fulfilled and at the same time, his human birth would be truly meaningful and blissful.

*****

[57]Brahman is one. His different powers are named as different personal godheads. From Sadguru we get knowledge ranging from Brahman to gross objects. Scriptures say that in this Creation there is nothing other than Brahman. Only Brahman exists. There is no second. His three main powers are named as Brahma, Vishnu and Maheswar. The sages and seers having realised Brahman have been imparting true knowledge to the mankind since time immemorial.

When Brahman willed to be many, first He became Guru. Thereafter the process of creation started. Everything in this Creation is getting regulated by Guru. We know that the divine powers are subtle. In our gross eyes we cannot experience the various godheads. On the other hand, Guru who gives us knowledge and raises us to realise Brahman, is seen by us. The personal godheads cannot give us liberation. Only Guru can lead us to

---

[57]*Odia Divyadhara Vol 6 Page 1*

liberation. Therefore, Guru is the highest and the most important God for us. All the personal godheads are with Guru. By serving at the feet of Guru, the virtues earned are more than the aggregate virtues earned through millions of pilgrimages. Since there are many godheads and we worship some specific godhead, we may get blessings from that specific godhead only. Others will not give us any blessings. But if we worship Guru, we get blessings from all the personal godheads also.

Guru means knowledge, greatness and heaviness. There is nothing bigger or heavier than Guru in this Creation. By taking shelter of Guru, one can do impossible things smoothly. We might have heard of many devotees and disciples whose Gurubhakti was par excellence.

Some of the names are Parshuram and Hanuman. Hanuman could accomplish lot of impossible tasks by chanting the name of Lord Rama. Because we do not understand the value of Guru, we are not attaching as much importance or weightage to Guru as we should.

Many devotees cry for God, but none cries for Guru. Unless we cry for Guru, we cannot get knowledge. Due to want of true knowledge, people are indulging in superstitious beliefs and various rituals. Sufferings do not wane. They are on the rise rather. Knowledge power is the greatest power and is the controlling power of all other powers. Knowledge power is Guru. Because we do not take shelter of Guru, our latent powers remain almost inert and do not get easily stimulated.

We have been worshipping various personal godheads for years together. We are not able to appease them. We are not able to get rid of sufferings. On the other hand, by worshipping Guru we can have His knowledge by which we can achieve wonders.

Ishta Mantra and Guru are one and the same. He, who has unwavering faith on Ishta Mantra and Guru, can do impossible things. God has no specific name or form. The only one God has manifested as various forms and qualities which are named differently at a subsequent stage. If we remember and worship Guru whole-heartedly the Gurushakti in us shall shine out. Ishta Mantra is a powerful Mantra. Never underestimate it. If Ishta Mantra is chanted daily with faith and devotion, everything would be achieved. It must be remembered that by receiving knowledge from Guru we are able to know Devas and ultimately Brahman. The sages had realised the value of Guru. That is why they were all worshipping Guru. Guru possesses complete knowledge. If Guru is satisfied with us, we can get His blessings and also from all the Devas. If Guru blesses the disciple, the disciple will be successful in all his endeavours. For this the disciple's thoughts, expressions and actions should be pure. This is the real spiritual efforts or tapas. The greatest thing for a man is Guru's blessings. All your efforts should be made for this. Now-a-days, since the people are not interested in knowledge and feel reluctant to approach Sadguru, they are getting deprived of the true knowledge. Guru-disciple relation is the most important relation. No kith and kin can be equal with Guru. There is nothing by which one can repay the debt owed to Sadguru in view of the enormous value of the monosyllabic mantra 'OM' which Sadguru imparts to the disciple.

How shall the disciple get released from the debt that he owes to Guru?

First by the monosyllabic mantra, the disciple gets benefited. When he becomes competent, he also passes on the mantra to others for their peace and bliss. Guru at that time feels that His 'Guru Dakshina' has been paid. By the blessings of Guru, the disciple gets protected from 'Tritap', the three kinds of sufferings such as Adhi-bhoutik (traumatic), Adhi-daivik (natural) and Adhyatmik (psychosomatic) sufferings.

Then who else is greater than Guru? There is nothing in the Creation which can be offered to Guru for repaying the debt owed to him. By making true relationship with Guru, a disciple attains God, the highest ever. Guru and disciple relationship is the best relationship. He, who knows this, accordingly pays respect to Guru, gets purified and gets Guru's blessings. Those, who ill-treat or under-estimate Guru, lose everything or get dispossessed of everything. After lot of virtues acquired in the previous births, one gets the opportunity to serve a Guru and pay respect to Guru. He, who loves Guru, would realise his Self. The fire of Brahman is always ablaze in the Guru–disciple relationship. Atman is not any gross object which Guru can pluck like a fruit from a tree and handover to the disciple. Guru is the embodiment of love and compassion. Guru loves the disciple day and night. If the disciple simultaneously reciprocates then realisation of Brahman may happen any moment.

Guru's words are power packed. If the disciple assimilates and remembers Guru's words, more and more power will be transmitted to the disciple. There is no doubt about it.

*****

[58]People at large do not know who Guru is. There are some Siddha Mahatmas who show miracles. There are some who wear some pattern of robes. There are some who wear ashes on their bodies and wear matted hair. Many people consider them as Guru. But they

---

[58]*Odia Divyadhara Vol 20 Page 15*

cannot help the disciples attain liberation. They may just teach some magical tricks to the disciples.

On the other hand, a Sadguru can dispel the ignorance of the disciples and enables union of Atman with Paramatman. Sadguru explains the difference as well as the unity among Paramatman, Prakriti and Jivatma. By doing so, a disciple can attain self-realization.

According to Sadguru Sri Sri Samarth Ramdas, the world is a Maya or illusion. Maya is like a tigress. This tigress has snatched us away from our mother i.e. Brahman. That means, the jiva is a calf. Brahman is the mother cow. Sadguru rescues the calf from the clutches of the tigress and unites it with its mother.

Those, who have not realised the Truth but on the strength of some miracles, try to impress us are like tigers who feast upon us. On the other hand, for those who are trapped in the worldly illusion, and getting washed away by the flood of desires, Sadguru is the only rescuer. You must know that a jiva suffers a lot when he is in the mother's womb. The jiva suffers a lot due to his ignorance as he goes on enjoying the fruits of his actions while undergoing the cycles of births and deaths. The wise men do not want to take any further birth. Rather they prefer to make intense spiritual efforts to realise Brahman in this birth itself.

Brahman is the Eternal Truth that has no beginning and no end. He is unborn and immortal. He, who realises Brahman, is always one with Brahman. Since we are suffering in the darkness of ignorance, He descends in the form of Sadguru to release us. Only Sadguru can rescue the ignorant men drowning in the ocean of Samsara by imparting them right knowledge. "Thou art Brahman." This is what the Vedas and the Upanishads reiterate. But since you have assumed jiva forms, you have forgotten your True Self, i.e. Brahman. He, who enables us to realise our True Self, is Sadguru.

I (Sadguru Sri Sri Arjun) am not showing you any miracle. Miracle is only a part of Maya. I am imparting self-knowledge. I have come to you to dispel all your illusions. I have come to release you from Maya. Sadguru is always one with Brahman. His mind as well as intellect is all Brahman. Sadguru takes sattvic food. He can empower the disciples to conquer their senses.

Brahman is Peace-Absolute, Bliss-Absolute and Freedom-Absolute. A sincere aspirant, who toes the footsteps of Sadguru, attains self-knowledge and reaches the Supreme.

*****

[59]Creation, preservation and dissolution are going on always in the kingdom of nature. This means, the tri-qualities such as Sattva, Rajas and Tamas are active in the kingdom of nature. Man is a part of nature. Therefore, the tri-qualities are also present in man. Man has to undergo pleasure and pain as long as he is in the nature. Man is affected by the tri-qualities or nature. If man does not reach sattvic stage, spiritual thoughts will not occur to him. Therefore, he will not be inclined to approach a Sadguru for true knowledge. Such persons will not get God's blessings. On getting instructions from Sadguru, a disciple starts walking on spiritual path and assimilates spiritual knowledge. Therefore, to take shelter of a Sadguru and to walk on right path with right knowledge is of utmost importance.

---

[59]*Odia Divyadhara Vol 12 Page 21*

There may be thousands of disciples of a Sadguru, but all cannot get His blessings. Only a few get His blessings. Guru's grace comes only on fulfilment of certain conditions.

To get Grace of Sadguru, a disciple must be very humble. He must have inquisitiveness for true knowledge. He should render service to Sadguru and be ready to carry out His instructions. Last but not the least, a disciple may get by heart all scriptures but if he does not possess good conduct and is not ready to surrender himself to Sadguru, he will not be eligible to receive Guru's grace. "In this gross body, subtle things like mind, intellect, vital energy and conscience belong to Guru. I have nothing to call my own." This conviction should overwhelm a disciple for getting Guru's blessings. Surrender means total surrender and not partial or piece-meal. Thereafter only, a disciple loses his individuality and realises Atman, that is, Self.

People now-a-days ask the question, "What is the necessity of spiritual knowledge? We are doing our duties and earning our livelihood. What does God do for us? What benefit shall accrue by knowing or thinking about God?"

In reply, this much can be said that most of the people now-a-days do not know what all their duties are. What for he is born? What for he is living? By whom he has come into existence and by whom he is able to survive? What is the goal of human life? He has been living a mechanical life without knowing the meaning and purpose of it. Answer to all these questions can be had from spiritual knowledge. Man is not conscious that his duty essentially involves truth, propriety, righteousness and many other divine qualities. He is also not aware that his duty is inextricably connected with the goal of his life. Duty is a stepping-stone towards the goal. In other words, without duty, goal is not achieved.

"If you want to live, be dutiful; if you want to live in the society harmoniously with peace and happiness, possess divine virtues; if you want freedom, acquire self-knowledge." – (Amritbindu – 16)

Where there is truth and righteousness, there shall be peace. Since the sages had this knowledge, they were not only living in peace and happiness, they were also attaining liberation.

The truth is that man cannot know his own mistakes by his limited knowledge. If one studies the scriptures and contemplates on the same, one can know where things go wrong. By mere study of scriptures, things may not improve until man corrects himself and conducts himself accordingly. Then only he will experience the truth. Attainment of truth brings in peace and bliss. Man is suffering which means he has been committing some mistakes somewhere. Rectification of mistakes is essential to get back peace and happiness. There is truth in everybody. Truth can be known by dint of inquisitiveness. It is not that easy to understand the truth. Hence it must be explained in a very simple and intelligible manner. The realisers can explain the truth in a simple and lucid manner. Hence such wise men must be humbly approached with inquisitiveness and serving attitude for getting true knowledge. Realization of truth is the aim of human life. It is the eternal abode of peace and bliss, where there is no trace of any suffering. It must be remembered that Brahman or Atman (Self) manifests as spiritual knowledge.

Brahman is Sat, Chit and Ananda (Existence, Knowledge and Bliss). He is all-pervasive. We are interacting with Him every moment. But we are not able to recognize Him. Due to ignorance we very often ask the question, "Where is God?" Once we know who God is, we shall not ask such question. When you come to know that God is all-pervasive, where shall you search for God? Once you understand Him well, there is no question of searching for God here and there.

Due to ignorance man thinks that it is impossible to realise God in this span of life. He is not aware that he is born for God-realization. A pickpocket takes so much risk and learns so many tricks to do pickpocketing. A householder takes so much pain to maintain his family properly with peace and discipline. The head of the family has to make so much sacrifice to maintain good relationship and good understanding among the members of his family. Comparatively, God-realization is less difficult. Spiritual knowledge has been compared with cotton (kapas), which is light, white and clean. In order to be like cotton, one must acquire spiritual knowledge.

Atman is always there within us. Atman is Bliss-Absolute and Freedom-Absolute. Therefore, everybody seeks bliss and freedom. Therefore, self-realization is of utmost importance. How can you know others if you do not know yourself? Therefore, it is the first and foremost duty and Dharma to realise Self. In other words, realization of True Self is Dharma. He, who does not try to know himself, is committing sin or *Adharma*. Man is bestowed with mind, intellect and conscience. The knowledgeable men are guided by intellect and conscience. The realised souls are guided by Atman. The tamasic people are guided by mind; the rajasic people are guided by intellect and the sattvic people are guided by conscience. In other words, sattva, rajas and tamas represent conscience, intellect and mind respectively.

Going deeper, Divya Darshan says that knowledge is the first manifestation of Brahman. Knowledge ranges from mind to intellect and from intellect to conscience. Conscience controls the intellect; intellect controls the mind. After self-realization, mind becomes reactionless, inert or extinct. A person with sattvic quality gets inclined towards truth and respects truth.

As told earlier, we are interacting with God always and every moment. We also speak to him. But since we do not know who God is, we are not able to identify Him. God can be realised by divine vision or divine knowledge. Therefore, we must enhance the level of our knowledge. Inquisitiveness is also a form of knowledge. The sages, in order to explain the spiritual knowledge, say that God is "Sat, Chit and Ananda (Existence, Knowledge and Bliss)". But after attainment of complete knowledge, the realiser shall realise that Brahman is different from Sat, Chit and Ananda. It means, He is neither Sat nor Chit, neither Ananda (bliss) nor grief. He is beyond all expressions. This is the ultimate state. The more one knows about God, the more one gets peace and happiness. Freedom means realization of the Supreme Brahman. There is no trace of any doubt and fear; there is no grief. Every human being is eligible for this state of freedom. Hence making efforts or spiritual practices to attain this state is Dharma of every human being. For this, the appropriate knowledge which is spiritual knowledge should be acquired. Spiritual knowledge deals with the subject of Atman. He, who does not evince interest in spiritual knowledge, is bound to suffer. In fact, spiritual knowledge is very much present in our day to day activities. It is to be remembered that Atman is there in everything at all times. If one loves or respects another person, it is also a subject matter of spirituality.

Who protects us? It is Dharma that protects us. To know and honour truth is Dharma. Dharma saves us from all misfortunes. Dharma is the basis of fulfilling all our basic needs and getting peace, bliss and freedom. Everybody should evince interest to know truth. This is the real worship. Observance of Dharma is a great spiritual effort that earns us virtues. Inquisitiveness speeds up the process of self-realization. Inquisitiveness is God-gifted and is there in everybody. If a person enquires about Truth or God, he is observing Dharma and doing his most important duty.

A man considers himself to be a jiva and therefore, limited or fragmented powers only find expressions in him. Because of this, he cannot detect deficiencies in him. He remains without trying to overcome the deficiencies. It is imperative that one must take the shelter of a Sadguru to arouse the latent power within. Everyone is swayed by the tri-qualities such as sattva, rajas and tamas within. Tamas drags us downward. Rajasic qualities make us active. Sattva takes us God-ward. The goal of life is to move upward for self-realization or realization of the Supreme Brahman. An external impressed force is necessary to break the inertia of the tamasic or rajasic man and redirect him towards the goal. It is not possible to break away from the inherent tamasic and rajasic qualities by own efforts. By surrendering to Sadguru, man comes under a great protective power that induces him towards the goal. There is power in Guru's instructions. If the disciples follow the instructions of Sadguru, they happen to possess more powers in them. Guru's good wishes bring inspiration to the disciples to move on the path of self-development. Those, who have forgotten Guru even after initiation, in them Gurushakti will not work. Those, who are awake and always remember Guru and Ishta Mantra with love and faith, will proceed faster towards the goal. All the sages had surrendered to Guru and reached the Supreme Goal. Guru signifies weightiness, preciousness and immensity. Guru protects us and sustains us all the time. Guru is immortal and free. He is eternal and all-pervasive. He is inseparably with us and within us. He, who knows and lives like this, regains Gurushakti.

A realiser always remains in transcendental state (State of Brahman) which is Nitya Loka. Sadguru comes from that state. His words are power packed. He also possesses all divine virtues and conducts himself accordingly. The highest state is called Pure Consciousness. Usually the word jnana or knowledge is applied in case of jiva, whereas the word Chit is used in case of the insentient. The sages have, in order to explain that inexpressible Existence, divided the same in the likes of fourteen Brahmandas or Bhuvans. Seven *Patals* and seven *swargas* make 14 bhuvans. Seven patals (hells) are named as *Atal, Bital, Sutal, Rasatal, Talatal, Mahatal and Pata*l. Seven swargas are- *Bhu, Bhuvah, Swah, Maha, Jana, Tapa, and Satya*. The common men usually live in Bhulok. They possess some ideas about the Bhulok. But the realised souls know about Satya Loka. Satya Loka regulates all lokas including Bhulok. Sadguru descends from Satya Loka to Bhulok in order to impart the true knowledge by means of gospels and instructions to the mankind as a result of which the disciples get enlightened. It is not necessary for Him to get by heart the scriptures and reproduce them. What they speak carries true knowledge. Parroting scriptures and chanting them is not an unmistakable sign of wisdom. The words of the sages have the undertones of advices and instructions since they have attained that divine power to speak so. He, who is guided by those advices and instructions, will one day rise to that state.

Those, who come in direct contact with Sadguru, can observe some of the unusual physical marks on his body. Only a realised soul can recognize another realised soul. In other words, the non-realisers cannot recognize a realiser.

A Sadguru perceives the Truth and the Law of Eternity functional everywhere, inside and in the surroundings. That is why He can explain things by picking up simple examples from this mundane world. He need not quote anything from the scriptures. His expressions and instructions are based on self-realization. His preaching becomes the scriptures subsequently. A Sadguru is quite simple and humble. Sadguru always wishes for the wellness of the entire mankind. It is not that easy to recognize a Sadguru. By the past good impulses or samskara, one approaches a Sadguru and surrenders to Him.

*****

[60]Brahman manifests as three powers. Those are Swarup Shakti, Ahladini Shakti and Jnana Shakti. The unitary and all-pervasive energy is called Swarup Shakti. It is Ahladini Shakti, where there is love and attraction. By this, we stay together and get attracted towards each other. The power by which we realise both Swarup Shakti and Ahladini Shakti is called Jnana Shakti. Jnana Shakti pervades everything everywhere. The same Jnana Shakti is also known as Consciousness. By jnana, we can explain and understand things. Hence jnana is a more appropriate word so far as man is concerned. In case of plants and animals, consciousness (chetna) instead of jnana is a more appropriate word.

The Creation is there since time immemorial. We understand the Creation by Jnana Shakti. Jnana Shakti is called Guru. Jnana Shakti is ever operational as a result of which the Creation infallibly moves on. Without Jnana Shakti or Gurushakti, there cannot be any Creation. When Brahman willed to be many, the Jnana Shakti or Gurushakti manifested as the Creation. By Jnana Shakti Brahman manifests as Jiva and by the same Jnana Shakti, the jiva can return to its origin or realise True Self. Changes are going on always in this Creation that emanates from its origin and ultimately merges in the origin. It is said to be rotating like a grand wheel.

---

[60]*Odia Divyadhara Vol 12 Page 30*

Brahman manifests as Jnana Shakti. The greatness of Brahman and His play is expressed through Jnana Shakti and is also understood by Jnana Shakti (knowledge power). In fine, Brahman manifests as the primordial energy that comprises the three aspects such as Swarup Shakti, Ahladini Shakti and Jnana Shakti. Whatever man knows or understands, whatever actions are undertaken by him, are all enabled by Jnana Shakti. Hence Jnana Shakti is so important.

A child gets attracted towards his mother. Mother also gets attracted towards her child. This becomes possible by Jnana Shakti. Jnana Shakti and Brahman are one and the same. Hence, one of the four greatest gospels is "Prajnanam Brahman." This means- Consciousness (Knowledge) is Brahman. Jnana does not imply any specific subject. It is inexpressible. It has no definition or synonym. Only by Guru's grace, Jnana Shakti can be experienced or realised.

The sages while trying to explain Jnana Shakti ask, "How are you able to know any subject?" It is due to the presence of Atman within. Hence Atman and knowledge are one and the same. It is by knowledge that the processes of creation, sustenance and dissolution are possible. Hence, He is called Guru. Guru implies preciousness, weightiness and immensity. In fine, it is only by Guru that the Creation exists. Without knowledge the personal godheads also cannot do anything. They cannot even exist without knowledge. Without knowledge, we shall not exist. Without knowledge nothing will exist. Knowledge is expressed through the body although it exists without a body. As told earlier, knowledge and Guru are one and the same. Hence, everyone, be he a human or a personal godhead, should take shelter of jnana. Only by knowledge we can observe our Dharma and perform our duties. The physical structure or body is not Guru. The Jnana Shakti that expresses itself through the body is Gurushakti. After Guru sheds his physical body, Jnana Shakti eternally remains as it is without any mutation. Hence, it is a blunder and great sin to think that Guru is no more. Guru is always there. He manifests Himself in different forms. He is also there in the tree because of which it collects its appropriate food and survives.

Jnana Shakti is also known as Chit-Shakti. Chit-Shakti is Atman or Self. The sages named the same differently and used the same for explaining the same truth in different ways. Gurushakti is same as Brahman. Jnana, Chit-Shakti, Brahman, Atman etc. are the different expressions of the unitary Supreme Power. Gurushakti has neither any form nor quality. How to express anything about Gurushakti! There is no language to express! He is the source of all powers and is all-pervasive, manifesting as everything. Even Brahma, Vishnu and Maheswar or any other personal godheads or deities cannot speak anything about Him. They are all specific powers of Gurushakti. Hence, they all meditate upon the formless Brahman. Without Knowledge, Brahma, Vishnu and Maheswar cannot do anything because for creation, sustenance and dissolution, application of knowledge is essential. Hence, Guru is a very sacred term. He, who understands Guru well, will shed blissful tears when he speaks about or remembers Guru. Brahman is Guru.

"I have come into existence by Guru, I am living by His power of sustenance and I am able to do all works due to Guru." This feeling should overwhelm all disciples. We fall into Maya after we take birth. It is only Guru who rescues us from Maya and takes us back to True Self which is our eternal and blissful abode. The sages know something about Guru Tattva. But the intellectuals are not qualified enough to speak about Gurushakti. Therefore, they cannot show the ways to realise Him, whom the sages have named as Jnana, Atman, Truth, Consciousness, Guru or Brahman.

The truth is that without the blessings of Guru, one cannot attain Him. He, who serves Guru, possesses desireless devotion, and follows His instructions, can get the blessings of Guru. Self-surrender is an essential pre-requisite for getting Guru's Grace. Only by Guru's Grace, complete knowledge of Guru is transmitted to the disciple and he realises his True Self. What he realises, he becomes that.

I (Sadguru Sri Sri Arjun) am speaking to you by Gurushakti. You are listening and understanding by the same Gurushakti. Whatever we have experienced, everything is by Gurushakti. He, who incessantly experiences Guru everywhere, gets overwhelmed with peace and bliss. With the remembrance of Guru, blissful tears roll down from his eyes. Gurushakti expresses itself as Swarup Shakti, Ahladini Shakti and Jnana Shakti. Since people now-a-days, do not know how to respect Guru, they do not get blessings of Guru. Ignoring Guru is same as ignoring jnana. It is stated in scriptures that he, who disrespects Guru, becomes a ghoul or an evil spirit and moves in an uninhabited arid region or a jungle. He, who loves Guru, attains the Supreme Brahman. Hence during practice stage, all seekers worship Gurushakti. By Guru's grace, a few of them attain the Supreme Knowledge. Therefore, everybody should prepare himself to get Guru's grace.

*****

[61]I am going to discuss something on Gurushakti. Nothing happens, nothing is possible without Shakti. This universe is a diversified manifestation of Shakti. Gurushakti is Energy-Absolute. What is Gurushakti cannot be explained. It is total Shakti. We have all experienced different kinds of shakti such as light energy, heat

---

[61]*Odia Divyadhara Vol 11 Page 3*

energy, sound energy, magnetic energy, mechanical energy, gravitational energy etc. We also know about power of speech, power of love, power of restraint etc. All types of energy by whatever names they may be called have come from Gurushakti. In other words, it is only Gurushakti that has manifested as such. Therefore, Gurushakti is beyond our imagination. How great it is! There is no language to express Gurushakti. When one experiences and expresses Gurushakti, one would be speechless, silent and still. Those, who have gone to that state, have realised Gurushakti. That is a state of trance. The more one knows about Gurushakti, the more one becomes powerful. While giving some indications about Gurushakti, some language is used. Just as I told, the gross or manifested state of that Shakti (*Apara Shakti*) is this entire Creation. This means, beyond the gross Creation there remains Para Shakti which cannot be explained through any language. To speak about Him, the sages just said, "He, who is the basis of everything, by whom this Creation has been made possible, He, who creates and at the same time sustains all, is Brahman". Here a name has been ascribed to Him. Brahman means great and the basis of all. There is in fact no language to express His greatness. The sages after realizing Him, called Him as 'Guru'. He is most precious and powerful; hence called Gurushakti.

Everything comes to light by Gurushakti. We can observe that in this Creation, the processes of generation, operation and dissolution go on every second. Who regulates all these? The answer is – Gurushakti. Happening of anything presupposes some shakti or power. The shakti which creates is known as Brahma. After the creation, things must exist for some days or years. The power that sustains the Creation is known as Vishnu. After some days or years, the things undergo changes or transmutation. The power that causes the transmutation or dissolution is called Maheswar. In other words,

Gurushakti is present in all the three phases as Brahma, Vishnu and Maheswar for taking care of generation, operation and dissolution. This means, everything is done by Gurushakti. All forms and qualities have been possible only because of Gurushakti. We can understand things and explain things by Guru or knowledge. Gurushakti is the creator, preserver and the terminator. We realise Gurushakti only by Gurushakti. The same Gurushakti is Jnana Shakti. All names and forms are the manifested states of Guru. Guru is the Supra-Causal factor of the Creation. We can understand Him by Him only. In future also whatever shall be created or destroyed, everything will be by Gurushakti. By Jnana Shakti, we understand everything. How can such a great power be explained through language? The subject matter of Gurushakti is so vast that it cannot be concluded even if ages run out. By whom, it rains? Before it rained, there was cloud. Before that, there was vapour. Before vapour there was water. Before water there were Hydrogen and Oxygen. All these were caused and conditioned by Gurushakti. Gurushakti is the basis of all, be it water or air, light or heat, potassium or phosphorous. Everything is manifested state of Gurushakti. There is no second thing other than Gurushakti i.e. Brahman shakti. Whatever we experience, whatever we see or come across, and whatever we do are all by Gurushakti. Gurushakti manifests as various forms and qualities. Gurushakti manifests as earth, water, fire and air, with the corresponding properties ingrained in them. Whether it is a plant or animal, the Sun or the Moon, the corresponding properties definitely appear in them. Qualities also change from time to time. For example, a child is different from a youth. An old man is different from a youth. A male is different from a female. If one describes Gurushakti in all its dimensions, ages and ages will not suffice. One life span will not be enough; many births are to be taken. Hence the sages call Brahman as inexpressible. We know the Creation within a certain period. But we do not know when it was created. We also cannot describe lot of things that have appeared and disappeared in the past. Lot of things and events shall also happen in future. Who can write down the myriads of past happenings? Future is also endless. The sages said, 'Brahman is inexpressible'. You should understand this much that all becomings and all happenings are caused by Him. By Gurushakti, you have taken birth. By His grace only, you can understand that you are human. You should remember that by Gurushakti you are surviving. By Gurushakti, you are able to see. You are energetic because of Gurushakti. As discussed earlier, when He takes the form of a male, all masculine qualities are seen in the male. When He takes the form of a female, all feminine qualities are seen in the female. When He takes the form of a transgender, different qualities are seen in the transgender. Gurushakti cannot be identified with any form or quality. Gurushakti cannot be said to be masculine, feminine or transgender. He cannot be particularly identified with the Sun, the Moon or a man or any other object. That means He is everything. He manifests as all without exception. When He is everything, whatever you point out, He is that. All powers and properties that are there in the Sun or a man, an animal or a plant, are manifestations of Gurushakti. He is called Guru. He is great because He manifests as all powers. Huge and infinite powers! It beggars all descriptions. His value is beyond our estimation. All powers are but one power. Brahman is all-powerful, beyond description. Shakti cannot be spoken about in a fragmented manner like this power or that power. Gurushakti is everything. Whatever you experience is His energy only. He, who realises Brahman in this manner, will not have any fear. People, after realizing His powers partially, say that by His grace, a lame man can also climb a mountain. But these are all very small or insignificant things so far as Gurushakti is concerned. At this also we wonder and disbelieve. By

His grace a blind person can also see. Brahman manifests as everything, which means He creates everything, organizes everything, maintains everything and transforms everything. For Him nothing is impossible. He is smaller than the atom even. Now you may try to find out the word which can appropriately describe Him. Nothing can be told about Him. He is therefore inexpressible. When that great power is contemplated upon by any aspirant, where is any fear for him? I am in Him. I am in His heart. I am on His lap. By His grace I have taken human form and got a Sadguru who is none other than Param-Brahman. He has gifted me with consciousness, knowledge and all powers. For Brahman nothing is impossible. If anyone thinks that something is impossible for Brahman, it is ignorance; it is sin. The more one knows about Gurushakti, the more one is benefited. When we do not know anything about Gurushakti, how can we be benefited from out of it? Things happen according to His Will. Due to our ignorance, we are not able to conduct ourselves properly and therefore we are deprived of His grace. Everyone should know that Guru or Brahman is the giver of knowledge and we are utilizing the knowledge gifted by Him to us. Gurushakti is there in my heart and outside everywhere. Gurushakti manifests as mother who gives birth to children. Gurushakti also manifests as father by whose support the children grow up. Gurushakti has manifested as my brothers and friends to give me company and play with me. Gurushakti has manifested as my wife to be an essential part of my worldly life. By Gurushakti I can see, hear, experience and do everything. Whatever I speak or think are all Gurushakti. The sages realised Gurushakti like this and therefore they became Guru. He, who knows Gurushakti, would become Guru. He, who does not know and does not evince interest to know, is ignorant. He, who makes enquiries to know about Gurushakti, is a disciple. Guru and disciple relationship is also a part of His Lila or play. The entire Creation is a manifestation of Gurushakti. Whatever we see are the gross forms of Gurushakti. Realization of this is true knowledge. It is called divine knowledge. This is otherwise known as divine vision. In the Shrimad Bhagavad-Gita, Lord Srikrishna demonstrated His Cosmic Form. He was reiterating that He manifested as everything visible and invisible. We talk of nine planets. They belong to this solar system. There are many such solar systems in this universe. Who has manifested as such? Guru only has manifested as such. Whole Creation is a Cosmic Form of Guru.

You should not consider just a specific name or form as God or Brahman. In that case your thoughts shall be limited to that form. When you say that this individual form has manifested as the entire Creation, bhava becomes confined to that specific form. This means that while seeing the Cosmic Form, you are bringing back your concentration to the specific form of Lord Sri Krishna as a human being. Our understanding is limited to the greatness of that specific form. Cosmic form goes out of mind. It should be remembered that the Cosmic Form contains all forms and not only a specific form.

On the other hand, if you realise that the all-pervasive, all-powerful, and formless Gurushakti, by its inherent greatness, has manifested as all forms and qualities, the gross and the subtle, your thought becomes all-embracing and infinite. "He is the Creation; He is the universe; He manifests as everything; He is all that I experience. He is inside and outside."

If you think that you are a jiva or a separate entity, you would be feeling that He is different from you. When all merge in one, there is no second to the One, no other individual entity. All individual entities are parts of the whole. In other words, all others are different forms of the all-inclusive and all-pervasive Brahman who is formless but omnipotent and omniscient. He, who understands Guru like this, sheds only blissful tears. When such feeling does not come to a disciple it means, he has not understood the significance and greatness of Guru. A child cries for a chocolate. A man cries for more money. We cry for kith and kin. Guru is all in all. By Him, everything happens. He is the very essence of our existence. We are so ignorant that we neither crave nor cry for Him. He, who would be eager to realise Guru, would attain and realise Him. Eventually he would be one with Him and become Guru. There is nothing higher or bigger than Gurushakti. Therefore, He is the Supreme. For such realization, no academic achievements or qualifications are needed. By Guru's blessings, one, who has got good samskara or past impulses, would be eager to know and realise Guru. He gets all knowledge by the blessings of Guru. If he yearns for Guru, Guru will always remain by his side and help him every moment. Guru would encourage and empower him. The knowledge that would be received from Guru shall enable him to tide over all sufferings and he would find himself liberated from all bondages. The subject matter of Gurushakti is endless.

When someone gets separated from his wife and children, tears come out from his eyes the moment he remembers them. But even though we stay separate from Guru, because we are not aware that Guru is the essence of our very existence, we do not think of Him, leave aside, crying for Him. He, who knows the greatness and importance of Guru, feels strengthened the moment he remembers Him. The strength and prowess of more than hundreds of lions will appear in him. Everything is possible. He, who understands Guru like this, enjoys Supreme Bliss. To explain this intricate subject to the people, different names such as Ishwar, Atman, Brahman etc. are ascribed. But the truth is that Gurushakti is all these. Guru should be realised like this. He, who realises Guru, becomes free and immortal. He becomes one with Guru or becomes Guru. Only eternal bliss prevails.

*****

[62]A, U and M- When these three alphabets get joined, it is pronounced as the monosyllabic 'Om'. These three alphabets represent creation, sustenance and dissolution. The dot at the top represents Brahman. The moon-like symbol is his potency. From there consciousness shines out. From there, the process of creation, sustenance and dissolution happens. These three phases are represented by Brahma, Vishnu and Maheswar. According to the Vedas, Brahman is same as 'Om'. In order to manifest as gross forms with the essential qualities in respective forms, He became Triguna (Tri-qualities – sattva, rajas and tamas). Brahman is 'Om'. His potency manifests as different qualities and corresponding forms. He and His potency are one and the same. The dot along with the crescent moon indicates His completeness and all His manifestations. 'Om' represents both the nirguna aspect and saguna aspect of Brahman. Sound is a modified form of vibration. Everything in the Creation has come from 'Om'. A sleeping person wakes up. An ignorant person becomes wise. Guru Nanak says, Guru is that 'Naada' which vibrates everything. He wakes everyone up. His words are the Vedas. Veda means knowledge. Veda is the store-house of all knowledge. For Creation as well as for maintenance, knowledge is essential. For transformation also knowledge is required. By

---

[62]*Odia Divyadhara Vol 10 Page 12*

knowledge, we can understand the processes of creation, sustenance and dissolution. In fine, knowledge is everything. According to Divya Darshan, knowledge is Guru and Guru is knowledge. He, who disregards Guru, disregards knowledge. He is no better than a rock or a wooden log. In whatever manner one follows Guru and to whatever extent one attaches importance to Him, one gets the results accordingly.

When we think of a snake, we immediately remember that there is poison in the snake. A snake may not be able to survive without poison. Brahman manifests as prana as well as poison.

Guru is in fact Veda or knowledge. He, who considers Guru as great, becomes great. Guru manifests as everything in the Creation. He, who considers Guru like this, would get knowledge. If you consider Guru as a human being, you will get only a human being as your Guru. If you consider Guru as Brahman, you shall become Brahman. Guru's knowledge is much more than yours. Hence treat Him with love and devotion. He would bless you. Guru is Knowledge-Absolute. This knowledge would enable you to attain liberation. When a disciple will be eager to acquire knowledge and shall cry for Guru, he would get.

Wherever there is faith, love and goodwill there is bliss. Guru is benevolent. Guru is the reservoir of peace and happiness, love and bliss. Guru transforms dead cells into living organisms. Guru converts the insentient into sentient. Guru transforms the weak as the most powerful. Knowledge is power. Power is knowledge. Hence the debt owed to Guru can never be repaid. What would you offer to Him, who gives you peace, bliss and freedom and takes away all your sufferings? Guru is your saviour; He is benevolent. If you remember Him like this, you will get peace, bliss and freedom. All sufferings shall vanish. All karma shall be burnt into ashes. No trace of it shall remain to cause your rebirth. There is no difference between God and Guru. Guru and God are one and the same. Guru has the power to create. Guru gives only those things to the disciples or devotees which are beneficial to them. Out of ignorance if the disciple asks for something, Guru will not give that. In other words, Guru gives things to the disciple not according to his desire but according to the need. The disciple does not understand this.

Just as a mother gives love and affection to the child and provides all the things necessary, Guru gives everything to His disciples and empowers them. Guru loves the disciples more than His own children. Guru is mother Durga, Kali, Saraswati and Laxmi. Just as a mother makes so many arrangements for the benefit of her children, similarly Guru also makes all arrangements for the disciples for their empowerment and self-development. But the disciples cannot understand the benevolence of Guru who has made comprehensive arrangements for one and all.

Guru has descended on this Earth only to give away all his knowledge to the disciples. This is the Law of Nature. Guru is always ready to give. Even when He is extending his hands, the disciple is indifferent and is unprepared to receive. Sages prayed to Sadguru, "Gurur Brahma, Gurur Vishnu, Gurureva Maheswar." A disciple, who understands this, can sincerely serve Guru. Service means carrying out Guru's instructions and taking care of Guru's physical body. By serving Guru, the disciple becomes a rightful recipient of Guru's blessings. But we are not conscious about Guru's blessings and good will. If a disciple can satisfy Guru, Guru would shower everything upon him. By receiving knowledge from Guru, the disciple can attain liberation and become immortal. It is difficult to express Guru's thoughts and feelings. He, who realises the greatness of Guru, can only express something about Guru's greatness.

We should make all efforts to acquire knowledge on the Unitary Existence. The more one knows about Him, the more one moves towards the goal. His sufferings shall gradually wane away. But the people seem to be indifferent to this highest knowledge i.e. self-knowledge.

*****

[63]Knowledge alone enables a man to know and understand everything. By knowledge, he knows about Guru and God. Since man knows truly little about God, he pays scant respect to God. All his worships become flawed. Similarly, one pays respect to Guru to the extent one knows about Guru. It is essential to know the relationship between Guru and God.

Quite a many worship God in some form or other. Some worship Him ascribing Him some form while some others worship Him as formless. God awards the fruits of actions to everybody. Hence God is said to be the maker of destiny. The idol we worship does not give us anything. We get the results according to our thoughts and actions. Guru in human form is far superior to the idol made of stones. We easily accept an idol as God whereas we do not give that much weightage to Guru. Why can't we consider Guru as God, if a form of clay or stone is considered by us as God? But the fact is that God has taken human form as Guru to give us knowledge. Hence Guru is none other than God or Ishwar. All the sages had considered Guru as God and that is why they could realise God. Some devotees consider themselves as servants of God and prefer to remain as servants. Guru is Brahma, Vishnu and Maheswar. When one respects

---

[63]*Odia Divyadhara Vol 16 Page 53*

Guru like this, he gets blessings from all Devas. Guru is Brahman. Guru is Atman.

Guru is the source of all powers. When somebody believes in God, that means, he has some idea about God. Wherefrom did he get this idea? Our Atman is Guru. Guru enables us to attain God because He himself has realised God. Brahman has become Guru in order to impart true knowledge to the mankind. Brahman is all-pervasive. Gurushakti is all pervasive. A disciple, who has got clear knowledge about the all-pervasive Gurushakti and possesses strong faith in Gurushakti, is fortunate because whenever he remembers Him, Gurushakti will be expressed in and through him. Since you do not have clear knowledge about Guru, you are not able to accept Him as God. To give us divine knowledge and divine thoughts, Gurushakti has taken the human form. The disciple who understands and accepts like this will be able to get His blessings and realise Brahman. You must conduct yourself according to Guru's instructions and indications. Do not contemplate on Guru's physical form. Contemplate on Gurushakti. Guru imparts us knowledge about the Supreme Truth. Hence, pay respect to Guru. Pay respect to your parents and superiors from whom you have been getting knowledge. You cannot give anything to Guru in return. Guru cannot be purchased by wealth. He is the basis and source of all powers and all wealth. All other Devas derive powers from Him. Shrimad Bhagavad-Gita lays emphasis on self-surrender. On the battlefield, when despondency overwhelmed Arjun, Lord Srikrishna gave a very thorough and analytical exposition about the unitariness of the Supreme Brahman. The Lord advised Arjun, "Surrender to me. I shall save thee from all sins." Surrender means relinquishing everything such as mind, intellect, conscience and even Atman. He will not be left with anything to call it 'mine'. When the part becomes the undivided whole, it means, the disciple is completely taken possession by Gurushakti.

*****

[64]After birth, man gets encased by illusions. He forgets his past impulses and knowledge. Only for his survival, whatever knowledge is essential, he remembers those things, i.e. about eating and drinking etc. A baby starts eating immediately after his birth, but his past impulses develop gradually as he grows up. He has been almost detached from Brahman and after passing through several births, has taken human form. Again, he would return to the source which is his goal. The sages and seers having attained the ultimate stage, return from there and declare that everyone has come from Brahman and shall ultimately merge with Brahman.

Unwavering faith, inquisitiveness and spiritual efforts are required for the man to realise True Self. To know about the Creation, the Creator and the Law of Eternity, there is need for initiation (Diksha). Even though man is superior to other animals, he suffers a lot due to illusory effects all around. Man has taken many births earlier. All powers and qualities acquired in the previous births are stored in him. Now that he is a human being, the relevant qualities corresponding to the human birth are seen in him. The knowledge pertaining to the previous births is in dormant state. To activate this dormant knowledge, initiation is of utmost importance. Mother is the first Guru. Father is the second Guru. Likewise, there are shiksha Guru (schoolteacher) and Karnna Guru who whispers God's name into our ears. Finally, Sadguru is most important in life. Sadguru guides the disciple to his goal of self-realisation. Man seeks happiness and bliss. Sadguru can make everything possible. Without true knowledge man cannot live properly and peacefully; he also cannot have a harmonious social living. In such a situation, how can

---

[64]*Odia Divyadhara Vol 4 Page 41*

he realise Brahman who is his ultimate goal? Sadguru's grace makes it attainable.

Man seeks liberation from all types of sufferings and worldly bondages. He wants to lead a fearless life full of freedom. By acquiring self-knowledge, he can attain this state by Guru's grace. Hence Sadguru is accorded highest value in the society. The sages and scriptures also reiterate the greatness of Sadguru.

There is energy (Shakti) in everybody. That lies dormant. As a man grows up, his dormant energy slowly gets activated by seeing, hearing and experiencing different situations. In absence of any conscious efforts, past knowledge and experiences come out very slowly and may even take many births to fully blossom.

One must acquire knowledge to be an engineer or doctor or teacher. To attain self-knowledge also, the related knowledge must necessarily be acquired. He, who has past impulses of very high standard, need not approach any Sadguru but such type of persons are very rare, not even one in millions. When the disciple approaches a Sadguru, it means, the disciple welcomes knowledge by which he can make intense spiritual efforts to realise True Self and get rid of all sufferings. If we welcome something, it will come. There is no doubt about it.

Even Lord Ramachandra and Lord Krishna whom people worship as God had surrendered to Sadguru for acquiring true knowledge. Lord Ramachandra had sage Vashistha as his Sadguru and Lord Krishna had sage Sandipani. All divine incarnates had had Sadguru. Without Sadguru, none has attained the highest state. Even Avadhut, although had no guru in human form, had twenty-four Gurus in the kingdom of nature whom he observed and learnt different types of lessons from them.

Guru means heavy, valuable, great. Knowledge of Sadguru gets transmitted to the disciple. Just as a student one day becomes a teacher, similarly a disciple also can become a Guru after acquiring right knowledge. A Sadguru gives knowledge of happiness, peace, bliss and freedom.

It should be remembered that without true knowledge, no peace or liberation is possible. Sadguru explains who God is. Where is He? How is He there? Why should we have devotion towards Him? What are His laws which we are supposed to follow? As long as we do not have clear answers to these questions, we cannot have happiness or liberation. We are to take birth after births and the Law of action would be keeping us enchained. Sadguru imparts the essential knowledge to the disciple so that he can come out of the bondages. Therefore, Sadguru is the vessel by which we can cross the world ocean full of sufferings. He is the ladder by which we can reach the highest. He is the basis of liberation. He, who appreciates this and surrenders to Him, gets happiness, peace, bliss and liberation.

By surrendering to Sadguru, Gurushakti is transmitted to the disciple and the dormant energy lying in the disciple gets activated. Due to ignorance, people waste their energy in wrong pursuits. Therefore, they suffer. We are also not aware of the latent energy in us. We consider ourselves as jiva (a living being with life force and ability to think). That is why the energy or power pertaining to a jiva only finds expression. By surrendering to Sadguru, we get to learn about the latent power in us. By His grace, the power within us gets activated and by that we can accomplish impossible tasks even. For example, when we feel lazy, at that time if we get instructions from our elders, we become active. This means there is power in the words of the elders. We, by ourselves cannot activate our idle energy. It requires some other external force to activate our inner idle energy. By the instructions of Sadguru, our power within gets activated and we become vibrant.

Compared to the ordinary man, Sadguru's power is extraordinary. Further due to Guru's love, affection and goodwill towards the disciple, the power of the disciple grows manifold very fast. Sadguru's instructions become very effective for arousing the inert power within.

Sadguru plays especially important role in the life of the disciple. Sadguru takes care of the disciple until the latter attains liberation which may take many births. Guru creates all congenial conditions every moment for the self-development of the disciple. Guru remains always alert and watchful for the peace and happiness of the disciple and for protecting the disciple from all miseries and misfortunes. Sadguru loves the disciple very much even more than his (disciple's) parents, brothers, wife and children do. Sadguru always creates suitable environment for the self-development of every disciple. From the point of view of Sadguru, there is no difference between Sadguru and the disciple. He knows that the disciple shall become a Guru sooner or later.

Sadguru has descended from Satya Loka to this Bhulok for the good of mankind. He is always keen to pass on all knowledge to the disciple. Hence, He works day and night for the good of humanity, more particularly for the disciples with all love and sincerity. By Guru's Will Power the disciple gets empowered. His purpose of descending gets fulfilled. Hence, He is ever watchful and active for the fulfilment of His noble mission. Sadguru is immortal. His mission is always on the go. Sadguru can understand the disciple well. Even if the disciple is unable to ask any question due to ignorance, Sadguru imparts all required knowledge to the disciple for his benefit. He bestows all powers on him for his smooth progress towards attainment of Self. He showers His grace always on the disciple. It is only Guru who is ever ready to impart all His knowledge and power to the disciple. No one else in the Creation, however close he may be, would impart everything to another. Even after Guru exits His mortal body, Gurushakti remains active in the disciple. This is how a disciple becomes a Guru one day or other. Even if he remains in the world, he is released from all bondages. He realises that he is immortal and free. Every person is Self-Absolute but due to Maya, he forgets True Self. He suffers although he is Bliss-Absolute. He suffers in the hell although he possesses nectar. Therefore, all freedom loving persons should surrender to Sadguru to get rid of all sufferings here itself by attaining self-realisation.

*****

[65]I am going to tell you something about the relationship between the body and the Atman. Even if a realiser is released from body consciousness, there remain some hurdles. The day he relinquishes the body, from that day he attains Nirvana. The physical body is an instrument used in the process of our sadhana. After enlightenment, the physical body seems heavier. Hence the liberated souls want to exit the body early. After attaining Supreme Knowledge there is no need of the body. A boat is required to cross a river but after crossing the river the boat is no longer required. Likewise, the liberated souls do not want to cling to the physical body any more.

Guru is always there in all conditions, in all forms and qualities, just as water remains somewhere as vapour and somewhere as ice. He is Rama, He is Krishna. Everywhere Guru can express Himself as and when necessary. The same Guru is now aged 52 years and

---

[65]*Odia Divyadhara Vol 20 Page 18*

imparting spiritual knowledge to you. Somewhere else he may be a child and somewhere he may be a youth of 20 years.

The relationship between the Guru and the disciple is close. With limited knowledge this cannot be understood. With our worldly obsessions, we crave for material wealth, children etc. All these are for this birth only, i.e. for a temporary period. But the relationship between Guru and disciple is forever. On the other hand, to attain liberation, how many births are be taken we do not know. But if Guru so wills, He can liberate us in one birth. When a disciple takes shelter of Gurushakti, by His grace, he attains liberation even within a short time. Guru wishes that the disciple should attain liberation as early as possible. But the disciple cannot understand what Guru is working for. The disciple sometimes makes very casual approach and even does opposite things. That is why the disciple's liberation gets delayed. If you remember what I (Sadguru Sri Sri Arjun) had told you on the day of initiation and if you are preparing yourself accordingly, you can attain liberation in this birth. When the disciple does anything wrong, Guru at times admonishes him. If the disciple proceeds in a wrong way, it becomes painful to Guru. He, who disobeys Guru's instructions, commits great sin. The disciple's behaviour of defying Guru's instructions amounts to confrontation with Guru. From the day of initiation, the disciple should endeavour to lighten the load of Guru.

He, who can meet the expectations of Sadguru, becomes eligible to receive His blessings. Guru always wishes that all His powers should be transmitted to the disciples. The disciple, who understands Guru well and intensifies his spiritual practice, becomes a Guru.

"Ignorance is a great sin." This gospel of Socrates should not be taken lightly. It should be our sincere endeavour to find out how the accumulated sins in us will be dispelled. Not willing to know is a great sin. It is imperative to know the ways to get rid of sins and the resultant sufferings. Contemplate on this deeply. Guru is ever prepared to impart you the required knowledge that washes away all your sins and sufferings. If the disciple has no keenness to receive the knowledge imparted by Sadguru, he is unfortunate and is trying to accumulate his sins instead of finding an early remedy. Human birth comes after millions of births. Having got human birth, if you do not evince interest in true knowledge, this means all your previous births as well as the present birth have gone in vain. Guru is calling upon you all to come and receive but you are apathetic. You are rather working according to your whims and caprices. How many more births you will take to prepare yourselves to receive this knowledge?

The relationship between the Guru and the disciple is more intimate than that between the husband and the wife. The relationship between the Guru and the disciple culminates in self-knowledge. Guru always wishes well to the disciples. But without following Guru's instructions, the disciple blames Guru for not doing anything good to him. The disciple does not understand the Guru due to ignorance.

The disciple takes initiation from Sadguru to attain liberation from the worldly illusions and sufferings. After taking initiation, if he does not follow Guru's instructions, he may not get this opportunity again. At the time of initiation, it has been told to you that you are lucky to have taken initiation from Sadguru. Hence do not throw away the opportunities you have got. Try to make the most out of it.

If Guru expresses his anger on any disciple, it is outward only and for a short duration. Guru has taken birth for the well-being of the disciple. Hence, at times Guru gets angry with the disciple to correct him. Guru's anger or even curse becomes a boon to the disciple. Guru always showers His grace on the disciple till his liberation. A disciple, who has gone astray, will come back to his present Guru or some other Guru again either in this birth or in the next birth for knowledge. All Sadgurus, irrespective of different names they assume, are of one class. This is also a grace of Guru. "I will acquire knowledge." This feeling in the disciple is activated by Sadguru. Hence the value of Guru cannot be measured. Guru descends in a physical body to save the mankind from the worldly illusions and sufferings. When you acquire true knowledge, at that time only, you will be able to understand the value of Sadguru and His grace. Jagadguru expresses Himself as knowledge. That means, Formless Brahman descends as Guru in physical form to save mankind from the snares of ignorance-generated illusions. Due to the grace of Guru, we learn something new always and are able to understand more and more. He, who remains obliged to Guru, gets more and more knowledge and enjoys bliss. But the ignorant people, because of their addiction to worldly matters, do not understand the greatness and importance of Sadguru. Guru always thinks how the disciple will peacefully live and get freedom from all sufferings. He is always of kind and loving nature. Those, who understand Guru well, can feel that Guru is their life. Guru is their Atman. Gurushakti will overwhelm him, who realises that Guru is there in him as his Atman.

All these things cannot be told to everyone. When Guru gets angry with a disciple or curses him, all the accumulated Karma of the disciple are destroyed. Even if you do not believe the Guru in a physical form, you must believe the Jagadguru who is formless. If you learn to love and respect Him, you will get His blessings. Those, who have strong past impulses, may not require Sadguru in a physical form since they strongly believe in the Gurushakti. They love and respect Gurushakti and therefore they get the blessings of Jagadguru, who is the Supreme Brahman.

*****

[66]After taking initiation from Sadguru, if one continues with idol worship, it is to be understood that he has neither understood God nor Guru. One has to at least believe that God is everywhere. In other words, He is all-pervasive. God manifests through knowledge which again manifests as forms and qualities. God is Sat-Chit-Ananda. Knowledge is involved everywhere i.e. in walls and woods, ants and animals, plants and planets. Guru means knowledge. Knowledge is Guru. When the unitary God willed to multiply Himself, at that time He remained as knowledge. Because when He would be many, He would be under the spell of the illusory effects of Maya. Hence, He remained first as knowledge or Guru so that jiva could get back to True Self. Guru shows us the way to get back to God. Father and mother are also called Guru. Teachers are also called Guru. Lastly Sadguru imparts the supreme knowledge that leads us to self-realisation. Thus, Guru is everywhere. He manifests as all. When a spiritual mendicant understands this, at that time, he would feel the presence of Guru everywhere. Once the level of our knowledge increases, we can realise Guru everywhere.

We see the gross form of Guru for a short period. He, who realises the presence of Guru everywhere, gets the blessings of Guru. Those, who worship and get some boons, get things according to their thoughts. Reflections happen according to our thoughts. Guru assumes gross form in order to impart knowledge to us. If you strongly believe that Guru is there in every form, you can feel Guru's presence even in the things you love and wish to possess. He is to be realised by knowledge. 'Darshan' does not mean only seeing by eyes. Guru is there unattached in demons and demi-gods, plants and animals. Guru is Brahma, Vishnu and Maheswar.

---

[66]Odia Divyadhara Vol 7 Page 26

God is a common word used by different people with varying levels of knowledge. Some people understand God as Brahman; some other people mean Ishwar or other divine beings while using the term 'God'. Vishnu is usually substituted by Ishwar or interchangeably used by the devotees. Many people belonging to different religions worship demi-gods. Some devotees worship Guru as God. The Sun is also regarded as God. He, who has more powers, is normally reckoned as God. The wise consider Brahman as God. The sages call Guru as Brahma, Vishnu and Maheswar. Guru is also Param-Brahman personified. For the devotees, Guru is God and for the wise Guru is an embodiment of Param-Brahman. Divya Darshan has been reiterating that whatever you see or feel all around, are nothing but manifestation of Guru or manifestation of knowledge. Whatever you see, Brahman manifests as such. If we call Guru as Bhagavan, then He is belittled. If you do not know that Guru's words are Veda Vakya (words of Veda), you will not get His blessings. He, who believes in Guru Vakya and conducts himself accordingly, obtains Guru's grace. He, who has faith on Guru Vakya, loves Guru. He, who loves Guru, is in turn loved by Guru. He, who is blessed by Guru, will get overwhelmed by love for Guru. He, who does not have love, would not get Guru's Grace. Love leads to union. Jiva would realise Brahman. The disciple would become Guru. He, who loves Guru, does not fear death even. He becomes fit to become a Guru.

*****

[67]Guru can, on the strength of his Will Power, get the disciples liberated. If Guru gives instruction to the Gurumaa, she can also get the disciple liberated because she is the consort of Gurudev. You may disown the embodied Guru, but you cannot disown the knowledge

---

[67]Odia Divyadhara Vol 7 Page 17

or Chit who has taken Guru's form. If a disciple disowns his Guru, Guru may forgive but the mother-nature would punish him. No one can escape the wrath of mother-nature. Knowledge power is the essence of Gurudev. He, who would cheat Him, cannot gain knowledge. How do you understand the greatness of God? By and through nature only, you can know the greatness of God. You can learn everything through and by nature. By the Will of Gurudev, the door of knowledge is opened. We do not have power to realise His greatness and great instructions. By His blessings only we can know Him. We are born in the lap of nature and live by nature. In the mother's womb we had direct link with the mother through the navel centre. Had He not designed like that, we would have become insentient. He has infused life energy into us. That is why, we all survive. When we have taken initiation, it means the mother-nature has paved the way clear to us to for getting initiated by Sadguru. If the disciple loves Guru, the mother-nature also blesses the disciple and opens the door to *Mukti* (liberation).

If parents are happy, the personal godheads also get propitiated. If the personal godheads are pleased, then God also is pleased. Guru also is pleased. If someone adores Guru and possesses single-minded devotion towards Guru, the mother-nature blesses him. Many sages adored nature and knew it well and ultimately, they realised Guru. Hence the mother-nature also favours and blesses the sages. Liberation comes only after Guru's blessings. The mother-nature puts the mendicant to test to ascertain whether the mendicant is having real faith and devotion towards Guru and whether he is observing the Laws or not. But we are afflicted by ignorance to such an extent that we try to win the blessings of Guru even by our fallible faith and deceptive devotion. The mother-nature observes us minutely. Mother-nature is ever watchful. Those, who try to destroy Guru's properties, will be punished by the mother-nature who will junk them to hell. The mother-nature keeps on eluding us even if we wish to approach Sadguru and acquire knowledge to attain liberation. When our faith, devotion and sincerity are seen to be well founded, the mother-nature guides us to Guru. Also as and when Guru instructs the mother to open the door, she opens it.

*****

[68]You may be thinking that Guru has given you some Mantra. You are chanting but no result comes from out of it. The reason is lack of samskara. By chanting Guru Mantra you can rise high. Higher than our Mantra, there is another Mantra which is given to the Sanyasis. By Guru Mantra one can become a rishi. Bhakta Kabir had risen to the highest state by Guru Mantra. The Mantra that has been imparted by Guru can take one to the highest level. That depends on one's samskara. Guru Nanak also lays lot of importance on Guru Mantra. A disciple can experience the play of God in this Creation. He can merge himself in the infinite ocean of divine bliss and experience the Supreme in himself. He, who realises that God is blissful, can be blissful. When a spiritual mendicant realises God's greatness manifested as this Creation, he would treat any kind of suffering as insignificant and transitory.

There is nothing equal to Guru Mantra. It is incomparable. If we are to get anything from Guru, it is Truth only. There is nothing bigger than Truth. Unless we realise the value of Truth, we cannot get bliss. It is only from Guru that the most valuable gifts such as Truth, Dharma and bliss are received. There is nothing more valuable than bliss. To attain this, one must forsake untruth. Everything starts from renunciation and ends up with renunciation. If one can renounce the untruth, one can attain Truth. Brahman is the Truth of all truths which means He is the Supreme Truth. That is your True Self. If we take recourse to falsehood, we cannot attain Truth. Realisation of

---

[68]*Odia Divyadhara Vol 9 Page 31*

Truth means realisation of Self. He, who takes recourse to Truth or takes shelter of Truth, can realise his Self. We are the persons who attain; we are also the persons who do not attain. Guru's blessing is already there. He wants everyone to attain Truth. Unless you make efforts, how shall you get? Guru always gives us. But if we do not receive, it is due to our ignorance.

Everybody would attain self-realisation. For this, God has made all sorts of arrangements and the Law of Eternity is functional with this end in view. Guru always inspires the disciples for their self-development. God does not want that anyone should suffer. Man reaps the fruits of his own actions. Children get the results according to their performance in the examination. The parents guide their children and make all sorts of arrangements for them so that they would not suffer. But the children cannot understand this intention of the parents. That is why, it is repeatedly told to you to quit untruth and regain your True Self.

Sages descend on earth to serve the humanity at large. They impart right knowledge to the whole of mankind and inspire them to tread on right path that leads to the goal. They show the ways that help one get rid of sufferings and achieve self-development. This is the best service they render to the mankind. But people are not able to know why the sages descend on the earth. When we chant Ishta Mantra, that means, we recollect His glories and greatness and remember His important role. Without knowing this, people wantonly question about what the sages are doing. They usually say, "The sages have not given them anything like gold or garments, money or matters. When people were in the grip of epidemics, the sages did nothing to serve or save them."

But if we analyse we will know that the present medical science owes a lot to the ancient sage named Charak. Now we are getting benefits from out of the knowledge he had imparted on medicines and medical science. Basing on the knowledge of the rishis and sages, we are being guided and that is how we live with peace and happiness. It is to be remembered that we are always getting the benefits from out of the knowledge imparted by the sages, our parents and elders.

Due to ignorance we are not able to understand all these aspects and we are not respecting them as much as they deserve. Hence the scriptures remind us that we are indebted to the rishis, to Devas and to our parents. We must free ourselves from the debts owed to them. Thereafter only, we can reach our destination. For this most important thing is the Ishta Mantra. If one chants Ishta Mantra with love and devotion, one would be able to get blessings from the Ishta. All his sufferings will vanish.

*****

[69]A Sadguru has realised Brahman or Atman. As told earlier Brahman and Atman are one and the same. When the all-pervasive Brahman remains in a body, He is called Atman. The common people cannot recognize a Sadguru. It is quite natural. How can a person of lower knowledge recognize a Sadguru! Some people believe Him after watching His conduct.

A Sadguru has extremely broad thinking like well-being of the entire Creation. He always remains in Truth and possesses divine thoughts. He does not think of any selfish gain. A Sadguru invests all His knowledge and power on the disciples for their self-development.

If we speak of His distinctive qualities, the first and foremost is that He should be possessing self-knowledge perfectly. He should be able to impart self-knowledge to the disciples in simple manner and

---

[69]*Odia Divyadhara Vol 17 Page 34*

in easy terms. If one does not possess self-knowledge perfectly, he cannot explain it to others perfectly.

A Sadguru should be perfect in Yoga. He should be able to impart knowledge on Yoga to the disciples for their good physical health and mental health. Through Yoga, the Sadguru can take the disciples to super-sensual state.

A Sadguru should also be perfect in Tantra science by which He can protect the disciples from the evil forces and impart true knowledge.

A Sadguru is an embodiment of Love. He always thinks of the well-being of everyone in the Creation. The disciples get attracted towards Him. It is not essential that a Sadguru should wear any special robes or should have matted hair. It is not essential that he should be well-versed in Sanskrit and be able to recite all scriptures. But the most important is that He should be well established in self-knowledge.

Since Sadguru has realised Brahman, divine qualities such as love and forgiveness are seen in him. Any time of the day you meet a Sadguru, is the most auspicious moment. For taking initiation from a Sadguru, any moment is an auspicious moment. He, who considers each word of Sadguru as a Mantra, progresses faster. For a disciple who has good impulses and who has strong faith on Sadguru, no other condition or any ritual is required. Forthe disciple who treats Guru as Brahma, Vishnu, Maheswar and the Supreme Brahman, no other mantra is necessary. Those, who have weak faith, get insignificant results. On the other hand, those who possess strong faith on Guru, move faster towards the goal.

During the process of initiation, the Sadguru tells so many things by which the faith of the disciple gets strengthened. A disciple gains a lot from out of the teachings of Guru. Divya Darshan lays stress on knowledge and divine virtues. The virtues should reflect in one's conduct. Those, who are committing sins, are to suffer. Love is a great divine virtue by which one gets divine blessings. Love brings bliss. God manifests as love. When you hate somebody, do you enjoy peace and happiness? Love is the basis of bliss. Love is the most important divine virtue of any spiritual mendicant. Without possessing divine virtues, none can realise Atman.

Many have attained the highest state of spirituality without any formal initiation. It is because they possessed divine virtues out of past samskara. One must possess divine virtues to get divine blessings and be one with divinity.

The relation between Guru and disciple: We normally consider our worldly relation as most important in our life. But this relation as between father and son, husband and wife, brother and sister, is for this birth only. The relation between Guru and disciple is the greatest because it is for several births. Guru is keen to impart knowledge to the disciple. Guru is everything in life. That is why the sages were chanting the following prayer.

Tvameva mata cha pita tvameva (You are my mother; you are my father)

Tvameva bandhuscha sakhaa tvameva (You are my relative and friend)

Tvameva vidya dravinam tvameva (You are the treasure house of knowledge and skill)

Tvameva sarvam mama DevaDeva (You are everything; you are my Lord)

Another very popular prayer runs like this.

GururBrahma GururVishnu Gurureva Maheswar,

Gurursakshat Parambrahman tasmai Sri Gurave namoh.

This means, Guru is Brahma, Vishnu, Maheswar and the embodiment of the Supreme Brahman. Salutations to Guru.

A disciple, who reposes strong faith on Guru, can attain liberation in this lifespan itself. A disciple must purify his heart in order to get Guru's blessings. He, who loves Guru, gets everything. No word to explain what he gets! Guru will express Himself in the disciple. The disciple will become one with Guru. Guru does everything for the disciple. The disciple must feel, "By His blessings everything becomes possible; I am an instrument only." Thus the disciple gets enlightened. There remains no separate existence of the disciple. Part is merged in the Whole. This means, the disciple becomes the Guru and imparts true knowledge to the whole world.

Guru fulfils all needs of the disciple. All sufferings are eliminated by the grace of Sadguru. A disciple does not know what all his wants are. He only thinks from a very narrow angle in terms of money or gold. The truth is that he needs knowledge. Lack of knowledge is his real problem. Hence everybody should pray for true knowledge. By knowledge, one can attain everything. One, who attains self-knowledge, is a perfect soul who needs nothing more. Guru can raise the disciple to that state.

In exchange of any amount of mundane properties, one cannot acquire self-knowledge. A disciple must completely surrender himself to Sadguru to get His grace. A disciple must try to know what he can offer to Sadguru to get His blessings. Those, who know how to make Guru happy, win His grace. A disciple should be keen to learn true knowledge thoroughly from Sadguru. Guru can easily know how keen the disciple is to acquire knowledge. Guru can easily know how much faith and love the disciple possesses. Therefore, the disciple must have strong faith in Guru's words. Although Guru's blessings are always there with the disciple, it is only by self-surrender that a disciple can get infinite bliss and liberation.

*****

[70]By the virtues earned in previous births and good impulses (past samskara) one gets Sadguru. Man yearns for happiness, peace and bliss all the time. But due to worldly bondages, he undergoes different kinds of sufferings. Sadguru can give the requisite knowledge to a disciple that enables the disciple to cut the bondages and get rid of sufferings. Therefore, to take shelter of a Sadguru is a good fortune. Life becomes worth living. By the knowledge received from Sadguru, a disciple gets everything and can get Guru's grace. Let us now discuss how to get knowledge.

A disciple's knowledge and samskara will improve fast if he remains with Sadguru and with a sense of inquisitiveness observes Guru's actions and behaviour. If he follows Guru's instructions and comes up to His expectation, he shall be blessed. Further the disciple should create such an environment as to receive the love and blessings from Guru. Unless he (disciple) loves Guru, whatever knowledge Guru gives would not be transmitted to the disciple. Knowledge bereft of love is incomplete. The disciple has to make him eligible to receive Guru's blessings.

There should be union of (disciple's) Atman with Guru (Paramatman) which means total surrender including intellect and conscience. When the disciple shall lose his self-identity, Gurushakti shall reveal itself in the disciple. On the other hand, if the disciple keeps on projecting himself and asserting himself, where is room for Guru to express Himself? The disciple may claim the body as his own, but the Shakti inside the body belongs to Guru. In other words, as long as jiva feeling overrules the aspirant, Guru shall not involve Himself or intervene in any manner. In other words, unless an aspirant overcomes his Jiva feelings, he would not be taken possession by Gurushakti.

---

[70]*Odia Divyadhara Vol 10 Page 20*

Love of Guru: Gurushakti is a great power. You may get your parents, sisters and brothers but you cannot get Guru. You may please or influence others in some way or other, but you cannot influence Guru by means of your individual proficiency, skill or cunningness. Hence you must completely surrender your individuality and welcome Guru heartily so that Guru shall take hold of the steering inside. Since there is no other wealth in the Creation which is more valuable than Guru, Atman must be sacrificed to attain Guru. Otherwise it is impossible to attain Gurushakti. Hence one among millions of the disciples attains Gurushakti. Without self-surrender Gurushakti cannot be attained.

Explanation: Guru loves everyone. Every disciple loves Guru. But there is some shortcoming somewhere so far as the love of the disciple towards Guru is concerned. Guru cannot be purchased by mind, intellect or conscience, not also by any gross matters or money. You cannot distract His mind to any beautiful form. You cannot attract Him by any outward glamour. He has relinquished everything and attained the highest state. Only by surrendering your Atman to Him, you can become That. That is real attainment. When Guru becomes happy, then only Gurushakti gets transmitted to the disciple. Without His grace, He cannot be attained whatever efforts you may make. Guru's grace is the greatest attainment of life. You may get the blessings of Devas but you may not get the blessings of Guru that easily. Hence Atman must be sacrificed. Gurushakti is the basis of all powers. Therefore, you may well imagine how much one must serve Him in order to get His grace?

Brahman is there everywhere. One need not search for Him here and there. By the knowledge imparted by Guru, Brahman can be experienced. The Guru-disciple bhava is such that it cannot be expressed. All powers are there in Gurushakti. That power is also there in the disciple. But it is less with the disciple and more with the Guru. Guru is God; Guru is father; Guru is mother; Guru is brother; Guru is teacher; Guru is everything. You know all these things but not to the full extent. There is inadequacy in your bhava. Due to ignorance, you are getting more attracted towards a beautiful form or appearance whereas Guru is not.

Guru has all powers. If you have an intense urge to stay connected, and realise Atman, Guru's power shall be transmitted to you and find expression in you. This means Atman gets merged with Atman. Unless this state of bhava comes, you will not experience bliss. When you heartily welcome Him, you will start enjoying bliss. Guru also becomes happy; the disciple becomes happy. As told earlier Brahman is not any object that Guru can pluck and hand over to the disciple. Thought of Brahman buoys up in and through the bhava between Guru and disciple. Guru's bhava is to give, and Disciple's bhava is to receive. When there is perfect harmony between the two thoughts, divine bliss prevails there. Brahman is Bliss-Absolute. As long as you are not blissful, you cannot attain the Bliss-Absolute. You may go on studying scriptures, enquiring on different subjects, and asking various questions to Sadguru, but ultimately you have to attain peace and bliss to realise Brahman. He, who attains the blissful state, gets liberated. To attain that state, it may take years. It may also take only a second. When one realises True Self, all accumulated sins in the previous births get dissolved. He, who has got some inkling of this riddle, can renounce everything. To get freedom from the bondages of samsara is no mean thing. Here lies the significance of the relationship between Guru and the disciple.

Brahman is there in the Guru as well as in the disciple. Unless that situation arises, the disciple cannot realise Brahman. This is the final say. This means, the state about which Guru would be speaking, the disciple should follow Him to that state to reach there. When Guru tells about Brahman or Satya Loka, the disciple should also be there with Him in Satya Loka along with Guru. Till Satya Loka, Guru and disciple would be together. Unless the disciple reaches Satya Loka, realization of Brahman would not be possible. The disciples may sometimes think, "After serving Guru for so long, why we have not realised Brahman?" That means there is something lacking in the disciple's service to Guru.

To serve the members of family such as parents, wife, and children, one has to work hard, earn money and provide for their necessaries as well as comfort. But it is easy and convenient to serve Guru. In the worldly life, one must arrange for money and wealth and undergo different kinds of difficulties to maintain the family. Despite all these, the members of family may not be pleased because it is difficult to fulfil all their desires. Hence, discontentment always remains. But when we serve Guru, He never complains about the service even if it is inadequate. Even if you do not give, or give less to Guru, He remains always satisfied. But if you have not fully surrendered yourself to Him, you would not be eligible to receive His grace. You cannot win His grace by your intelligence and conscience. Knowing this, a sincere disciple surrenders his Self to Guru and becomes one with Him by getting His grace. The fact is that unless one has that much of samskara, he cannot surrender to Guru totally. An intelligent disciple by serving Guru may move on the path of self-development. The disciple has to come to that state where he can get Guru's grace. Guru is always willing and ready to give. He has descended to liberate the aspirants. But the disciples are not able to receive the same. Due to good samskara, a disciple reposes faith in Guru, serves Him sincerely, and gets devoted to Him. Due to good samskara, we pay respect to our parents. For this, no academic qualification is necessary.

After getting Guru, the happiness and peace of a disciple should be on the rise. For getting Guru's grace, try to have more faith, devotion and love towards Guru. You shall receive His grace in this birth itself.

*****

[71]Now a days, people are so much engrossed in their material pursuits that most of them do not take interest in the study of scriptures, nor they understand the value of Guru. Therefore, they are deprived of true knowledge. In absence of true knowledge, they are bound to suffer. They do not get mental peace. There remains disquietude and various types of disturbances. Even basic needs of man cannot be fulfilled in absence of true knowledge. Man is chasing the mirage instead of trying to reach the goal.

Divya Darshan imparts true knowledge for the wellness of the mankind. We are all children of God who is unitary and all-pervasive. God is omniscient and omnipotent. By the grace of Sadguru, true knowledge comes to the disciples and ultimately, True Self is realised. Knowledge is essential not only for individual survival, but also for a harmonious social living with peace and happiness. Life to fully bloom and be blissful, Guru's grace is essential. Guru should be respected always. By Guru's guidance and grace, everything is attained including Brahman. After that nothing remains to be known; nothing remains to be attained.

There is no other friend and well-wisher like Guru in this world. By His grace, the disciple attains the Supreme. No other relation is as great and pure as that between Guru and the disciple. Our blood relations accompany us for one life but the relationship with Guru is forever. Guru remains with the disciple and guides him to liberation. Guru gives the invaluable monosyllabic mantra to the disciple. There is no language to speak about the greatness and significance of the mantra. In order to get released from the debt, the disciple has to surrender himself to Guru. By doing so, the disciple not only gets all benefits including peace and happiness, he also becomes suitable to spread the divine knowledge among others for their wellness. There

---

[71]*Odia Divyadhara Vol 15 Page 44*

is no difference between Guru and Brahman. They are one and the same. It is by Guru that we can know who Brahman is. The disciple is saved from tritap (three kinds of sufferings) due to Guru's Grace. "Guru is life; He is the very essence of life. My existence is impossible without Him. He is great, my nearest and dearest. There is none equal to Him or comparable to Him". He, who respects Guru like this, becomes eligible to win His Grace. Those who disrespect Guru, ruin themselves. Due to virtues and past impulses in course of several previous births, one gets the chance to serve Guru. He, who serves Guru, gets knowledge and realises the Supreme Brahman. All sins are washed away. All worldly bondages are shattered. All illusions vanish.

Self-knowledge is so important and indispensable that the spiritual aspirants with intense inquisitiveness were leaving their homes and moving to the jungle in search of sages. In this scientific age, it is not necessary to go to jungle for doing any sadhana. Sadhana is possible while being in samsara (world) and leading worldly life. The only key to self-knowledge is inquisitiveness. There is bliss and freedom in self-realization. Ignorance is the cause of sufferings.

By God's grace, the great divine virtue of love dawns upon the spiritual aspirant. By means of love, one can attain Brahman. Love culminates in desireless devotion and consequently Para jnana. Para jnana is Mahabhava. Blessed is he who attains this Supreme state. Without knowledge, karma cannot be accomplished well. Without knowledge bhakti will not mature. Without knowledge one cannot distinguish between good action and bad action. Since the ignorant men do not know how to perform karma, they reap the results of their actions and mostly suffer. Brahman manifests as knowledge.

Creation, sustenance and dissolution become possible due to knowledge. Behind all these changes there is an unchangeable existence who is Supreme Brahman. Living for realization of truth is Tapas.

*****

[72]There are two ways for the disciples to acquire knowledge.

The disciple should possess the quality of inquisitiveness. He should be with Guru always and observe Guru's conduct and activities. He should follow the instructions of Guru with love. Guru is always imparting knowledge, but the disciple is not able to assimilate the same fully due to want of unconditional love. Hence, he must conduct himself in such a manner that he will be eligible to get Guru's blessings.

By applying his intelligence or even his conscience, a disciple will not be able to get Guru's blessings. Self-surrender is essential for the purpose. The disciple must shed his individuality or ego so that Gurushakti will find expression in the disciple. If you hold onto your ego, how can Guru be there in you? You may be having a body but all powers inside you belong to Guru. When jiva feeling has kept you overwhelmed, how Gurushakti will be active in you?

When we love somebody and if he scolds us or hurts our feelings, we do not get affected so much by that. Since we love him, our mind is attached to him. Gurushakti is the greatest power. You may get your wife, parents, brothers and sisters etc., but it is not that easy to

---

[72]*Odia Divyadhara Vol 19 Page 7*

get Guru. The more your mind gets attracted towards Guru, the more you will be nearer to Him and shall get His blessings.

Man may impress others by his cleverness. But Guru cannot be attained by means of individual intelligence or knowledge. As told earlier, without self-surrender, Guru cannot be attained. When a disciple surrenders himself completely with love, Guru will bless the disciple. There is nothing more valuable than Guru. That is why Self has to be surrendered to Him. Without this, Gurushakti cannot be realised. There may be millions of disciples but out of them one or two only may get His Grace.

Guru always loves everyone. Guru cannot be bought by money or any other wealth. Guru cannot be influenced by your beautiful appearance. Mind, intelligence and conscience cannot reach Him. Guru has relinquished everything and has attained the highest state. Even if you offer heaven to Him, he cannot be bought. One has to surrender one's self and nothing less than that. Unless you get His Grace you cannot attain Him. Remember, Gurushakti is the source of all powers.

Brahman is there everywhere. He need not be searched outside. You can experience Guru by the knowledge you get from Him. Guru possesses all powers. But the disciple has truly little power. Guru is God. Guru has come as your parents and teachers. But the disciple is not aware of all these. If you be in contact with Guru, all powers will be transmitted from Him to you. It means Self is getting united with Self. Love rules in the relationship between Guru and the disciple. Unless this feeling is there, one cannot attain bliss. When Guru's thought and the disciple's thought become one and the same, Self is experienced.

Brahman is not an object which Guru may handover to the disciple. Bliss is present in the highest state of bhava between the Guru and the disciple. Guru gives; the disciple receives. It is all Self-Consciousness. Brahman is Bliss-Absolute. Unless you get peace and bliss, how can you attain Him, the Bliss-Absolute? After knowing or understanding Guru, you should experience bliss. If that is not there, even though you go on asking questions to Guru and get all answers, you cannot get bliss. He, who gets bliss, shall get liberation. You may take years and years to get bliss; you may also take only a second. All sins accumulated in several births will be washed away at a trice.

He, who knows the importance of this mysterious knowledge, can relinquish everything to acquire it. By this, he can be released from the worldly bondages. Brahman is there in Guru. Brahman is also there in the disciple. Guru has realised whereas the disciple has not. For realizing Brahman, that level of knowledge is essential together with Guru's grace. During the discourse, the disciple follows the Guru to whichever Loka He goes. When Guru speaks about Brahman, He is in Satya Loka, and the disciple also follows Him to Satya Loka. Guru is always with the disciple till the disciple reaches Satya Loka. Unless the disciple reaches Satya Loka, he cannot realise Brahman.

In the society, we serve our parents and children etc. These are all worldly affairs. Craze for comfort, selfishness and ego are there in these acts of service. For extending these types of services, money, physical labour and time are required. Even after all these also, sometimes we get frustrated to find that our children are not satisfied. It is because, they all have greed and desires which can never be fulfilled. On the other hand, it is very easy to serve Guru. Guru is free from desires. He will never feel for any kind of deficiency in our services to Him. He does not expect anything from us. He remains satisfied with whatever little service we extend to Him. But it must be remembered that as long as the disciple has not surrendered to Him, he cannot get His blessings. As I told you earlier, serving the family members is more difficult. Guru observes the disciple's attitude of serving Him. Without samskara a disciple will not come forward to serve Guru nor will he get any opportunity to serve Him. Samskara means believing in the Guru; keenness to serve Him, serving the parents and believing in God. For this, no educational qualification is necessary. By serving Guru, a disciple gets elevated to higher planes of consciousness. Guru is always ready to bless the disciples. He has come to liberate the disciples. But the disciples are not able to attain the same. The deficiencies are with the disciples and not with Guru.

*****

Shakti Tattva & others

[In the following discourses Sadguru Sri Sri Arjun explains about many a Tattva (Theory) like Shakti Tattva, Srishti Tattva, Prakriti Tattva, Panch Kosa, Theory of Void, Theory of Space and the all-inclusive Om etc. The purpose is to understand the mystery behind the Creation and arouse inquisitiveness and curiosity in the minds of the readers. The brief presentation of these Tattvas will reinforce the belief and understanding of the readers, it is hoped.]

[73]**Shakti Tattva:** Changes are going on incessantly in this Creation. It is essential to know Him who is there at the background of all changes and has been effecting all changes. If He remains unknown, sufferings would be there. After realisation of Brahman, all sufferings would vanish. Sufferings shall be there till we have doubts and fear. We shall discuss here about the Creator, who is making all changes that include the processes of creation, preservation and transmutation.

Shakti (Energy) has neither a beginning nor an end. Energy gets transformed. Shakti is there in everything. Shakti is there in all of us because of which we can do different work. Brahman eternally remains in His formless state. He is subtle. He manifests as gross objects. That energy has manifested as Prakriti (Nature). That Shakti is everywhere. I possess strength. That also is a form of energy or

---

[73]*Odia Divyadhara Vol 9 Page 51*

Shakti. You can see, hear, taste, touch and smell. Everything is possible because of Shakti. Hence Shakti is God. We ourselves are That. Whatever all we come across, the visible as well as the invisible, are That. We owe our existence to that Power. Every one of us is a manifestation of that Shakti. Whatever you speak about, He is that. Whatever we experience He is that. Realisation of Shakti is realisation of God or Brahman. We are there. He is also there. He is ever existent. There is no question of His non-existence. When we are there how can we deny the existence of our Creator? There is nothing second to Shakti. That Shakti is Guru. That Shakti is the disciple. Shakti is there in everything. Shakti manifests as everything. By putting faith on Guru's words, one can realise that Shakti. Shakti plays different roles in different forms. Shakti can never be destroyed. He manifests as different forms. By what, we can know Him? He expresses Himself as Energy (Shakti). He manifests as forms and qualities. Shakti Tattva is an important Tattva. Shakti is everywhere. Brahman is Conscious Energy. He is Energetic Consciousness, omnipresent, omnipotent and omniscient. Brahman expresses Himself eternally. Everything is Brahman. Brahman pervades everywhere. He is the only Existence. Realisation of Brahman is siddhi. After realisation, one gets equal vision. "I am there in everything as Atman." This realisation is siddhi. In the Shrimad Bhagavad-Gita, Lord Krishna, while presenting Himself in His Cosmic Form, explained to Arjun thus- "I am the Sun, the Moon, river and mountain etc." The sages live blissfully on realising this Shakti and become Bliss-Absolute. They do not undergo any type of sufferings. He, who realises Self, becomes Self-Absolute. On realising Shakti or Energy, one becomes Energy-Absolute. On realising Brahman, one becomes Brahman.

Shakti cannot be spoken about. Whatever is spoken about Shakti, there would be lacunae in it. Shakti has no name, no form, and no quality. Shakti is realised by sages as nameless, formless and unqualified. Only the realisers have full knowledge about Shakti. Ignorance about Shakti is weakness. If you arouse your knowledge, you can also realise Shakti. Sages have realised Para Shakti. You are That. Shakti is God. This Creation is full of Shakti. Shakti is all-pervasive and therefore, it is present in everything. People worship Shakti as Goddess Durga. Brahman manifests as Prakriti composed of three qualities viz- sattva, rajas and tamas. God remains as intellect and consciousness and does everything. He manifests as Will Power (*Ichha Shakti*), Knowledge Power (*Jnana Shakti*) and Active power (*Kriya Shakti*). The Creation is the manifestation of the primordial energy. Primordial Energy or mother Durga remains at the root of the Creation. By knowledge we can know Brahman's all-pervasiveness and worship Him accordingly.

Shakti must be experienced everywhere. "He is my Guru by whom I can understand and experience. He is there inside me." This should be the feeling of the disciple. The experience that Guru is there everywhere is the best upasana. This sort of upasana can be carried out for 24 hours. In this kind of upasana, the thought of Brahman remains always. Shakti is all-pervasive. I am on Her lap. Realising that Mother Durga is always inside us is the best worship. Obervance of the Law of Eternity is the best sadhana.

"Get rid of all fear in this world. Shakti is God. In this Creation full of Shakti, muster up Shakti and be one with Shakti."

He is Brahman by knowing whom everything becomes known; nothing else remains to be known. He is Brahman by attaining whom everything is attained; nothing else remains to be attained. This is called Param Siddhi. Nothing remains to be contemplated upon. He is called Brahman by whom everything works or in other words, everything becomes possible. Brahman is neither Truth nor Untruth.

Brahman manifests as consciousness. Consciousness manifests as forms and qualities. Man can know the forms and qualities but not the Consciousness who manifests as such. He, who expresses Himself through Consciousness, is Param-Brahman. Para Shakti manifests as forms and qualities. The attributes that are expressed through the forms come under *Apara Shakti*. From Triguna onwards, it is all *Apara Shakti*. Man experiences bliss in the gross body as well as in the subtle body. Even after the gross body is destroyed, subtle body remains. After the subtle body is destroyed, causal body remains. Self- Consciousness can be experienced after transcending the above three states. One can experience bliss because of the causal body. Transcending the causal body means moving to Transcendental (Turiya) state which is beyond any attributes or qualities. At that time, he can say, "I am the Bliss-Absolute." Transcending the causal state is *Mukti* (liberation).

All spiritual efforts end here. Brahman is Shakti. Shakti is Brahman. Shakti and Shaktiman are one and the same. Brahman is omnipotent and omniscient, the cause of creation, operation and dissolution. Entire Creation is regulated by Him. That power manifests as the Sun, the Moon, stars and planets etc. Brahman pervades everything everywhere. In other words, the entire Creation is His manifestation. He is inside everybody as Antaryami and regulating everything but due to ignorance man considers himself as the doer of everything.

*****

[74]**Srishti Tattva:** The theory of Creation is a very mysterious and important subject of spirituality. This knowledge cannot be appreciated without complete knowledge on spirituality. Unless you know the mystery of the Creation, you cannot know how the Creator Himself manifests as the Creation. Therefore, every spiritual aspirant should try to understand the Theory of Creation. Many things are visible while many more things are invisible. While the matters, plant kingdom and the animal kingdom are visible, the subtle things such as personal godheads, subtle bodies and qualities are invisible. According to the scriptures the visible world is only one quarter whereas the invisible world constitutes three quarters. The invisible universe is not separate from the visible universe. The invisible world is also there inside the visible universe just as the subtle body is there inside the gross body. The causal body is there inside the subtle body. In other words, the subtle body and the causal body are there inside the gross body. Whatever would come to light in future, are also present now, but they are all in invisible states. Those are all present in knowledge. That means the Creator has made all arrangements ab initio, for whatever all are needed for the Creation. For the plant kingdom all pre-requisites such as earth, water, air and light were all available much before the plant kingdom came to exist. Man knows truly little about the Creation. Of course, man knows more than the animals know. The personal godheads know more than the man. God knows everything about the Creation. Hence it is said that God is the knower of everything. Creation includes everything such as matter, plants, animals, birds, personal godheads and God. When such a beautiful and well-planned Creation is there, this means the Creator is also there. If a baby is there, his parents are also there. Hence definitely there is a Creator who has made this

---

[74]*Odia Divyadhara Vol 7 Page 29*

Creation. The Creator is named differently. Once we know certain things their ancillary subjects also are known gradually. Therefore, once we collect knowledge on the Creation, we can ultimately know about the Creator. Scriptures say that Brahma is the Creator. We may refute the existence of Brahma but we cannot refute the power or energy that is involved in the process of Creation. That power is named as Brahma.

In the preliminary stage, to explain things the scriptures have described about Brahma, Vishnu and Maheswar who are the causal powers for the creation, sustenance and dissolution. In other words, the process of creation, sustenance and dissolution happen due to the three qualities such as sattva, rajas and tamas. From the three primary qualities, many other qualities come out. The sages and seers named them as personal godheads. Above all these, there is Brahman, the Supreme. He is the Supra-Causal factor or the basis of all invisible and visible things. Hence there is no doubt that Brahman exists eternally. The sages have realised Him, and they use the word 'Sat' to affirm His existence. He has no specific name, form or quality. By His self-glory, He manifests as all names, forms and qualities. Those, who do not know Him, neither understand the cause nor process of Creation.

According to the scriptures, Brahman willed to be many. This means, first He manifested as subtle and then gross. The qualities are subtle whereas the forms are gross. There is quality involved in every form. The qualities correspond to the forms. The basis of all forms and qualities are the primary three qualities such as sattva, rajas and tamas.

Now the question is- whether forms have come from qualities or qualities have come from forms. Everything is created from energy or Shakti. Qualities being a form of energy or Shakti, all forms have come from qualities. The primary three qualities are invisible. So are all other qualities. The visible universe has come out of the invisible energy or Shakti. The primary three qualities ultimately get merged in a state which is attributeless. Hence Jagadguru Shankaracharya realising this Supreme state said, Brahman is real, and the universe is unreal. The attributeless Brahman has manifested as attributes. Hence, we should make efforts to realise the eternal Brahman instead of getting attached to the changeable universe of names, forms and qualities which ultimately, through the process of transformation, gets merged with the attributeless Brahman, the Supreme. But we get attached to the visible things with names and qualities which are easily available and usable. We attach more importance to the forms but do not try to know the qualities therein. The energy that manifests as forms and qualities comes under *Apara Shakti* (lower energy). Para Shakti has neither any form nor quality.

One would get some indication of Para Shakti if one knows *Apara Shakti* (forms and qualities) well. While Samkhya Darshan lays more emphasis on the primary three qualities, Vedanta Darshan goes to the cause of three qualities. The answer is Brahman. This means Brahman has created everything.

Divya Darshan asks, "Who is there who manifests Himself, regulates Himself and reveals His own identity?" When we say Brahman has created all these, it is just for a preliminary understanding. Brahman is the cause of whatever has happened in the past, is happening now and shall happen in future. This foregoing statement is of a little higher stage. But to say that He Himself manifests as everything, everywhere as forms and qualities is a thought of highest level. It is a mysterious thing to know about the greatness and True Self of Brahman. Knowing His greatness and True Self is siddhi or self-realisation. He is the basis of everything, yet He is not involved in anything. He remains unattached with all becomings. He does not limit Himself to any specific object or subject, since He is the source of all energies. Due to His self-glory, He is there as the Sun, water, air, plant, creatures and man. After realising this, the sages have been reiterating that He is the only One that exists eternally although appears many. But we speak of the unitary Brahman and at the same time, we worship many. Brahman manifests as all these. When this is said, there is a bridge established between monism and dualism. His greatness is 'Mahimaa'. He who realises His greatness can ultimately be merged with Him. In this Creation, whatever one comes across knowingly or unknowingly are nothing but Brahman's greatness. In other words, Brahman alone expresses Himself. When Brahman takes various forms, the corresponding qualities also find expressions in the forms. A man also undergoes different situations. He gets angry, he grieves, he gets entrapped by infatuation and on the other hand, his happiness at times knows no bounds. These are various forms of man. A subtle body has taken the gross form. The causal body has taken the form of subtle body. Man is Sat-Swarup, Chit-Swarup and Ananda-Swarup but due to ignorance he forgets this and suffers. Different conditions or forms of a person are nothing but various states of the Sat-Chit-Ananda. Man, in reality, is Bliss-Absolute.

Whatever we see or experience in this Creation, are only the manifestations of Brahman who is unitary, infinite and eternal. He, who can open this knot, can realise Him. This is the Cosmic Form of Brahman which is explained in the Shrimad Bhagavad-Gita. That means, we see only Brahman all around. According to Divya Darshan we are seeing the manifestation of Brahman everywhere. This idea is also reiterated by Vedanta. The Jagat is filled with Brahman. In other words, the whole universe is pervaded by Brahman as the basic substratum of one and all. By knowing this, man can get rid of all sufferings. Differentiated knowledge would bring in sufferings.

The inquisitiveness to know Brahman is real worship. By this, Self can be realised. Nothing is left to be known or attained after knowing Brahman. Hence everyone must try to realise the Supreme, the attributeless Brahman.

*****

[75]The mystery of the Creation should be fully unravelled in order to know Brahman. When the Creation is there, the Creator is also there. Unless we know the Creation well, we cannot know the Creator. The sages and seers in their state of samadhi had realised Brahman. Even after returning from samadhi, they cannot describe Brahman fully. From scriptures, we gather some knowledge about Brahman, but that is very insignificant.

We see and experience innumerable forms and qualities. All these forms and qualities are created from out of Brahman and ultimately, they merge in Brahman. It would not be correct to say that whatever things we see, or experience were all in Brahman. The scriptures say that Brahman is pure, untainted, uncontaminated and divine. He is immutable or unchangeable. He is eternally one. Nothing else is there other than Him. But He possesses so much power or energy that He can manifest as everything. The waves are created from water. The quality of water and the quality of waves are apparently different. The waves again merge with water. The Law is that whatever is created shall merge ultimately with the source from which it was created. In this way everything we see or experience remains for a temporary period and again due to process of change

[75]*Odia Divyadhara Vol 7 Page 34*

everything goes back and gets merged in the source that is Brahman. When a pot is broken and becomes clay, at that time the quality of the pot also vanishes. It should be remembered that at the time of mingling gradually, the qualities of the pot should be totally lost, and it should be transformed well to mingle with the source material. Let us discuss about the five gross elements. From Space, air is created; from air, fire is created; from fire, water is created and from water, earth is created. While mingling also, first earth mingles with water; water with fire, fire with air and finally air with the space. This process of creation and again going back to the source becomes possible only due to His greatness. Hence man, in order to be Brahman, is to purify and divinise himself through the process of sadhana by acquiring knowledge, and observing the Law of Eternity. Man must free himself from six internal enemies (Desire, anger, greed, attachment, pride and ego) and inculcate divine virtues in order to be eligible to merge with Brahman. It is certain that man would ultimately merge with Brahman but quite a many, due to lack of knowledge of spirituality, do not believe it.

To explain things, it is stated that the Creation has started from Brahman. The scriptures say that Brahman has neither beginning nor end. Something which has a beginning has an end too. Every moment, we witness the process of creation and dissolution. Some examples may be cited here. Take the case of water cycle. Water becomes ice. Ice again becomes water. Water becomes vapour and again in a specific situation, it becomes water. This process is going on incessantly. This has neither beginning nor end. Brahman is attributeless and formless. Still man can realise Him by jnana and bhava. There is something called Brahmi state. There is nothing in that state but still the same has existence. When we are experiencing the Creation, it means we always come across creation, sustenance and dissolution. The sages said, "Brahman willed to be many." This is just to make somebody understand the greatness of Brahman. We humans also wish certain things. It would be a mistake to ascribe the same wishful thinking to Brahman. This is all about Pure-Consciousness. Without knowing this state, people enter into unnecessary arguments and end up with confusions and conflicts.

Now let us discuss about the evolution of this Creation. Brahman willed to be many. From this, we shall proceed further. Before creating, He became Guru or kept Himself in Guru State. That State is different or is beyond the Creation. Because of Guru's grace, man can know, understand and ultimately, he can realise True Self. By whom we can understand and make others understand is called Guru who is Knowledge-Absolute. Knowledge is Chit-Swarup. The consciousness by which we understand and explain things to others is called Guru. Hence, Divya Darshan says, knowledge is Guru and Guru is Brahman. One of the four Mahavakyas as highlighted in the Vedas and Upanishads is "Prajnanam Brahman." That means knowledge is Brahman. Since He remains unattached to and independent of the Creation, it becomes possible for Him to create, sustain and transform. By consciousness, new things are created through the process of change. This entire process of change is called Creation. That the jiva is originally and eternally Brahman is explained by Guru. By Guru only, man can penetrate the intricacies of the Creation and unravel the mystery of Maya to ultimately get back True Self. To know the Creation, one must necessarily approach a Guru. It is to be remembered that the unitary state of Brahman is called Guru. He, who can realise Gurutattva, can overcome the cycle of birth and death, and become free. The sages in order to explain the Creation speak of the noumenon and the phenomenon (Purusha and Prakriti). Purusha is there in everything as attributeless. According to Divya Darshan, it is not correct to consider Purusha different from Prakriti. Prakriti is the inherent greatness or potency of Purusha. Due to the greatness of Purusha, Prakriti plays its role. Divya Darshan further says that it is only Purusha that manifests as Prakriti. Or, Purusha himself has become Prakriti. At times, to explain others we talk of self-glory of Purusha by which Prakriti expresses itself. When everything is Brahman, how can Prakriti be different from Brahman? An example may be cited here. Man makes a machine and he himself operates it to his benefit. Man's knowledge and skill has taken the form of the machine. Brahman manifests as various forms and qualities. Remaining unattached, He controls and regulates all forms and qualities.

Another name of Prakriti is 'Om' or 'Pradhan'. Earlier it has been discussed that Brahman is the source and basis of everything. Whatever forms and qualities we see, Om is there in all. When Brahman willed to be many, He became three qualities such as sattva, rajas and tamas. Thereafter all other forms and qualities were created. Those three qualities are also called Brahma, Vishnu and Maheswar. By rajas, the creation takes place; by sattva, sustenance takes place and by tamas the process of transformation or dissolution takes place. These three powers belong to Om. At times, the name Ishwar is also used. All powers or energies, all forms and qualities come from Om and it is Om who controls everything. Hence, I (Sadguru Sri Sri Arjun) have all along been advising you that unless you get the blessings of Om, you cannot reach Brahman. Om is also known as Prakriti or Hiranyagarbha. Without the blessings of Om, it is impossible to get liberation. She is known as Adya Shakti.

In the Samkhya Darshan, Prakriti is depicted as insentient. The three qualities (sattva, rajas and tamas) manifest as all forms and qualities including insentient objects. The insentient objects are also diversified states of the three qualities. These three qualities supported by Consciousness have vast powers inherent, by which all forms and all qualities, whatsoever, blossom out in phases and according to the need of the Creation. This means, everything has been created from Triguna, also known as Pradhan. From Pradhan to jiva, whatever things are created come under Mahatattva. Pradhan is also known as Mulashakti and causal body. Intellect and mind come under Mahatattva. There are five tanmatras such as sound, touch, sight, taste and smell followed by the five gross elements such as ether, air, fire, water and earth. The 17 tattvas such as five sense organs, five organs of action, five tanmatras, mind and intellect constitute the subtle body. Considering Ahamkar (ego), it comes to 18 tattvas as depicted by some scriptures. All these are called Jiva. But since we possess gross bodies, we do not have idea about subtle body. But the intelligent or wise men, knowing the presence of subtle body inside the gross body and knowing that the gross body is regulated and guided by the subtle body, give more importance to the subtle body and causal body.

In everything starting from nature to the jiva, Brahman is there. Everyone is controlled and guided by Brahman. Brahman controls and guides the Creation. That state of Brahman is called Ishwar. This means that Ishwar is also guided and controlled by Brahman. The gross body is controlled and guided by the subtle body. The subtle body is guided by the causal body or Ishwar. The causal body is ultimately controlled and guided by Brahman who is the Supra-Causal factor. A man can know everything from jiva to Brahman by the grace of Sadguru.

If we do not follow the instructions of Sadguru, we cannot realise Brahman. Guru is everywhere in everything. He, who knows Gurutattva fully, can know everything. Kabir said, "By the grace of Guru I could know Guru and Brahman." Without Guru's grace, it is not possible to go back to that state from which we have come. He, who can realise Guru, can know his Self. All divine powers (such as- Laxmi, Saraswati, Durga, Kali) are there with Guru. It is Guru who takes care of the disciple even after the death of the disciple, for his further self-development hereafter.

*****

[76]**Prakriti Tattva:** Man is the best of all creatures in this Creation. You all know why man is considered superior to others. But man has some weaknesses due to which he considers himself as Jiva and is unable to justify his superiority. It is only man who can think, "Who I am and where I have come from." Man is in the ambit of nature. Due to Maya, he is unable to know himself. He alone, who contemplates on who he is and where he has come from, can know. He, who does not want to know himself, can never know the truth about himself. The sages had realised this and through various scriptures they have imparted true knowledge. Man has come from Brahman and one day he will go back to Brahman to be one with Him. Now that man has got a human form, human qualities are seen in him. Due to this specificity, he cannot realise his infinite and formless existence which is the True Self.

Brahman has become Jiva. Whatever are existing in the universe, are there in the Jiva. Forms may be different, but the essence is same everywhere. There is unity in diversity. The subtle body is there inside the gross body. This subtle body is called jiva. When the subtle body expresses itself through the physical form, its power becomes limited or finite. When the subtle body relinquishes the physical covering, it remains subtle and regains more power. There is causal body in the subtle body. The causal body is more powerful than the

---

[76]*Odia Divyadhara Vol 15 Page 9*

subtle body. Jiva transcends the causal body to realise self-consciousness which is Supra-Causal. When man attains this state, the gross, subtle and causal forms get merged into one.

You know that in the subtle body, there are, mind, intellect, tanmatras etc. Conscience radiates from the causal body. You are not different from Brahman. Everything is in you. Since you identify yourself with the gross body, limited powers are expressed through you. Generally, nature is considered as an unconscious entity. But such idea is not correct. Jiva is conscious; nature is also conscious; both have come from Brahman who is all pervasive Pure Consciousness. When Atman is ever-present in the jiva, how can he be without consciousness? Every moment, changes are taking place in the nature. This indicates that there is consciousness in the nature. Jiva is Sat-Chit-Ananda. But due to ignorance, he identifies himself with his physical body and therefore he is unable to realise True Self. Such identification with the physical body is very strongly impressed in his mind since distant past over several births.

Prakriti (Nature) is a combined state of tri-qualities such as sattva, rajas and tamas. 'Om' manifests as nature. The other side of 'Om' is Nirguna (the first quarter). 'Om' is the second quarter. From 'Om' to Tanmatras (Sound, touch, sight, taste and smell) is the third quarter. The visible universe made of five gross elements is the fourth quarter. Thus, Brahman is said to be having four quarters, as explained in the scriptures.

The third quarter is from 'Om' to Tanmatras. It is the state of the Devas. The fourth quarter is the visible universe, constituted of the five gross elements, such as space, air, fire, water and earth. We are not able to see space and air. Brahman is subtler than the subtlest, unimaginable for the mind. Devas come under the ambit of nature. Brahma, Vishnu and Maheswar have also come from 'Om' or nature.

From 'Om' to Tanmatras, is Mahatattva or Buddhitattva. It is the abode of all Devas. When the subtle body assumes physical form, its power gets reduced. Thus, when Brahman manifests through various stages and becomes Jiva, limited powers are expressed in the jiva. Jiva is unable to know Brahman who is the True Self. Jiva is unable to understand the changes and happenings in the subtle state (From 'Om' to Tanmatras) and gets shocked and surprised by their effects on his nearby surroundings as well as on the gross universe.

People carry with them some good samskara and some bad samskara by which they get affected. Since we identify ourselves with our bodies, we attach more importance to the physical bodies. It is to be remembered that from the subtle state, we have assumed gross forms. From the gross forms, we will have to go back to the subtle state and then merge in the causal state. In the causal state, the impact of the gross and subtle (From 'Mahatattva' to Tanmatras) will not be there.

Causal state is the equilibrating state of the tri-qualities such as sattva, rajas and tamas. This is Sat-Chit-Ananda state. The sages remain in this state which is a union of blissful state and nirvikara state. From this level, they impart true knowledge to the mankind.

Sufferings are there for everybody irrespective of whether one is a ruler or the ruled, a master or a servant. Three broad categories of sufferings are there. They are- Adhyatmic, Adhi-daivic and Adhi-bhoutic. The source from which tri-qualities come into play is called Adyashakti or Maya. Maya has got two powers; veiling power and projection power. Due to veiling power of Maya, the truth gets veiled and due to projection power, one thing appears as another. (The popular analogy of the snake super-imposed on the rope can be recollected here)

Goddess Durga is called Mahamaya. According to Tantra science, there are three powers namely, Kali Shakti, Laxmi Shakti and Saraswati Shakti. He, who will get the blessings of the three powers, will get rid of all sufferings. According to Yoga Sastra, once one realises the tri-qualities, he can realise the unqualified Brahman.

Samkhya Darshan lays emphasis on 25 tattvas including Purusha to explain the Creation as follows.

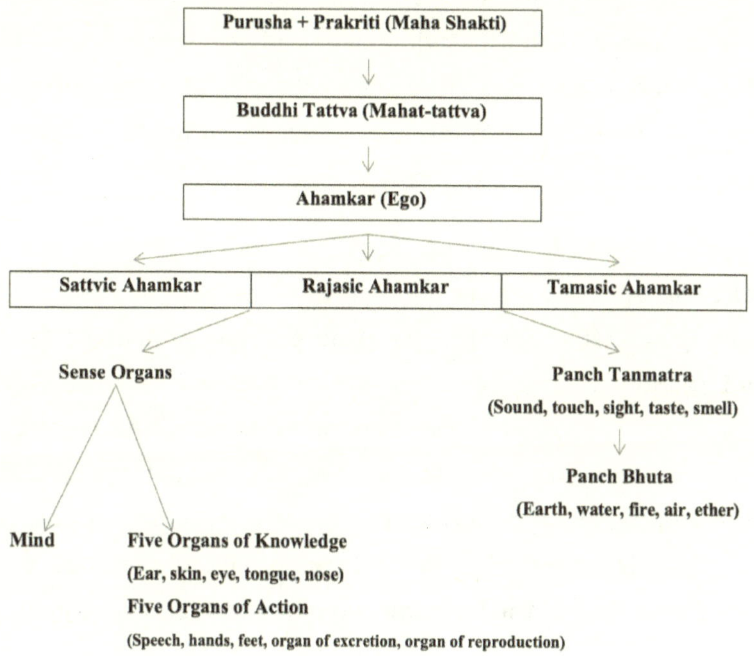

Prakriti Tattva must be understood well before realization of Brahman. Unless Prakriti Tattva is understood properly, Maya cannot be comprehended. Maya is nothing but the play of Prakriti. According to Divya Darshan, Purusha expresses Himself as Prakriti. As such, Purusha and Prakriti are one and the same. In other words, they are non-dual. Prakriti is the potency of Purusha. Since we all are in the peripheral region of manifestation, we are not able to know our source. Once we know mother Durga, all our negative qualities which are known as the six enemies such as desire, anger, greed, attachment, pride and jealousy will disappear.

*****

[77]Panch Kosha Sadhana:

Everyone experiences sufferings. Man has been suffering from time immemorial and struggling to get rid of sufferings. Lord Buddha said, "There is suffering. There is a cause of suffering. Suffering has come; it must go also. If the cause of suffering is known, its eradication becomes possible."

Same type of suffering does not remain always. After one suffering goes away, another suffering comes. In the process of fighting against sufferings, one explores knowledge and attains bliss and freedom. Finally, he comes to know that he is the Bliss-Absolute. Man must try to realise the Supreme Brahman. The Law of Eternity is ever at work. According to this Law, man must attain the Supreme Brahman to get rid of sufferings. By material fulfilment, he can get happiness for some time, but it does not last long. Hence, the wise take the shelter of the Supreme who manifests as everything.

All scriptures have tried to explain this to the mankind. According to them self-surrender is the highest form of Bhakti. Without trying to know who God is, it is futile to hope for peace and bliss. Divya Darshan says, "Ignorance is the cause of sufferings." God has endowed man with knowledge. By knowledge man can survive. By knowledge, he can make a harmonious social living and live in peace

---

[77]*Odia Divyadhara Vol 16 Page 5*

and happiness. But for getting rid of all sufferings and getting peace and happiness man must take recourse to spiritual knowledge. Self-knowledge must be acquired to get permanent bliss. Brahman is there as Self who is present in all beings. Not knowing the Self is ignorance. It means, not knowing the power of one's own Self is ignorance. Not knowing the Law of Eternity is ignorance. Not knowing the Truth is ignorance. Brahman is all-pervasive, full of consciousness and energy. He is eternal. He manifests as the Creation and knowledge. But due to ignorance, (ignorance means not absence of knowledge but limited or incomplete knowledge) man has forgotten True Self. He is impacted by the past impulses collected in all his previous births. He remains complacent by knowing some essential mundane matters which are temporal and partial truths, but not the Supreme Truth. Man is endowed with all potentialities to realise Brahman and come out of the cycle of birth and death. Man is endowed with body, vital energy, mind and intellect so that he can live in bliss. These are all divine provisions to attain True Self. But man identifies himself with body, mind and intellect and remains bound by them as a result of which he suffers.

Taittariya Upanishad discusses about the five sheaths present in the body. From the spiritual point of view, every spiritual aspirant should know how this body is composed of. These five sheaths are physical sheath, vital sheath, mental sheath, intellectual sheath and blissful sheath. Brahman is Bliss-Absolute. He resides in every being as Bliss (Ananda). He remains veiled by other four sheaths as a result of which it becomes difficult to realise Him.

We know that there are five gross elements such as- space, air, fire, water and earth. From space, the other four gross elements have come. Akash or space is very subtle which cannot be seen by eyes. Space is present in the other four gross elements. When our knowledge level goes up, we can know more about the presence of space in atoms also. When a man dies his physical body is destroyed. This is Annamaya Kosha (Physical sheath). Inside the physical sheath, there are other sheaths such as vital sheath, mental sheath, intellectual sheath and blissful sheath. When the physical sheath is burnt or destroyed, the other sheaths are not destroyed. He, who acquires knowledge about the sheaths, can feel that he is not the physical body constituted of bones, marrows, flesh etc. He will realise the blissful state. Brahman is eternal as He is without beginning and without end. He is different from this body as He witnesses the physical body as well as senses, mind and intellect. The physical body is made of five gross elements. The physical body is made by the food we take. The food gets transformed into various substances in the body and gives energy to the body. The physical body cannot exist without Prana or vital energy. It is Prana that regulates the physical body. Brahman also manifests as the gross elements. He manifests as the food materials. The physical body is transient whereas Atman is eternal. With the destruction of the physical body, only the five gross elements go away but the subtle body remains and assumes some other form in due course.

It must be remembered that you are not the physical body. Because of the presence of the subtle body inside the physical body, the physical body becomes functional. To satisfy your senses, you keep on collecting more and more things. Some of you are killing animals to satisfy the tongue. By doing so you are committing sins and inviting sufferings.

Those, who will try to realise the Supreme Brahman, the Bliss-Absolute, will succeed one day.

Annamaya Kosha (The Physical Sheath): The outermost or the gross body is the physical sheath or Annamaya Kosha. This body is made of food. This body is itself a food. But the subtle body is different from this physical body made of food or anna. It means the physical sheath is the outermost covering of the subtle body. The subtle body acts through the physical body. The physical body is subjected to injuries and pain. But the subtle body goes on adding to its knowledge and experience. The subtle body has been making its spiritual efforts through the gross body for realization of True Self. That is why Devas also prefer to possess human bodies when they happen to come back to the Bhulok.

The gross body is well equipped with sense organs, organs of action etc. and is quite suitable for making spiritual efforts. But man does not understand the great purpose of this human body. Unaware of the spiritual goal, he spends his life only for survival and acquisition of some mundane things. According to Taitteriya Upanishad, Bhrigu, then a young boy, prayed to his father Rishi Varun to instruct him about his duties. Rishi Varun replied, "Try to know the Supreme Brahman by whom you have come into existence, by whom you survive and in whom ultimately you will merge."

By the virtues collected in previous births, you are born as human. Knowledge is necessary to know that all the karma you undertake is sadhana to reach life's goal. For this purpose, you are maintaining your body and acquiring knowledge. Due to ignorance, you perform all your actions for survival and some material pleasures. Deviated from the destination, man suffers. For maintenance of the physical body God has made necessary arrangements of food materials. Different animals take different foods. Man must know the appropriate food by which he can remain fit to carry on his spiritual efforts. Hence it is the first and foremost duty of everyone to take care of the body. Various instructions are laid down in the Ayurveda regarding the time by which one should get up from bed, daily routine, exercise, yoga and pranayama etc. A sound body with a sound mind is extremely helpful for going ahead with spiritual efforts. If the body suffers from different ailments, it will be difficult to do Sadhana and attain the goal. Mind of a sick man will not remain stable or concentrated. Therefore, it is imperative that everyone must take care of the body first in order to progress faster on the spiritual path.

*****

[78]**Pranamaya Kosha (Vital Energy Sheath):** Inside the physical sheath, there is vital energy sheath. This sheath keeps the body and sense organs active. This vital energy is not visible, but everyone can experience its existence and functions. When we are sick, we are not able to see properly, hear properly or walk properly. In other words, our senses become weak when we fall sick. The sages were living for hundreds of years because they knew how to take care of the body, vital energy and mind.

Strong vital energy is essential for spiritual sadhana. Speech becomes powerful and effective due to strong vital energy (Prana Shakti). Inspiration and courage are also due to Prana Shakti. By spiritual efforts, Prana Shakti gets strengthened. Prana Shakti or vital energy gets spent due to bad doings, bad thoughts and bad tendencies. Hence, the spiritual mendicants should maintain a restrained lifestyle with good and positive thoughts for faster movement on spiritual path. For this, celibacy is especially important for enhancing the vital energy.

---

[78]*Odia Divyadhara Vol 16 Page 10*

Persons with more vital energy are generally fearless. They are not idle. The energetic persons love others, live happily and can inspire others. On the other hand, a weak person cannot even laugh. He has no interest in anything. Due to ignorance, we waste our vital energy on undesirable lines. Due to negative thoughts and also due to intake of improper food, vital energy gets drained out. A selfish or egoistic person with jealousy and anger etc. wastes his vital energy. Laughing with an open mind is a blessing of God. On the other hand, the vital energy of a stressed person gets reduced. Too much of indulgence in worldly matters distances one from self-consciousness and keeps one engrossed in the mundane objects. Too many worries and anxieties adversely impact the vital energy. The more one gets connected with divine thoughts or spiritual pursuits, the more one radiates with vital energy.

But due to ignorance, we indulge in wrong doings and carry negative thoughts by which our vital energy gets misdirected or wasted and life's goal remains unattainable. The greater the vital energy, the greater is the will power. According to our thoughts, different rays are emitted from our bodies that can influence others. Taking sattvic foods, doing yoga, pranayama and meditation etc. boost the vital energy.

Therefore, remain conscious of your divine nature and divine goal; be elated that the ever-blissful Atman is inside you; love others, serve others, remain humble and respect others so that you can be more vivacious and energetic that will help you cross any hurdle during your spiritual journey.

*****

[79]**Manomaya Kosha (Mental Sheath):** The vital sheath is inside the physical sheath. Inside the vital sheath, there is mental sheath. Healthy body and a healthy mind are essential for spiritual journey. Mind either impels one to the goal or it may impede spiritual progress. Mind can be helpful for reaching the blissful state inside. When one reaches the blissful sheath, peace and bliss will be expressed in and through the other four sheaths such as intellectual, mental, vital and physical.

We are suffering which means we are in darkness of ignorance. God is known as Bliss-Absolute. Since we confine ourselves to the physical sheath and identify ourselves with the body, we are not able to attain bliss. When man reaches the blissful sheath, he will realise that he is neither the physical sheath, nor the vital sheath, neither the mental sheath nor the intellectual sheath. A sage, established in wisdom, has a physical body. The ignorant man also possesses a physical body. While the former lives in bliss, the latter undergoes sufferings. That is why the sages always instruct us to delve inside. When we meditate, we forget the physical body. When we sleep, we also forget the physical body.

In the blissful sheath, as the term indicates, there is bliss and bliss only. But an ordinary man does not experience the blissful sheath. Divya Darshan says, “Ignorance is the cause of sufferings.” Mind is usually inclined towards the objects and mundane pleasure. But things it enjoys are short-lived. There is intellect present inside. Intellect controls the mind. He, who will contemplate on True Self, will get bliss. We are given this physical body to help us realise the Self. But by identifying ourselves with the physical body, we forget

---

[79]*Odia Divyadhara Vol 16 Page 12*

the True Self. We must realise that this physical body is not the True Self. In other words, Self is independent of the physical body.

You must have a clear choice. Whether you want to live in peace and bliss, or you want to undergo sufferings? When you suffer, you start blaming others, even your parents, friends and relatives. Whether you believe in the presence of God or not, it is immaterial; but if you consider yourself as Bliss-Absolute and enjoy bliss, that is enough. There are various ways to attain bliss. When you get perturbed, at that time it may so happen that your intellect shows you some way to come out with some solution. All your worries go away. Similarly, sufferings will go away if you realise the bliss within you.

Brahman manifests as various forms and resides in all these forms. He is named as Atman when He resides inside any form. While explaining who Brahman is, the sages consider it necessary to start from 'Lila' or divine play by Brahman in innumerable forms and qualities. In this way they explain the greatness of Brahman. Finally, they indicate about the True Self of Brahman. The Mandukya Upanishad explains consciousness in four states such as waking, dream, sleep and transcendental. Brahman is present inside the jiva. At this state, He is called Atman. Even if He is Bliss-Absolute, he has four outer coverings such as intellectual sheath, mental sheath, vital sheath and physical sheath. In other words, the vital sheath is there inside the physical sheath, mental sheath is there inside vital sheath, intellectual sheath is there inside the mental sheath and blissful sheath is there inside the intellectual sheath. All the four outer sheaths are the manifestation of blissful sheath. Because of the presence of Atman, these sheaths become functional. Atman is there inside the blissful sheath. Ultimately, the blissful sheath also is to be transcended for realization of Brahman.

*****

[80]**Vijnanamaya Kosha (Intellectual sheath):** Intellectual sheath is there inside the mental sheath. There are certain things on which mind gets perplexed or confounded but by application of intellect, the problem gets solved. Intellectual sheath is the first covering of Atman. The physical sheath is the outermost covering of Atman. He, who can go deeper and deeper, can unravel the coverings and realise Atman who is eternally blissful. There is nothing called suffering so far as Atman is concerned. The entire Creation is the manifestation of Bliss. Bliss pervades everywhere and everything. Therefore, everything has some utility value. Brahman is therefore Bliss-Absolute. A child may ask "Why there is air or water? Why there are trees?" An elderly person knows the answers. Can anybody ask why there is mother or why there is cow or why there is rice? We get happiness and bliss from all these because there is bliss in everything. Both the Creator and the Creation are full of bliss. He, who realises this, attains Sajujya *Mukti*. As told earlier, beyond the blissful sheath, there is nirvikara state which is Nirvana. Some sages have gone up to Sat-Chit-Ananda state on realizing all-pervasive Bliss. Some sages have attained nirvikara state on transcending the blissful state. Common people cannot distinguish the different levels attained by the sages. Only a sage can recognize another sage.

Man gets both pleasure and pain. He speaks truth; and at the same time he also tells lies. He possesses some divine qualities as well as some demoniac qualities. For most of the persons, the suffering is more and happiness is less. Unless one surrenders to God, one will not get the bliss desired by him. The surrendered person gets God's blessings. Man must awaken his divine nature to attain Brahman. After unfolding the mysteries about the outer and

---

[80]*Odia Divyadhara Vol 16 Page 18*

inner sheaths, one realises the divinity within. There are some sages who speak about Brahman. Some sages speak about Truth. Some sages do not speak about Brahman but they impart knowledge on how to get rid of all types of sufferings.

The ordinary men in their quest for happiness and bliss run after material possessions. But those men, who have attained blissful state, realise the greatness of Brahman and enjoy bliss. No external object is necessary for them to enjoy bliss. No external situation is relevant for them to earn bliss. Bliss comes from within. They remain in blissful state irrespective of whether they sleep on the floor or on a cosy bed.

But pleasure seekers as we are, we run after different varieties of sense objects throughout our life and end up in sufferings. But the sages have minimum requirements that are essential for their living. They enjoy bliss everywhere and in all circumstances.

Although Guru is keen to impart true knowledge to the disciples, they do not evince much interest as a result of which their learning process gets slowed down. The physical body represents the Annamaya and Pranamaya kosha. There are Manomaya kosha and Vijnanamaya kosha representing the subtle body which are inside the physical body. Blissful sheath or Anandamaya kosha is the causal body. Brahman always remains in unqualified state, i.e. beyond the forms and qualities. He is the Supra-Causal factor. Due to our ignorance, we identify ourselves as the physical body only. He, who goes a little deeper, will know that he is the subtle body operating through the physical body. Further, he will know that he is the causal body. As one goes deeper and deeper, one's sufferings will get reduced.

During childhood, the children cry for chocolates and crave for impossible things. At the adult stage, those kinds of cravings and sufferings go away. There come new sets of desires and sufferings. Due to lesser knowledge, man gets attracted towards appearance. As his level of knowledge goes up, he gets attracted towards the qualities. When he goes on increasing his level of knowledge, he no longer gets attracted towards the forms and qualities. Intellectual sheath is the place of Devas. Man, by his conscience (Viveka), gets indications about the existence of a Supreme Power. Brahman manifests as knowledge by which man can get rid of all his sufferings. There is no other way for man to get rid of sufferings. Guru imparts only true knowledge to all.

He, who reaches Vijnanamaya kosha, gets a glimpse of Brahman just as we see the brightened sky at the horizon before sunrise. He starts enjoying bliss at that stage. As told earlier, the blissful sheath is the causal body. Beyond that, it is infinite Supra-Causal Existence which is unqualified (attributeless) and formless.

If you will intensify your spiritual efforts, by Guru's Grace, you can realise that you are That.

*****

[81]**Anandamaya Kosha (Blissful Sheath):** Blissful Sheath is the subtle-most sheath. Beyond this state, there is still higher state which is that of the Supreme Brahman. In this state nothing else is there, not even the 'I' sense. There is no second. Hence no comparison is possible. This state is the True Self. A spiritual mendicant after his spiritual efforts and acquisition of more and more knowledge attains this state where all paths end and merge, nothing more remains to be attained and nothing more remains to be known.

---

[81]*Odia Divyadhara Vol 16 Page 25*

Coming to the blissful sheath, the realiser enjoys untold bliss. He enjoys the manifestation of Truth in innumerable forms and qualities everywhere. Fears, doubts or anxieties are totally absent there. The jiva feeling goes away. This state is the equilibrating state of three qualities such as sattva, rajas and tamas. This is Sat-Chit-Ananda stage when he blissfully realises the Cosmic Form. The most sought-after valuable possession in this Creation is Bliss. It is the greatest attainment. There remains nothing other than peace and bliss. After transcending intellectual sheath, one attains blissful sheath.

The next higher state is Brahmi state. In this state there is no bliss and no thought. It is Pure Consciousness, ever wakeful. It is beyond pain and pleasure, weal and woe, monism or dualism, Chit or Achit, Sat or Asat. It cannot be expressed. The great Rishi Yajnavalkya had remained silent after telling 'Neti, Neti.' It means, "Not like this, not this much."

Now I am giving you some hints about Samadhi state. On realizing the Supreme Truth, the realiser gets astounded and remains unmoved there like a wooden log. This is called kashtha samadhi. In case of bhava samadhi, a realiser remains engrossed and concentrated in the thought of Brahman without having any other thought about any object or circumstance. Bhava is the essence of Jnana. Such realiser realises the state of bliss. Body consciousness is absent there. Another kind of samadhi is Dhyana Samadhi. While meditating on the Lila, greatness of Brahman or True Self, one gets established in Dhyana Samadhi through continuous contemplation on Brahman.

Consciousness manifests as Prana. Prana becomes inert at the time of death. When somebody dies, it means all activities done by Consciousness come to a stop. It is by Consciousness that all activities are done. He, who will contemplate on Consciousness, will get lost in that. Brahman or Atman is the MahaPrana. It is to be understood and appreciated that Brahman manifests as innumerable forms and qualities to fulfil all our needs and give us happiness. The sages can remain in samadhi state for a long time because during that period they enjoy bliss.

Divya Darshan says, "The more we know the value of certain thing, the more we like it and the more our mind gets attracted towards the same." Brahman is Supreme, most precious and all-powerful. He is the life, vitality and everything of every being. One will be inclined towards Him once one knows this. Due to want of spiritual knowledge, man is suffering. The more one knows about Brahman, the more one gets attracted towards Him. Hence Divya Darshan emphasizes on acquiring knowledge about Brahman. He is the basis of everything in the Creation. One must know about Brahman in order to get peace and bliss. There is no other way. Why should you ask for anything from Him before knowing about Him, His importance and indispensability? Through the Law of Eternity, He has made all arrangements and provided everything since our birth for fulfilment of all our needs. Nothing remains to be asked for. Only knowledge is necessary to make use of the things that are already in place. Divya Darshan says, "By acquiring knowledge, man can know about Brahman's perfect pre-arrangements, and fulfil all his basic needs." Only by knowing Brahman's greatness, man can quickly move into samadhi state. The Creation is all blissful. It is Brahman's manifestation. There shall be no discrimination between the small and the big. When one realises this, he enjoys permanent and infinite bliss. This is called Brahmananda. This is the state of Mahanirvana or *Moksa*. In other words, man has the potentiality to become Deva and thereafter Brahman. This means, after attaining divine nature, he will be merged in Brahman.

*****

[82]**The mystery of Om:** Subtle state of sound is *Naada*. *Naada* expresses itself as sound through vibration or waves. When our eardrum gets vibrated, we experience sound. Sound exists in the space in the form of waves. *Naada* is the cause and basis of vibrations and sound. *Naada* is a self-impelled spontaneous power that causes vibrations. *Naada* is subtle and inaudible whereas sound is audible.

In the Om above, there is a crescent moon symbol and on the top of it there is a dot. The crescent moon symbol represents Naada and the dot above is Bindu symbolizing Brahman. Naada is an expression of the Pure-Consciousness. It implies the inherent thought or will power of the Unitary Existence, i.e. Brahman. It is Naada that causes vibrations or waves that manifest as sound. While the common men can hear the sound, the wise men realise the Naada which is Brahman's Will that involves creation, sustenance and dissolution. In the invisible Creation, whatever exists are all waves caused by Naada. This means, the Unitary Existence pervades everywhere as Shabda-Brahman. It is Brahman who manifests as Naada, vibrations, waves and sound. In order to explain things, the sages divide this in two stages- Brahman and His manifestation. Hence the sages assert that there is nothing in this Creation, other than Brahman. He is not different from His manifestations. Example of fire may be cited here. Fire is nothing but light and heat. There remain heat and light

---

[82]*Odia Divyadhara Vol 15 Page 17*

inseparably in fire. Without light and heat, there is no substance called fire.

Brahman is Consciousness-Absolute. He wills. That is Naada. In other words, the Creation is the manifestation of Naada.

*****

[83]The mystery of 'Om' is the mystery of the entire Creation. Everything has emanated from 'Om'. When we talk of Creation, we mean the visible and the invisible, all forms and qualities. 'Om' has been treated by the scriptures as the eternal symbol of Paramatman. 'Om' is all inclusive. It means creation, sustenance and dissolution. It includes gross, subtle, causal and Supra-Causal existence. A-U-M together is pronounced as 'Om'. 'A' and 'U' represent forms and qualities respectively. The subtle state is the place of the Devas. This is the second quarter. The state 'M' from which all forms and qualities have emanated and are regulated is the third quarter. Let us discuss this in greater detail. It also represents the fourth state.

Brahman is there in everything. It means He manifests as all forms and qualities. Hence 'Om' includes everything from Brahman to the gross object. Nothing in the Creation is excluded from 'Om'. Hence meditating on 'Om', is as good as meditating on one and all. 'Om' manifests as all (inclusive of the gross, the subtle and the causal).

Brahman has neither form nor quality. He expresses Himself as 'Om'. It means, everything is well taken care of including creation, sustenance and dissolution. Brahman has two aspects viz: Nirguna and Saguna. He is essentially formless but manifests as forms. He is attributeless but manifests as attributes. But 'Om' includes both the

---

[83]*Odia Divyadhara Vol 10 Page 16*

aspects. It is all in one and one in all. Upanishads say, the entire Creation is full of Brahman or full of 'Om' which includes both visible and invisible universe, with attributes and without attributes.

As told earlier, 'Om' contains three alphabets such as A, U and M.

'A' represents gross world, which is described in scriptures as Virat, Agni, Prithvi, and Vaishwanara.

'U' represents the subtle world, which is named by the sages as Hiranyagarbha, Vayu and Taijas.

'M' represents the causal state which sages have named as Aditya, Praajna.

A- In the Creation, God is Supreme. Hence, He is called Virat. Virat in the form of Agni holds this gross world. All objects in this gross world are regulated by Agni that remains in everything as thermal energy. That is why plant kingdom as well as the animal kingdom is sustained. Even the minerals exist in their forms as they are supported by thermal energy.

U- This represents the subtle world from where the gross world has emanated and where every gross matter eventually gets dissolved. Hiranyagarbha is infinite. Anything created from out of it does not diminish it. Anything getting dissolved in it does not increase it. The plant kingdom as well as the animal kingdom lives on air. Taijas means Jyoti, Shakti, Prana, strength. Paramatman is Taijas.

M- M stands for Ishwar. He does everything including creation of any form, its sustenance and dissolution through the process of change. He is also called Aditya or Surya. Both Vayu and Agni are there in Aditya. Due to Surya, the plant kingdom as well as the animal kingdom is created and sustained by deriving energy from it. Hence, He is called Prana also.

'Om' is the greatest Mantra. All Devas, the animal kingdom and plant kingdom have emanated from 'Om'. All Mantras start with 'Om'. The wise people and the advanced aspirants meditate upon 'Om'. Not only humans, Devas also meditate upon 'Om'. Brahma, Vishnu, Maheswar, Laxmi, Saraswati and Durga etc. meditate upon 'Om'. Ishwar also meditates upon 'Om'. 'Om' manifests as Brahma, Vishnu and Maheswar. Brahma creates, Vishnu sustains the Creation and Maheswar modifies or dissolves the Creation. According to the Vedas, 'Om' is the chief name of Param-Brahman. Param-Brahman became 'Om'. Chanting 'Om' has got so many beneficial effects. Even the Devas get attracted towards 'Om' and descend to join Satsang where 'Om' is chanted, and its greatness discussed. It is to be remembered that wherever God's name is chanted, all bad things go away. If 'Om' is chanted with devotion, all sufferings vanish, and peace prevails.

It is said that thirty-three crore Devas reside in us, but we are searching for them outside. He, who delves deep inside, would get the answer. If we do not know the value of a currency note, we cannot make use of the same even if we possess a bundle of notes. It is like not having any. If you know the Devas, you will get blessings from them. If you do not know the Devas, how do you expect that you would get God's blessings? In order to know more and more about God and get His blessings, you should attend Satsang regularly. He can only save you from all sufferings since He is the Supreme.

*****

[84]We just now chanted 'Om' three times before beginning this spiritual session. By chanting 'Om' with devotion, a lot of benefits accrue to everyone. Its vibration is so powerful that all evils go away from the area. Even the Devas get attracted towards it. Devas also attend spiritual session or satsang being held anywhere. We get their blessings. Some Devas also get liberation in the process of listening to the high-level spiritual subjects. It is stated in various scriptures that wherever God's name is chanted, all bad things and harmful elements go away. While starting any auspicious work, we blow conch which gives the sound of 'Om'.

To remember and welcome God, one may chant His various names but His first and foremost name is 'Om'. By knowing the significance of 'Om', if someone chants this monosyllabic 'Om', all his sufferings go away. 'Om' is the dearest name of the Supreme. 'Om' is God, Ishwar, Brahman and Atman etc. He is inside all beings and everywhere. Since we do not search for Him inside, we do not get Him. That is why we are not getting the desired results from Him. We do not know about the gods, whom we worship. That is why we do not get the blessings of the gods and goddesses. Since we do not know about them, we do not have real devotion towards them; even we do not fully believe them. Even though we are always helped by the Devas, we are not able to know their contributions. We do not evince interest to know also. This is regrettable. Hence our first and foremost duty is to know about the Devas who are manifested forms of 'Om'. We must know about 'Om'. Hence, we should attend spiritual sessions and gather more and more knowledge in order to reinforce our devotion and love towards 'Om'.

---

[84]*Odia Divyadhara Vol 16 Page 43*

'Om' is the Supreme Lord of the Creation. He is the basis of all. Everyone should take shelter of this greatest power. He is the power of all other powers. He only can save us from all sins and sufferings. When we remember, chant or worship 'Om', all other gods and goddesses are automatically worshipped. He, who always remembers God, will not suffer. The moment he remembers God, he is near God or God is near him.

People have almost forgotten God in these days. In the Satya yug, people were having strong belief in God. They were living in peace and harmony. But now-a-days, people have either no idea or faint idea about God. Without God, how can we live in peace and happiness? Sanatan Dharma is based on the unitariness of Brahman, the Supreme. He, who will know the subject matters relating to Atman, will conduct himself in accordance with the Law of Eternity and will get rid of all sufferings. Although we suffer and lament, we do not try to find out how to come out of it. We neither try to know the cause of our sufferings nor try to find remedies to the same. The sages have handed down to us so many scriptures dilating on various ways to get rid of sufferings and earn peace and happiness. We also do not evince interest in the scriptural instructions.

The moment we chant 'Om', a divine feeling vibrates in us. If it is chanted with devotion and love, divine power is aroused. Collective chanting of 'Om' has still greater impact. The power centres in the body get activated. The greatness of 'Om' is ineffable. Before undertaking any work, we should remember 'Om'. By doing so, we stay connected with the Almighty throughout all our endeavours. Everyone should contemplate and meditate on the primordial energy, the Matrishakti to get blessings. Let all sufferings vanish. Let everyone live in peace and happiness.

*****

[85]**Aakash Tattva:** Before coming to this topic, we should know what the Aakash (sky) is. We normally think that the sky is above us and it is a blue canopy of heaven. Sky is void, colourless and formless. The scriptures categorise Akash under the five gross elements such as earth, water, fire, air and space (Aakash). From space the other four elements have come out. Many may not accept this. The sky is stated to be void which means shunya. Our doubt mainly hangs around how the visible universe could come from shunya which means void. But space is not shunya. Many stars and planets exist in the space. These stars and planets are of different shapes and sizes, different colours and different speed although some are stated to be stationary. But the space is not having any shape or colour. It does not move. It is everywhere. According to physical science, matter has three states-solid, liquid and gaseous. There is also a fourth state of matter. It is subtler than the other three states. Space contains all these. In other words, all these are in the womb of space. Entire universe takes shape in the vast womb of space. No example can be cited to explain the space. It is because any example, which is more often a known material, is picked up from out of the subsequently created gross world of matters. If question is raised as to whether the space is gross or subtle, the answer may be 'subtle'. But how much subtle it is, there is no answer to it.

Atom is not visible. Inside an atom so many protons, neutrons and electrons are on the move. There is also space inside atom. Otherwise the high-speed electrons could not have revolved. Still the scientists have been able to cognize and count them. To explain the subtle atoms they have said that in a drop of water if all atoms are labelled and mixed with the ocean, and subsequently a glass of water

---

[85]*Odia Divyadhara Vol 4 Page 8*

is collected from the ocean, it would be seen that the glass of water contains some labelled atoms. Further space is subtler than electrons otherwise electrons would not have moved.

Among the rays such as Alpha, Beta and Gamma, Gamma rays have the highest penetrating power. It can penetrate a 6" thick lead plate very easily which indicates that the space is subtler than the Gamma rays. Because space is subtlest it is all pervasive. It is the base of everything else. According to Upanishads, Gargi asked Rishi Yajnavalkya, "Basing upon what the plant kingdom, the animal kingdom, all stars and planets exist?" The answer given by Rishi Yajnavalkya was "Aakash"- the Space. Brahman is attributeless and also with attributes. Nirguna tattva is known as Para and Saguna as Apara. Nirguna is subtle and Saguna having forms and qualities is gross. *Apara Shakti* has taken the form of the visible universe. The different powers of Brahman are called personal godheads. When *Apara Shakti* gets transformed from the subtle to the gross we come across different forms. It is a well-known scientific fact that energy gets transformed to matter and matter to energy. The invisible universe is packed with and made of energy. This is called super-sensual state. Preta tattva, Devata Tattva come under this state. The visible universe is always influenced by the invisible universe. Everything in the visible universe is controlled and impelled by the invisible universe. The invisible state is the source of everything in the visible universe. The stars and planets are created from Nebulae. Those nebulae are created from space. They come from the space and get automatically dissolved in the space. Everything we come across such as stars, planets, five gross elements, five subtle elements, all gases, all matters, different forms of energy, mind, intellect, animal kingdom, plant kingdom, mineral kingdom, the personal godheads and Brahman etc. are all in the space.

That is why Brahman is compared with space. While trying to hint upon Brahman normally the example of space is cited relating to His greatness, all-pervasiveness and true nature. If Aakash or space is completely understood the subject matter of Brahman can also be understood.

The ancient sages knew about the space and its contents. The creation of various rays, their radiation, their effects, magnetic effects, various waves such as magnetic, light and sound were all known to them. They also knew about stars and planets. That is why they have dealt with Astronomy, Astrology and Tantra etc. It is said that Rishi Vishwamitra had created one more heaven in the space by the powers of his Tapas. It is also said that they were using spacecrafts in which the rays were used as fuels. They were soundless crafts because of which Ravana took away Sita in the aircraft named Pushpak. The aircraft could be made invisible as and when required and could reach any destination, even a remote place named Panchavati.

All these things are normally discarded by the intelligent men as mere myths as these are beyond their intellectual and logical powers to conceive any such thing. But how such imaginations could occur to Rishi Valmiki if such concepts were not present at all in those days?

In the Kali Yug, all the ancient knowledge has almost lapsed into oblivion. In our modern scientific age, again we are trying to explore things by employing different methods and technologies and carrying out various experimentations. Whatever we know about the space, are minimal or too little. A lot more remain to be explored. The sages had mastered the knowledge on space and therefore they had supernatural powers. They could ultimately realise the Param-Brahman who is the basis of all.

*****

[86]**Shunya Upasana (Worship of the void):** I shall tell you how to worship the void. There are different types of worship undertaken by different types of devotees. Worshipping the void is also another way. Some classes of devotees lay emphasis on worshipping the void. The common people are surprised to hear about void worship. They consider it absurd. They cannot even think of void worship. Worship is not possible without some form, they believe. But void worship is important and useful. Void worship is the best kind of worship. Those who are making spiritual efforts are to necessarily resort to worshipping the void.

Some think that single pointedness would come only if some form is kept before them. But the fact is that mind shall be stilled, or single-pointedness of mind would be achieved better while worshipping void. Void means nothingness. Still there is something which the sense organs cannot reach. In the scriptures Brahman is stated to be only one who should be meditated upon. According to the Advaita Philosophy, only One must be meditated upon since One is the only Truth. All others are transitory. That unitary existence has no specific form or quality. He is beginningless and endless. He is all-pervasive. An idol is not all-pervasive. Mind gets restricted to the form of idol only. Single-pointedness cannot be achieved by idol worship. On the one hand, we know that God is all-pervasive and at the same time when we meditate upon an idol in a limited area or surrounding, our mind would not be able to discard others and remain restricted to the idol only. The thought of all-pervasiveness would not easily come while meditating on a specific idol or idols. Mind can think of only one thing at a time and not many things. It

---

[86]*Odia Divyadhara Vol 7 Page 45*

moves from point to point amazingly fast. Sense organs distract the mind from one thing to the other. This is fickleness of mind

When we meditate on an idol, we see the whole body of the idol. There are many parts of the idol such as eyes, nose, ears, forehead etc. Where to concentrate? On the mouth or on the forehead; on the eyes or on the ears? Mind would shift from one limb to another. Concentration may be better when we focus ourselves on a flame or one point.

Since God is all-pervasive, we cannot restrict Him to any idol. Hence if we meditate on the void, we will have better concentration. God is formless, hence limitless. This is why real meditation is to meditate on True Self.

Void is not nothingness. It is all-pervasive and eternal existence. It has neither forms nor qualities. It has no comparison or simile. Brahman is one and secondless. Close your eyes or keep them open, it is immaterial. The Paramatman is always Shunya. While meditating on Shunya, all thoughts and imaginations of the mind shall also become nil. By meditating on the Shunya, we transcend the forms and qualities. Play of the mind also stops. Generally void (Shunya) is compared to Aakash (space). What shall we say about Aakash; small or big? Is it long or wide? Is there any upside or downside? Is there any colour? Hence Brahman is likened to Aakash. Space does not indicate any specific area or region. It means all-pervasiveness. God should be meditated upon as Shunya. This thought of Shunya is endless. It will not be completed even after hours, days, months and years. Shunya is beginningless and endless. Hence whole life is inadequate to meditate upon Shunya which is inexhaustible. Even births after births would not be sufficient to assess the magnitude and extensiveness of Shunya. When we meditate upon a limited form, our thoughts on size and shape, beauty or ugliness of the object of meditation, may disturb the mind. Therefore, meditating on Shunya will bring in concentration faster. The spiritual mendicant can reach Nirvikalpa Samadhi (non-dual state) quicker through Shunya meditation. In fact, the unbridled thoughts of our mind distract our attention and therefore obstruct our meditation. Hence, one must bear in mind that Paramatman has neither forms nor qualities. He is Shunya...Shunya....MahaShunya!

The sages and seers in order to explain things to the common persons descend to a lower level and express Shunya or space as Brahman. Common people may not be able to meditate upon Shunya. In Shunya meditation, all thoughts and imagination of the mind shall get annulled. All the past feelings and ideas gathered in several births would be deleted. The sages and seers were doing this type of meditation on Shunya because of which they were able to realise the Supreme Truth.

Brahman is compared with Akash (Space). We possess some knowledge on Akash (Space) but not fully. Now let us discuss about Akash (Space).

Out of the five gross elements, Akash is the first element from which other four elements have come forth. Air is created from out of Akash, fire from air, water from fire and the earth is created from water. While we are able to perceive and feel the four elements, we are not able to perceive Akash (space). Air also cannot be seen. At times, we can see the gaseous state. All these four gross elements were initially in invisible state. At a subsequent state when they got condensed and assumed gross forms at that time, we could see them.

In and around all stars and planets, the force of attraction is ever at work. Atmospheric layer is also there surrounding the planets.

Atmospheric pressure is different in different planets. Somewhere there is thick layer and somewhere thin. Up to that limit i.e. the atmospheric area, we call Akash and beyond that, we call Mahakash. We experience the changes within the atmospheric area or where the force of attraction is at work. Wind blows in this area. The birds fly in this area. Clouds are formed to come to us as rain. Aeroplanes also fly in this area. Man's feet are on earth, but he moves in the sky.

Mahakash: Where there is no air or no force of attraction, that area is known as Mahakash or Antariksha.

Scriptures while explaining about the Creation say, "Brahman willed to be many." Brahman is formless and is without any quality. The Akash is also formless and is without any quality. From this state only, all forms and qualities have come out. From the space, the other four elements such as air, fire, water and earth have come out. This indicates that from the formless, all forms are created. From the attributeless, all attributes are created. There is no form or quality ascribed to the space. All the stars and planets have been created from out of the space. Even if we say there was nothing, it means that there was something. 'Nothingness' signifies absence of forms and qualities. According to Science all stars and planets have come from nebulae. Then where nebulae have come from?

Nebulae are created from out of space. The Rishis say that Brahman is like the space. First manifestation of Brahman is space. Brahman is all-pervasive like the space. Hence, when a spiritual mendicant meditates upon Brahman as Shunya, there is nothing wrong in that. If we ascribe any form or quality to Brahman, it means we are restricting or limiting the infinite Brahman. When everything is created from out of space, what else it can be other than Brahman?

The more we expand our thoughts, the more knowledge we would get. Hence, why should we not meditate upon Brahman considering Him to be all-pervasive like the space which is Shunya?

There is also Brahman in the forms or idols. But since the idols are limited by forms, our thoughts also get restricted accordingly. Hence it is much better to meditate on Brahman as Shunya where there is no boundary or limitation.

Shunya meditation amounts to direct worship of Brahman, without any other personal godhead in between. The Devas represent different powers of Brahman. If we meditate upon the limited, the results shall also be limited.

While doing Shunya meditation, there is no need for any gross objects or offerings like fruits, flowers and incense-sticks. Shunya is such a vast expanse of existence that even after meditating upon the same for years and years, it shall not end. Inside Shunya, how much fruits, flowers, sandal wood paste and incense sticks are there, one cannot imagine.

Oh Lord! How beautiful is your temple! How divine and how much vast the same is! I cannot imagine even how much treasure and beautiful things are there inside your temple! All these are yours. I have nothing to call my own which I can offer to you. How can I express the greatness of the Shunya Mandir!

Oh Lord! You do not have any form or quality. You have nothing but you are there everywhere as everything. Everything means whatever one can imagine. Therefore, Shunya Worship is the best worship by which the goal can be realised faster.

*****

[87]**Concept of Time (Kala):** Because of time we come to know about something. Because of time we can see something. The knower and the known, the seer and the seen are possible because of time. Without time nothing exists. Time measures the distance between birth and death, creation and dissolution of anything. Whatever we come across are all within the ambit of creation, sustenance and dissolution. Normally the gap between the two events or occurrences is measured by time. For our convenience we have divided time into year, month, week, day, minutes, seconds and moments.

Whatever happens whether the same is within time? Whether time comes first, or God comes first? With our limited knowledge we say that everything happens in the womb of time. Now the question is who created time? God is eternal and all-pervasive. Kala or time comes next. God has manifested as the Creation. Whatever we come across in the Creation are all names and forms arising due to continuous changes. Whatever is being created remains for some time and thereafter it gets dissolved. Due to these changes we experience time. If there is no change, the question of time does not arise at all. God has made time; otherwise the creation, sustenance and dissolution could not have taken place. Since God is there, his Creation goes on and his play goes on. It is to be understood that time is also there.

When the time distance is big, man at that time cannot measure the same. His arithmetic does not work. At that time man uses the term 'Kala'. Just as God has neither any beginning nor end, similarly time is also beginningless and endless. God and 'Kala' are co-extensive. Hence Kala is construed as Shakti or power and is named

---

[87]*Odia Divyadhara Vol 4 Page 13*

as the Goddess Kali. Kali is considered as immensely powerful in whom everything happens and gets dissolved in due course.

Goddess Kali is dark in complexion wearing garlands made of human skulls. This is symbolic presentation of Kala which dissipates everything. The process of dissipation goes on always. Kala is unknown and unknowable. Hence people worship Kali as a Goddess possessed of great powers.

The idea behind worshipping Kali is to conquer Kala. The personal godheads are all there within Kala. Personal godheads come and go within the vast expanse of time. Unless one transcends time, one cannot get rid of time. To worship Kali for this purpose, she has been assigned a form which has a dark complexion, elongated tongue and her neck is laced with a garland of human skulls.

Changes do take place always; something changes slowly and something very fast. The birth and death occur within one moment in respect of certain things. Some of the things are created and destroyed within a minute. It takes millions of years for swamp forests to become coal. For creation of diamond also it takes thousands of years. There are certain matters which get transformed to other forms in thousands of years. Arithmetic fails when we consider the age of the Sun and other stars. Our intelligence makes a retreat. Then, it is called 'Mahakala'. The Suns and other stars which have been created will also be dissolved in Mahakala one day.

Within our limited knowledge we try to measure time using various units. Mahakala is that where knowledge cannot reach. Everything gets manifested in the womb of Mahakala. Who can escape this Mahakala? Who can surpass Mahakala?

It has been explained in various scriptures that the Creation took place when Brahman willed to become many. Various forms came into being. The difference or gap in the process of change is called time.

Brahman is there. Atman is there. God is there. Because He is there, the Creation is also there. Because Creation is there full of changes and is made of changes, the question of time becomes relevant.

He, who realises True Self, experiences, "I am always there; I have no death". It is to be understood that he has surpassed time. Death occurs in the time frame. What is death? It is the end of a specific form. He, who realises that he always exists, is above the timeframe. He is the conqueror of death and time. He, who thinks, "I am mind, I am intellect, I am the body", has birth and death. In the time frame he is born, undergoes changes and ultimately dies. Those sages and seers, who have reached the highest state, assert that they have conquered death and conquered time too. Even after destruction of the body also a realised soul can appear in any form. What do we call Him who is ever-present? He is always there as Atman.

Hence the realised souls are God in forms. They can do anything they like. Hence the sages are conquerors of death. Such sages are incomparable. There is heaven and hell difference between a sage and a common man although both are in human forms. Time kills us moment by moment whereas the sages have conquered death as well as time. Time is always wakeful. Time never takes rest. Due to ignorance we are not able to know this. Whatever names and forms are there in the kingdom of nature shall one day be lost in the nature itself. There is Kala present in nature, and it sustains nature.

"But I shall rise from nature and shall get back my True Self." He, who is always eager to realise Atman or Brahman, is awake. He, who is awake, alone can realise Brahman and conquer death and time.

He, who is unconscious about this, is asleep. Kala tramples over him who is asleep. We all have seen the picture where Kali is dancing over Lord Shiva who is asleep. We are all asleep. That is why Kala is annihilating everyone including plants, animals and humans. He, who will conquer Kala, would get rid of all sufferings, shall enjoy bliss and shall realise Brahman. In other words, even if we are having all powers latent in us, due to our ignorance, Kala tramples over us. Therefore, the advanced souls are conscious and with single pointed devotion engage themselves day and night on spiritual practices. By merely chanting some mantra, death cannot be overcome. One must acquire right knowledge and possess divine virtues. He, who possesses divine virtues, would have more God-consciousness. Such a person can get rid of all sufferings and realise True Self.

*****

[88]**Astrology and space science:** Astrology is a space science. Astrology is an extension of astronomy. Astrology is important because by this study, everything like past, present and future can be known. Many people believe in astrology. Astrology is quite popular in Egypt, Babylon and Greece. But the critics discard astrology as blind belief. Astrology was developed in India 4500 years ago. Even many texts are available which are dated back to 300 and 1700 BC.

Astrology is one of the six limbs of the Vedas. The sages of yesteryears had linked astrology to observance of Dharma. Stars, planets, solar position and lunar position in relation to the earth are also linked to some festivals and Dharmic rituals. Everything has effects on others. So are the stars and planets whose movements or positions affect the plant life, animal life and our planet as a whole.

---

[88]*Odia Divyadhara Vol 4 Page 3*

What is the basis of astrology (Jyotish Vidya)? Jyoti means rays of light. Jyotishka means stars and planets. Since rays of light come out from the stars and planets, it can be said that they are all forms of light. Effects of the light rays are different from one star or planet to the other.

According to science, every matter is made of atoms and molecules. They are all changing always because inside the atoms, the electrons, protons and neutrons are changing position continuously. Because of changes, we come across the Creation, its sustenance and dissolution. Different forms and qualities are also seen due to changes. For example, changes occur in the iron atoms on heating of iron and different types of rays are emitted by iron particles. The emitted rays such as light and heat have effect on other matters. Due to this light the nearby objects or air gets heated up. These effects vary from matter to matter. The rays are also different from matter to matter. Astrology is mainly based on the effects of changes of planetary positions. In other words, astrology is mainly based on the rays emitted by different planets and stars. Rays are of different colours. The nature of rays also depends upon the intensity of changes and type of the matter. Although these rays are not visible its effects are there.

Even the sunrays are not visible. We see the sunrays only when they are reflected on any matter. Light appears white or bright even though it carries seven colours such as V~I~B~G~Y~O~R. The effects of different colours are also different. In this Creation starting from stars and planets to the plant kingdom and animal kingdom, there are heterogeneities. They are also composed of different ingredients. The Earth where we live in is surrounded by various stars and planets.

We all know that every matter including birds and animals, human body, stars and planets are made of five gross elements. According to science, they are made of innumerable atoms and molecules. That is why it is said that whatever is there in the Creation is also there inside us. Whatever is there in the universe is also there inside the individual body. It is quite natural and true. Since everything is built of atoms and molecules whatever occurs outside, their effects will also be there on us. Everything has effect on others. Somewhere the effects are perceivable and somewhere not. It should be remembered that in respect of all created things, their sustenance and dissolution also take place in the source from which they are created. In other words, any matter which is created based on something, on that base it rests and ultimately in that it gets dissolved. The past, present and future of any matter are all linked to the base from which the same is created (Example-The pot and the clay)

By Sunlight, the plants and animals survive. Where there is no light, there is neither plant nor animal. The plants grow and bear flowers and fruits of different colours because of Sunlight. At the time of Sunset some plants close their leaves and reopen at Sunrise. Some flowers get their sustenance from moon beam. The humans are also quite dependent upon sunlight. Their waking up, working and sleeping depends upon the Sun. This shows what an intimate relationship we have with the rays. We make intense use of X-rays. Radium rays are used to treat cancer. In other words, the invisible rays are doing so much for us. The rays coming from every matter according to their nature or qualities have the power of creating, sustaining and dissolving. The ancient sages had studied the effects of every mysterious ray and the combined reactions of multiple rays of various stars and planets from different directions and distances on the Earth and its inhabitants.

Accordingly, the sages were conducting themselves and could find out ways and means to escape the wrath of the harmful rays. For example, the time of birth and place of birth have different dynamics in relation to the planetary and stellar positions. Their effects will be there on the bodies constituted of the five gross elements particularly of a new-born whose appearance, complexion, mental and intellectual powers were foretold. According to the rays the new-born would have different smell and shall have different qualities. On examining these aspects, the male and female horoscope matching is done for marriage purpose. It is clear from the above that the rays of the different planets and stars are impacting the life on this planet. Aryabhatta, Varah Mihir, Khana etc. have made great contribution in this field. The pyramid of Egypt was built based on Astronomy. Great scientist Galileo had invented telescope. Science has contributed a lot to space science in recent years. Nine planets and 27 stars are normally considered for astrological studies. Any change in the Sun and its periphery greatly impacts the earth as a result of which earthquakes, volcanic eruptions, tornado and landslides etc. occur impacting the lives and properties on this earth. Astrology can be compared with a mirror. By the knowledge of astrology, we can remain alert and know about favourable and unfavourable situations happening and which are yet to happen.

Human body is constituted of five elements such as Earth, Water, Fire, Air and Space. The Earth which is also constituted of five elements has close connection with the Sun and the Moon. Hence a man's mental and physical states are always impacted by the changes taking place in them. Therefore, to escape from diseases, disasters and natural calamities and to maintain mental balance, knowledge of Astrology helps a lot.

It is to be remembered that there is a cause behind every effect. In other words, no effect will be there without a cause. Once we can analyse the cause and know the cause, we may also be in a position to control the effects to some extent. We are all bound by the cause and effect relationship. The Almighty can only release us from the bondage of cause and effects. Astrology is a great help to us in this regard.

*****

[89]**Devata tattva (The Personal Godheads):** Man can understand God's greatness by acquiring more and more knowledge about God. Based on knowledge, he loves and respects God. Soon he realises that everything is done by God. Behind all activities in this Creation, God's role is there. On knowing all these, he finally surrenders to God. Without knowing the greatness of God, how can anybody surrender to God?

It is therefore essential for the man to acquire spiritual knowledge. Without spiritual knowledge, man cannot live in a proper manner. By acquiring true knowledge, man finally realises that he is the Self-Absolute or Pure Consciousness. We should therefore transcend all other levels to reach the level of Pure Consciousness. By knowledge, we come to know that there is God. The realisers have direct experience of God. Many people, even without acquiring knowledge about God, have faith on God due to their past impulses (samskara). On the other hand, there are many qualified persons who have mastered different branches of knowledge but cannot believe in the existence of God. They do not bother to know the truth about how and from where the five elements came into existence

---

[89]*Odia Divyadhara Vol 18 Page 35*

before we were born; how nature (prakriti) was there before we were born and how consciousness (chetana) was there before the nature came into being. After taking birth, how we grow up? How food gets digested and how the blood circulation process in us is always on? How the respiratory system works so perfectly? Who has made all provisions for all creatures to be born, to grow and live with happiness? Who has created all the required minerals, water, fire and air for the Creation to come into existence and continue to exist? Who is the unchangeable essence triggering all changes silently and unnoticeably? Knowing all these things is called true knowledge.

In absence of spiritual knowledge many people turn out to be non-believers. Anybody who will know about the greatness of God and the essential role He plays for our creation, survival etc., will start believing in God. It is the duty of all of you to spread true knowledge among the people so that they will take to divine path and will reach the divine goal. By acquiring knowledge one can move from tamasic quality to rajasic quality and from rajasic to sattvic quality. When a man will reach sattvic quality, he will hesitate to do wrong things and will prefer to walk on the path of Dharma. He would like to sacrifice for others and render services to them. Unless men possess sattvic quality, how will Satya Yug come? How will the people live in peace and happiness? Hence, it is our duty to spread the spiritual knowledge among the people for their well-being. It is not enough if you alone become knowledgeable. You must also try to spread this knowledge so that others will also learn. With this purpose, Divya Darshan has come. For the cause of peace and happiness in the society and to welcome Satya Yug, all of you should try in this regard.

Now I (Sadguru Sri Sri Arjun) will tell you something about the Devas. You should know layer after layer and ultimately realise the indivisible Pure Consciousness.

With limited and fragmented knowledge, man thinks that he is the doer of everything. Who can say this? He, who has realised the Supreme Consciousness, can say this. If someone says so with limited knowledge, it is sheer ignorance only. The sages who have realised the Supreme state can say so. Everything is done only by God.

From the point of view of highest spiritual knowledge, the different powers of Brahman are named after different Devas. The Devas play important roles for the creation of human beings also. All activities of the Creation such as rain, light, sunrise and sunset etc. are all done by the Devas. But man, due to his ignorance, is unable to understand that the Devas are doing so many things for our survival and happiness.

We have named the fire God as Agnidev, water God as Varunadev, air God as Vayudev, and the Sun as Sun God. The Devas are vested with various powers because of which we are benefited by them. Like this there are Gods like, Indra, Varuna, Kuber, Brahma, Vishnu, Maheswar, Ganesh, Kartikeya, Laxmi and Saraswati, Durga etc. We shall now discuss how we are always benefited by the Devas.

When we want to cook rice, first we decide for how many persons we shall cook and how much rice is required. Accordingly, we choose the utensil of appropriate size. We decide how much water is to be put and how much fire is to be used and how long. This is called knowledge about cooking rice. The presiding duty of knowledge is Goddess Saraswati. Buddhi also plays a role here. The knowledge and buddhi you have applied do not belong to you. They belong to Goddess Saraswati and Lord Ganesh respectively. Whatever water and fire you use, belong to Varuna and Agni respectively. For the fire to burn, the support of Vayu is indispensable. It can be seen from the above that the food is cooked with the help of divine powers. But without giving credit to the divine powers, we say that we have cooked the food. The strength we have used to make all these arrangements belongs to Mother Durga. Nothing is ours. By whom it rains? The blowing of the wind, the burning of the fire are all divine powers. Certain visible things become invisible and invisible things become visible due to divine powers. In the darkness, we cannot see any object. It is due to the presence of light or the Sun God only that we can see any object. Because of the fire within us, our food gets digested. The excretory system in our body has been made possible because of Vayu. In absence of water, fire and air we cannot survive. The vital parts of our body cannot function. The foregoing discussions are only indicative. Long or endless list is there about the role functions of the divine powers. Whether it is the kingdom of nature or even our own physical bodies, all processes are active due to the divine powers. Without the strength or power bestowed upon us by the divine powers, we could not have lifted our hands even. The various divine powers are named after different personal godheads. They are here to execute the powers delegated to them by the Supreme Lord. They have been serving everyone in the Creation. That is why we survive. Behind all happenings in the Creation, the Supreme Lord's perfect or most efficient system of planning, organization, direction and control is at work. But due to ignorance, we are not able to understand His designs. We consider ourselves to be the doers of everything.

Since everything is gifted to us by the divine powers, it is our duty to express our gratitude to the gods and goddesses by performing different rituals, sacrifices, worship and chanting of mantra. We try to appease Agni, Vayu, Varuna, Indra, Vishnu and Maheswar etc. We worship Durga, Kali, Laxmi and Saraswati as a mark of our respect, love and devotion to them. As told earlier, those are all names of different divine powers. He, who realises the role functions of the divine powers, will spontaneously love and respect the personal godheads. We cannot live without water, but we do not want to know about Varuna Deva. We inhale air but we do not want to know about Vayu Deva. We use heat and light, but we do not respect Agni Deva. The more we love and respect the personal godheads the more shall we be benefited by them. Those, who get blessings from Devas, will get blessings from the Supreme Lord. You might have heard that the sages can do wonderful things. It is because Devas are pleased with them. They all do things for the sages.

Those, who do not understand Devas, cannot understand the Supreme Lord. Knowledge is essential to know about Devas and their Creator, the Supreme Lord. He, who acquires knowledge, realises Brahman and thereafter Param-Brahman, realises True Self. Do you respect the concerned Deva while taking bath? Remember that by taking bath, you are cleaning your body and remaining healthy. By taking water, your thirst gets quenched. Pay respect to water. Conserve water. Do never disregard water mistaking it for just an ordinary or worthless material. Devas do not have any form. For example, Agni Dev does not have a specific form. When He manifests, we see Him in different forms. Unless we recognize the divine powers by which we get all direct benefits always, how can we know the Supreme Lord who is there at the background of everything? In other words, without acquiring knowledge we cannot realise the Supreme Truth who is Bliss-Absolute, Freedom-Absolute, Eternal, Infinite and the Indivisible Whole. He is the True Self.

*****

Epilogue

Divya Darshan is full with philosophy of life and teaches the very purpose of life. The secret of divine knowledge is explained in a very simple manner.

Divya Darshan lays stress on divine virtues and knowledge to get rid of all sins and sufferings. Human life is a rare opportunity to move from ignorance to wisdom.

We are intrinsically divine but have taken human form temporarily and we have forgotten that. By spiritual efforts and Sadguru's Grace, we can regain our lost paradise.

A man must know how to live, what to do and what not to do, what goal is to be pursued, from where his journey began, what are the laws/rules to be followed and which path is to be followed to reach the destination, what should be his thoughts, what should be his conduct and how shall he maintain his social life to earn peace and happiness. A man must know what truth is and what righteousness is. Further he must know his duties and responsibilities.

Divya Darshan says, "If you want to live, be dutiful; if you want peace and happiness, possess divine virtues; if you want freedom, acquire self-knowledge." In the path of knowledge, all the three (apparently three but essentially one) such as Karma, Bhakti and Jnana get synchronised, enhanced and perfected so that the seeker can attain the Supreme who is formless, attributeless and blissful. In other words, all the three such as Karma, Bhakti and Jnana as they come under the purview of knowledge, should happen simultaneously and not by trying on the same one after another.

Ignorance is a great sin. Ignorance is the cause of sufferings. Knowledge of Brahman is essential to come out of doubts, despair and all sorts of sufferings. Brahman being all-pervasive need not be searched for in any specific place outside in any forest or mountain. He will listen and respond wherever you will remember Him. He, who searches for God here and there, has not understood the all-pervasive Brahman. We all shall be merged with Him one day. One manifests as many. Many will be merged in one. This is the Law of the Universe. This is the theory of monism. Every form is a form of Brahman. Every quality is a quality of Brahman. Every name is a name of Brahman. Every power is Brahman's power. Every consciousness is Brahman's consciousness. All knowledge is Brahman's knowledge. Every truth is a manifestation of Brahman, the Truth-Absolute. Brahman must be realized to get rid of all sins and sufferings, to be released from all the worldly bondages, and to get bliss and freedom. Brahman is the Supreme Truth. He is the goal.

People now-a-days ask the question, "What is the necessity of spiritual knowledge? We are doing our duties and earning our livelihood. What does God do for us? What benefit shall accrue by knowing or thinking about God?" In reply, this much can be said that most of the people now-a-days do not know what all their duties are. What for he is born? What for he is living? By whom he has come into existence and by whom he is able to survive? What is the goal of human life? He has been living a mechanical life without knowing the meaning and purpose of it. Answer to all these questions can be had from spiritual knowledge. Man is not conscious that his duty essentially involves truth, propriety, righteousness and many other divine qualities. He is also not aware that his duty is inextricably connected with the goal of his life. Duty is a stepping-stone towards the goal. In other words, without duty, goal is not achieved.

Finally, Sadguru Sri Sri Arjun gives loud message to the entire mankind as follows: "Oh, mankind! Forgetting your true self and mistaking this stage as your abode and unreal role as your 'self', how long will you continue to be tortured in the frying cauldrons of lust and greed, pride and prejudice?

Arise! Enkindle the flame of awareness within. Get ready to return to your peaceful, immortal and heavenly abode and get back your eternal, true and pure self. Then only you will free yourself from all miseries and fears.

Remember! You are the immortal and emancipated soul."

*****

Reference to Divyadhara (Odia)

Prologue

1. Divyadhara - 11, Divya Darshan Vichara Dhara, Page -19

2. Divyadhara - 15, Shanka o Samadhana-1, Page -26

Chapter - 1 (The Supreme Truth)

3. Divyadhara -18, Satyabodha, Page -46

4. Divyadhara - 20, Satya O Maya, Page -36

5. Divyadhara -13, Amrit Bindu 42, Page -8

Chapter - 2 (Self-Knowledge)

6. Divyadhara -4, Mun Kiye, Page -21

7. Divyadhara -17, Atma Jnana, Page -30

8. Divyadhara -10, Adhyamtika Jnana (Introduction), Page -1

9. Divyadhara -19, Durlabh Manisha Janma, Page -45

10. Divyadhara -6, Adhyamtika Jnana Sambandh, Page -6

11. Divyadhara -19, Shanti, Ananda *Mukti*, Page -49

12. Divyadhara -8, Atma Tatva Sambhandera, Page -17

13. Divyadhara -7, Jiva Brahman Samparka o Brahman nka Avadana, Page -7

14. Divyadhara -7, Atma Dvara Atmanku Labha Kara Jaye, Page -12

15. Divyadhara -15, Sthula o Sukhma, Page -23

16. Divyadhara - 20, Sthula o Sukhma, Page - 36

17. Divyadhara -15, Shanka o Samadhana-2, Page -30

18. Divyadhara -15, Veda Vedanta ra Araparira Katha, Page -40

19. Divyadhara -17, Advaita siddhanta, Page -25

20. Divyadhara -8, Mahakarana, Page -9

21. Divyadhara -8, Chetana o Satya, Page -12

22. Divyadhara -8, Shakti, Page -14

23. Divyadhara -14, Indriya Sanyama, Page -42

24. Divyadhara -12, Gita Saransh, Page -35

25. Divyadhara -18, Srimad Bhagavad-Gita o Adhyamtika Jnana, Page -50

26. Divyadhara -17, Dharma o Sv*Adharma* Palana, Page -40

27. Divyadhara - 20, Jnana Yoga, Page -42

28. Divyadhara -17, Siddhi, Page -4

Chapter - 3 (Dharma in the Context of Spirituality)

29. Divyadhara -1,Dharma Kana, Page -3

Chapter - 4 (The Greatness of God)

30. Divyadhara - 20, Atma Chetana, Page -12

31. Divyadhara -17, Bhagabana nka Abadana, Page -53

32. Divyadhara -5, Atma Puja, Page -40

33. Divyadhara -5, Adhyamtika Achara o Adhyamtikata, Page -45

34. Divyadhara - 20, Amrit Bindu 82, Page -59

35. Divyadhara -12, Atma Samikhya, Page -5

36. Divyadhara -13, Amrit Bindu 56, Page -32

37. Divyadhara -3, Bhagbata Upalabdhi, Page -16

38. Divyadhara -3, Bhagbananka Astitva o Parichay, Page -37

39. Divyadhara -8, Bhagbananku Anubhava Kariba Kipari, Page -25

40. Divyadhara - 20, Grace of the Supreme, Page -6

41. Divyadhara -10, Bhagaban Kiye, Page -34

42. Divyadhara - 20, True knowledge & Brahman, Page -9

43. Divyadhara -2, Brahman jnana kana kahuchi, Page -21

44. Divyadhara - 20, Amrit Bindu 60, Page -53

45. Divyadhara -6, Bhagbananka Parichaya o Abadana, Page -13

46. Divyadhara -15, Amrit Bindu 67, Page -53

47. Divyadhara -13, Amrit Bindu 64 65, Page -42

48. Divyadhara -6, Maya Achi o Nahin Madhya, Page -39

49. Divyadhara - 20, Srimad Bhagavad-Gita, Page -39

50. Divyadhara -8, Bhagbananka Mahanata Abadan o Svarupa, Page -4

51. Divyadhara -10, Jnanara Mahima, Page -7

52. Divyadhara -10, Yoga, Page -39

53. Divyadhara -15, Jiva o Iswara, Page -14

54. Divyadhara -17, Brahman nka Atmaprakash, Page -21

55. Divyadhara -9, Guru Nanak Vani, Page -25

Chapter - 5 (Gurutattva)

56. Divyadhara -9, Gurutatva, Page -39

57. Divyadhara -6, Gurutatva, Page -1

58. Divyadhara - 20, Who is Guru, Page -15

59. Divyadhara -12, Adhymtika Jnana o Sadguru Kripa, Page -21

60. Divyadhara -12, Guru Tatva o Guru Shakti, Page -30

61. Divyadhara -11, Guru Shakti, Page -3

62. Divyadhara -10, Omkar o Guru, Page -12

63. Divyadhara -16, Iswara o Guru, Page -53

64. Divyadhara -4, Dikhya ra Abasyakata, Page -41

65. Divyadhara - 20, Taking charge of the disciple, Page -18

66. Divyadhara -7, Biswas, Page -26

67. Divyadhara -7, Guru o Guruma, Page -17

68. Divyadhara -9, Gurumantra, Page -31

69. Divyadhara -17, Sadguru nku Chinihba Kipari, Page -34

70. Divyadhara -10, Sisya Jnana Paibar Saral Upaya, Page -20

71. Divyadhara -15, Guru nka Tatparya o Shisya Shisyaa nka Pratharna, Page- 44

72. Divyadhara -19, Guru Seva O Guru Asirvad, Page -7

Chapter - 6 (Shaktitattva and others)

73. Divyadhara -9, Sakti Tattva, Page -51

74. Divyadhara -7, Srusti Tattva-1, Page -29

75. Divyadhara -7, Srusti Tattva-2, Page -34

76. Divyadhara -15, Prakriti Tattva, Page -9

77. Divyadhara -16, Annamaya Kosa o tara Sadhana, Page -5

78. Divyadhara -16, Pranamaya Kosa o tara Sadhana, Page -10

79. Divyadhara -16, Manomaya Kosa o tara Sadhana, Page -12

80. Divyadhara -16, Vignanamaya Kosa o tara Sadhana, Page -18

81. Divyadhara -16, Anandamaya Kosa o tara Sadhana, Page -25

82. Divyadhara -15, Sabda Brahma, Page -17

83. Divyadhara -10, Omkar Rahasya, Page -16

84. Divyadhara -16, Omkar Dhvani ra Mahanata, Page -43

85. Divyadhara -4, Aakash Tattva, Page -8

86. Divyadhara -7, Sunya Upasana, Page -45

87. Divyadhara -4, Kala Vijnana, Page -13

88. Divyadhara -4, Jyotish Shastra o Mahakasha Vijnana, Page -3

89. Divyadhara -18, Devata Tattva, Page -35

*****

www.ingramcontent.com/pod-product-compliance
Lightning Source LLC
LaVergne TN
LVHW041139150826
845673LV00001B/40

* 9 7 9 8 8 8 7 8 3 5 6 9 3 *